Latin America:
Struggle for Progress

Latin America: Struggle for Progress

Critical Choices for Americans
Volume XIV

James D. Theberge
Roger W. Fontaine

Lexington Books
D.C. Heath and Company
Lexington, Massachusetts
Toronto

Library of Congress Cataloging in Publication Data

Fontaine, Roger W.
    Latin America, struggle for progress.

    (Critical choices for Americans; v. 14)
    Includes index.
    1. Latin America—Foreign relations—United States. 2. United States—Foreign relations—United States. 3. Latin America—Foreign economic relations. 4. Latin America—Foreign relations. I. Theberge, James Daniel, joint author. II. Title. III. Series.
F1418.F67   327.8'073   75-44732
ISBN 0-669-00428-6

Foreword

The Commission on Critical Choices for Americans, a nationally representative, bipartisan group of forty-two prominent Americans, was brought together on a voluntary basis by Nelson A. Rockefeller. After assuming the Vice Presidency of the United States, Mr. Rockefeller, the chairman of the Commission, became an ex officio member. The Commission's assignment was to develop information and insights which would bring about a better understanding of the problems confronting America. The Commission sought to identify the critical choices that must be made if these problems are to be met.

The Commission on Critical Choices grew out of a New York State study of the Role of a Modern State in a Changing World. This was initiated by Mr. Rockefeller, who was then Governor of New York, to review the major changes taking place in federal-state relationships. It became evident, however, that the problems confronting New York State went beyond state boundaries and had national and international implications.

In bringing the Commission on Critical Choices together, Mr. Rockefeller said:

As we approach the 200th Anniversary of the founding of our Nation, it has become clear that institutions and values which have accounted for our astounding progress during the past two centuries are straining to cope with the massive problems of the current era. The increase in the tempo of change and the vastness and complexity of the wholly new situations which are evolving with accelerated change, create a widespread sense that our political and social system has serious inadequacies.

We can no longer continue to operate on the basis of reacting to crises, counting on crash programs and the expenditure of huge sums of money to solve our problems. We have got to understand and project present trends, to take command of the forces that are emerging, to extend our freedom and wellbeing as citizens and the future of other nations and peoples in the world.

Because of the complexity and interdependence of issues facing America and the world today, the Commission has organized its work into six panels, which emphasize the interrelationships of critical choices rather than treating each one in isolation.

The six panels are:

Panel I: Energy and its Relationship to Ecology, Economics and World Stability;

Panel II: Food, Health, World Population and Quality of Life;

Panel III: Raw Materials, Industrial Development, Capital Formation, Employment and World Trade;

Panel IV: International Trade and Monetary Systems, Inflation and the Relationships Among Differing Economic Systems;

Panel V: Change, National Security and Peace;

Panel VI: Quality of Life of Individuals and Communities in the U.S.A.

The Commission assigned, in these areas, more than 100 authorities to prepare expert studies in their fields of special competence. The Commission's work has been financed by The Third Century Corporation, a New York not-for-profit organization. The corporation has received contributions from individuals and foundations to advance the Commission's activities.

The Commission is determined to make available to the public these background studies and the reports of those panels which have completed their deliberations. The background studies are the work of the authors and do not necessarily represent the views of the Commission or its members.

This volume is one of the series of volumes the Commission will publish in the belief that it will contribute to the basic thought and foresight America will need in the future.

> WILLIAM J. RONAN
> *Acting Chairman*
> Commission on Critical Choices
> for Americans

Members of the Commission

EDWARD TELLER
   Senior Research Fellow, Hoover Institution
   on War, Revolution and Peace,
   Stanford University

ARTHUR K. WATSON*
   Former Ambassador to France

MARINA VON NEUMANN WHITMAN
   Distinguished Public Service Professor
   of Economics, University of Pittsburgh

CARROLL L. WILSON
   Professor, Alfred P. Sloan
   School of Management,
   Massachusetts Institute of Technology

GEORGE D. WOODS
   Former President, World Bank

Members of the Commission served on the panels. In addition, others assisted
the panels.

BERNARD BERELSON
Senior Fellow
President Emeritus
The Population Council

C. FRED BERGSTEN
Senior Fellow
The Brookings Institution

ORVILLE G. BRIM, JR.
President
Foundation for Child Development

LESTER BROWN
President
Worldwatch Institute

LLOYD A. FREE
President
Institute for International Social Research
_____
*Deceased

Preface

In the present period of international fluidity, the success of Latin America in industrializing, as well as the form and nature of the political and economic instruments of progress, will have ramifications, not only for the balance of power within Latin America and the Western Hemisphere, but for the world.

National successes and failures are already raising new problems which cannot be considered solely in bilateral or hemispheric terms. The increasing tendency of the republics of Latin America to identify their interests with the "non-aligned" nations will affect the complex relationship between the industrialized and industrializing nations.

This new direction in foreign policy, coupled with Latin America's efforts to expand its diplomatic activity and define its national interests, is changing the nature of relations within the hemisphere. Specific security problems, the renegotiation of the Panama Canal Treaty, as well as Cuba's insistence upon the exportation of revolution, can affect stability not only on bilateral and hemispheric levels, but within the international sphere.

The United States and the other nations of the Western Hemisphere have entered upon a new, less stable but challenging period in their relationships. While the outcome cannot be predicted, options exist which can change the nature of the hemisphere.

Latin America: Struggle for Progress focuses on these options and discusses the choices available to the United States in its relations with Latin America. It is one of seven geographic studies prepared for the Commission on Critical Choices for Americans, under the coordination of Nancy Maginnes Kissinger. Other volumes examine Western Europe, the Soviet Empire, the Middle East, China and Japan, Southern Asia, and Africa.

The organization and direction of the research embodied in this report on Latin America prepared for the Critical Choices Commission was initially the responsibility of James D. Theberge, when he was Director of Latin American Studies at Georgetown University's Center for Strategic and International Studies. In this task, he was assisted by Roger W. Fontaine of the Center staff, as well as a number of other scholars who contributed background papers on several issues. In June, 1975, Mr. Theberge was nominated U.S. Ambassador to Nicaragua and Mr. Fontaine subsequently assumed responsibility for the report. Therefore, Ambassador Theberge does not necessarily agree with all the facts, interpretations or recommendations presented in this volume.

W.J.R.

Contents

List of Tables

Introduction

New global and regional realities require major changes and adaptations in United States policy toward Latin America. The United States no longer enjoys overwhelming power and resources in the world and must marshal both with greater wisdom and economy than ever before in the promotion of its interests. United States policy must be reappraised in the light of Latin America's socioeconomic transformation and can no longer afford to waiver unstably between active interventionism and imprudent neglect of our interests.

What is needed now, as in the past, is a policy towards our Latin American neighbors that is sympathetic and responsive to our mutual development and security requirements; that can be pitched at a sustainable level of effort for the rest of the decade; and, that is tolerant of a degree of diversity.

This report attempts to examine new Latin American realities; to identify and explore the important trends and issues that will likely affect hemispheric relations over the next decade; and, to specify a reasonable range of choices and their consequences available to United States policymakers. It also offers suggestions concerning the practical and moral limits to U.S. policy. The approach adopted in this report is to reject the extreme notions that the United States can, or should, do nothing to shape events in the hemisphere in our interests or that the United States has the capability and obligation to impose its own ideals and standards on other peoples.

The report is divided into five chapters. Chapter I, "Latin America in the World Arena," documents the region's shift away from dependence on the United States for aid, trade, and investment toward new and greatly widened ties with Japan, Western Europe, Canada, the Communist countries, and the Third World. It also examines those resources which Latin America can use to exploit its new position in world politics. These include food, petroleum, and minerals, as well as conventional and possibly nuclear weapons. The section also assesses the opportunities for greater regional integration. At the same time, it tests the limits of the region's new internationalism.

Chapter II, "The Quest for Order and Progress," analyzes the political and economic currents that are running through most of Latin America. There will likely be more economic and social progress than political peace and tranquility in the region, with the return to civilian and constitutional rule a distinct possibility in several countries.

Chapter III, "Latin America: The Critical Choices for Regional Issues," relates most directly to United States policy. It addresses specific issues that are either regional in scope or bilateral in nature. They cover those political, economic, and security problems that likely will have the greatest impact on United States-Latin American relations in the coming decade.

Chapter IV, "Latin America: Critical Choices in Key Countries," is devoted to those countries that are of special interest to the United States: Argentina, Brazil, Cuba, Mexico, and Venezuela. In each paper, the critical problems are discussed, United States current policy assessed, American goals enumerated, and policy options laid out along with some of their probable consequences.

Chapter V offers some conclusions. Finally, we are including a detailed analysis of a key country Venezuela which has only recently emerged in importance, written by Dr. Philip B. Taylor, a longtime observer of that country.

It may be useful at this stage to describe some of the most general policy options or postures open to the United States in its relations with Latin America. It is sometimes assumed that the United States has only one serious choice: to be more accommodating and responsive to Latin demands and to transfer more financial and other resources to Latin America for development purposes. There are, however, a broader range of options open that also deserve consideration.

The Special Relationship. The assumption underlying this alternative is that a special relationship exists between the United States and Latin America that entails reciprocal obligations and considerations. The United States has an acknowledged responsibility to support economic development and provide security protection for friendly countries.

In the economic sphere, Latin America is given special treatment in aid and trade matters, including commodity agreements.[a]

The Latin American countries are expected to give reasonable consideration to United States interests. The special relationship also implies a revitalization of

[a]The special relationship, though rarely called that, is rooted in the belief that the hemisphere is a community of nations dedicated to similar political and social ideals. This view was most widely shared (at least in the United States) during World War II, and enjoyed a brief revival in the early years of the Alliance for Progress.

hemispheric organizations like the Organization of American States (OAS) and the preservation of traditional markets.

The Balanced Relationship. The major operating assumption of this policy option is that the United States does not have exclusive or predominant responsibility for Latin American welfare or security. There is only a residual recognition of the important historic, geographic and cultural ties between the United States and Latin America and an awareness that United States relations with Latin America are characterized by elements of both conflict and cooperation.

In this alternative, Latin America's special place in the world system is recognized because of its unique characteristics. It belongs neither to the First, Second, or Third Worlds. It is not developed or democratic enough for the First World; it does not (except in the case of Cuba) have enough Marxist police state regimes to belong to the Second World; and, finally, Latin America has been independent too long, and is too developed, economically, politically, and socially, to fit easily into the Third World. Thus, because it is not yet committed to any of them, the United States has an opportunity to encourage Latin America's adherence to the First World by promoting new aid, trade, and investment relationships with Western Europe and Japan as well as with North America.

Latin America on Its Own. This choice stresses the absence of any kind of special relationship between the United States and Latin America. The importance of historical, geographical, cultural and political ties is considered to be vastly exaggerated and no longer of consequence. This option assumes that the United States has no special responsibility, grants no special privileges, seeks no sphere of influence, and treats Latin America as just another part of the Third World. Hence, Latin America is encouraged to expand its relations with the rest of the world while reducing its dependency on the United States. United States-Latin American relations are placed on a strictly businesslike basis. The inter-American system is downgraded or abandoned.

These general policy options obviously do not exhaust the possibilities and various combinations are possible. But they do provide some notion of the range of choices open to policy-makers in the hemisphere. These choices, have been the subject of considerable debate in recent years throughout the hemisphere, a debate that has by no means been settled to everyone's satisfaction.

Acknowledgments

The authors would like to thank particularly those who directly contributed to this study. The list is short, but the depth is great. First, we would like to thank Nancy Maginnes Kissinger for extensive comments and criticisms of the original draft. We would also like to thank Anne Boylan, Charity Randall, and Cathy Abshire of the Commission staff for their patience and editorial wisdom and management. Among our academic debts, the largest are to Philip B. Taylor and Milton Barall. Finally, we must add a special thank you for Mary Park who typed all versions of this report, usually with finished-by-yesterday deadlines.

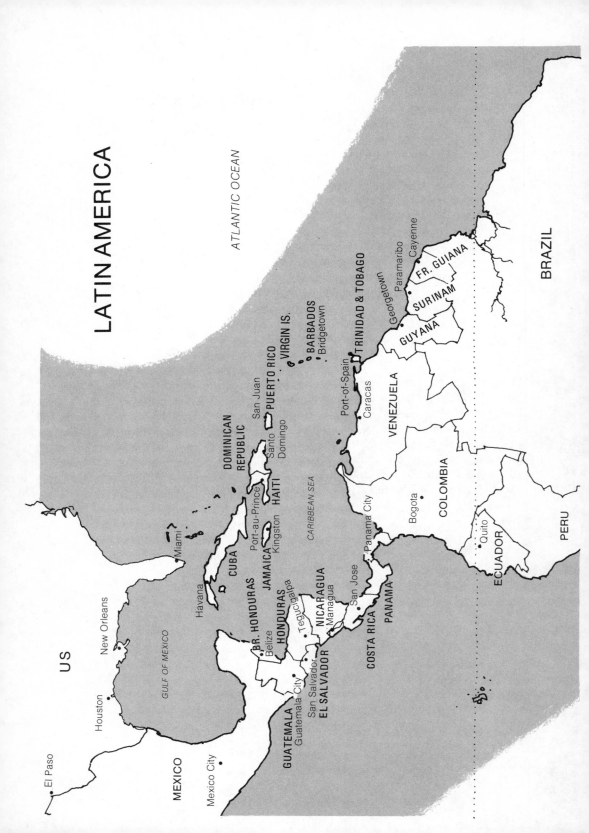

LATIN AMERICA

US

MEXICO

El Paso

Houston

New Orleans

Mexico City

GULF OF MEXICO

MEXICO

GUATEMALA

Guatemala City

EL SALVADOR

San Salvador

BR. HONDURAS

Belize

HONDURAS

Tegucigalpa

NICARAGUA

Managua

COSTA RICA

San Jose

PANAMA

Panama City

Havana

CUBA

Miami

ATLANTIC OCEAN

JAMAICA

Kingston

HAITI

Port-au-Prince

DOMINICAN REPUBLIC

Santo Domingo

CARIBBEAN SEA

PUERTO RICO

San Juan

VIRGIN IS.

BARBADOS

Bridgetown

TRINIDAD & TOBAGO

Port-of-Spain

Caracas

VENEZUELA

COLOMBIA

Bogota

ECUADOR

Quito

PERU

GUYANA

Georgetown

SURINAM

Paramaribo

FR. GUIANA

Cayenne

BRAZIL

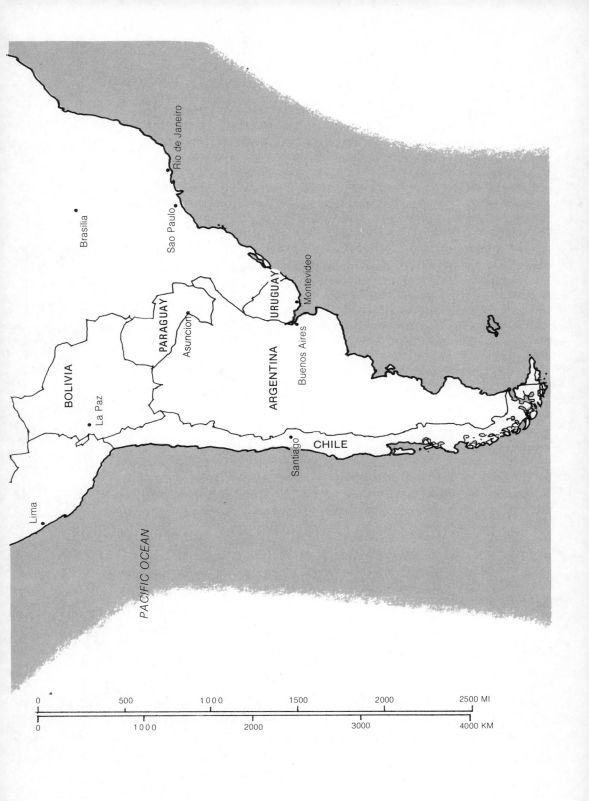

Brasília

Rio de Janeiro

Sao Paulo

Lima

BOLIVIA

La Paz

PARAGUAY

Asunción

URUGUAY

Montevideo

ARGENTINA

Buenos Aires

CHILE

Santiago

PACIFIC OCEAN

| 0 | 500 | 1000 | 1500 | 2000 | 2500 MI |

| 0 | 1000 | 2000 | 3000 | 4000 KM |

I

Latin America in the World Arena

Latin America: The New Diplomacy

Latin America is slowly altering its traditional patterns of international relations. For centuries these were focused on North America and Western Europe. But now, an increasing number of Latin American countries are establishing diplomatic and commercial relations with regions of the world with which they previously had little or no contact.

The expansion of Latin America's world ties should come as no surprise. Inevitably, the Latin countries are becoming further integrated into the global political and economic system. Neither should Latin America's new diplomacy be exaggerated. The North Atlantic trading area (plus Japan) will still remain the major economic partner of Latin America for decades.

Furthermore, it should be remembered that the special economic relationship between the United States and Latin America is of relatively recent origin. Until Latin American independence, the region's economic relations were virtually monopolized by Portugal and Spain, and in the nineteenth century post-independence period its political, economic and cultural ties were primarily with England and France. It was not until World War I that the United States became Latin America's chief economic partner. Indeed, as late as 1938, the United States accounted for 37 percent of the region's imports while Western Europe (including England) maintained a 40 percent share. Only after World War II did the United States achieve dominance by supplying, for example, 59 percent of Latin America's imports in 1948 while Western Europe sank to below 20 percent.[1]

Moreover, the Latin American nations have coupled an aggressive bilateralism with a wide reaching multilateralism. Many of the region's republics began first attending and then aggressively participating in Third World forums such as the

1

United Nations Conference on Trade and Development (UNCTAD), the Group of 77, and the so-called nonaligned movement.

But playing an important role in such gatherings also revived the old Bolivarian dream of Latin (in fact, Spanish) American unity. Without that, it was felt, the region's influence and ability to protect its interests would remain scant no matter how many international conferences were attended.

Hopes for reuniting the old Spanish empire and transforming the weak, fragmented Latin countries into a powerful bloc of nations has never completely died in spite of numerous disappointments. Attempts were made during the independence period and continued through much of the nineteenth century. Numerous and often ambitious projects were proposed, discussed, and accepted on a wide range of economic, political, cultural, and security matters. Nevertheless, they all failed to create a politically or economically cohesive and unified Latin America.

Latin American unity proved to be a durable aspiration, however. After World War II, regional economic integration became popular once again in Latin America. The success of Benelux, the European Economic Community, and the European Free Trade Association in particular played a special role in reviving such hopes. And, although they are far from being realized, they remain at the heart of Latin America's new diplomacy.

Latin American Integration and Cooperation

The first serious attempt at economic union was the creation of the Latin American Free Trade Association in 1960 (LAFTA).[a] Subsequently, subregional common markets were tried in Central America (CACM), the Andean area (ANCOM), and the Caribbean (CARICOM).

However, after nearly two decades of experimentation, LAFTA itself may only be judged a qualified success. Moreover, it is not likely that large-scale integration will be achieved for the foreseeable future. The indifference of the larger nations, coupled with the fear of the smaller countries that benefits will be unequal, present formidable obstacles to any regional scheme.

Coordination of economic policy outside of LAFTA, has also proved difficult. Thus far, despite repeated efforts, it has not been possible to create a Latin American organization capable of establishing an overall regional position of any of the major issues of trade, finance, and development. The Special Commission for Latin American Coordination (CECLA), established in May

---

[a]LAFTA was designed as a free trade area for all of Latin America. All trade barriers were to be eventually removed but there was no provision for a common external tariff. But even this modest goal was not achieved as trade negotiations proved slow and often unproductive. By the mid-1960s the smaller republics of South America, led by Chile, formed a subregional Andean Common Market which provided for a faster rate of trade liberalization and the erection of a common external tariff wall.

1969 at the Viña del Mar Conference, was designed to produce common policy positions before confronting the United States at regular OAS meetings. But CECLA was not given a permanent organizational structure; it met instead on an ad hoc basis to discuss issues of regional interest. Thus, despite achieving some common positions—notably in September 1971, when Special Commission members issued a protest against the United States' 10 percent surcharge on all U.S. imports—CECLA soon fell into neglect after members found policy coordination difficult and time-consuming.

More recently, Mexico and Venezuela have taken the initiative in creating a new regional organization—the Latin American Economic System (SELA)— which would provide a forum to discuss problems and positions vis-à-vis the industrial countries in general and the multinational corporations in particular. According to the joint declaration of March 1975, signed by Presidents Luis Echeverría of Mexico and Carlos Andrés Pérez of Venezuela, SELA's aims include the defense of prices and markets for the area's raw materials and manufactures, the establishment of Latin American multinational companies, and fostering regional financial, technical, and scientific cooperation. But SELA does not enjoy the backing of all Latin American countries. Some (Argentina and Chile) believe the Mexican-Venezuelan effort serves those nations' interests exclusively while others (Brazil, for example) fear that SELA will become a weapon of confrontation with the United States and achieve nothing of substance. Thus, SELA may prove to be only another gesture at continental unity, although high-level attempts are still being made to make SELA permanent.

Latin American disunity is not the result of "U.S. imperialism" or multinational corporation manipulation as is sometimes falsely alleged. The lack of unity is partially a result of the region's varied nature: it is composed of countries at different stages of development, (with competing rather than complementary economies) and ruled by rival ideologies. Moreover, the region is still plagued by an inadequate (but improving) regional transport and communications infrastructure. Furthermore, the regional ambitions of certain Latin American heads of state constitute another permanent obstacle to economic integration and cooperation since these men are often perceived to be, despite their lofty rhetoric, merely pursuing their own country's interests.

The four major competitive centers of political influence and economic strength—Argentina, Brazil, Mexico, and Venezuela—also pose significant barriers to regional cohesion. Each of the Big Four believes it is large enough (or rich enough, in Venezuela's case) to secure by itself the basis for its own national economic integration and development. And each has created, or is creating, its own sphere of influence in its immediate neighborhood. Therefore, these four are often less interested in regionalism and at times opposed to it, in contrast to their smaller and poorer neighbors.

Argentina has competed with Brazil for influence in the southern cone of

South America since the nineteenth century, although it is only recently that Argentina has had to take Brazil's territorial, demographic, and economic expansion seriously. At the same time, Argentina's chronic instability has reduced its ability to act decisively (unlike Brazil) in regional and world affairs.

At present, Brazil is the only country in the region which has the economic strength and political cohesion to carry out a global foreign policy. Brazil is confident of its national identity and destiny, and appears capable of overcoming present problems such as the oil crisis by continuous economic growth. Brazil's newfound strength, however, is creating a power imbalance in South America that causes concern in neighboring countries. Over the past decade, heavy investments in major hydroelectric and irrigation projects on the upper Parana River, including joint projects with Paraguay and Uruguay, have created tensions and conflicts with a less dynamic Argentina.[b]

Mexico, under President Echeverría, has pursued a foreign policy designed to reduce economic dependence on the United States by the diversification of its relations, which, it is believed, will in turn convert Mexico into a significant force in Third World politics. The United States' immediate neighbor has also been extending its economic and political ties with the countries of the Caribbean basin and Central America. It is precisely this diplomatic activism, coupled with a growing economic presence in the Caribbean-Central American area, that provokes the suspicions of the smaller, weaker countries within Mexico's sphere of influence.

Venezuela has obviously benefited greatly from its membership in the organization of Petroleum Exporting Countries (OPEC), but it has been at the expense of the oil-importing countries of Latin America (particularly in Central America and the Caribbean), whose already precarious economies were ravaged by the fourfold increase in oil prices in 1972-74. Venezuela has blunted criticism by promising to help in the formation of OPEC-type cartels for other mineral and tropical commodity exports, and by recycling surplus petrodollars to Jamaica, Peru, the Central American countries, the World Bank, the Inter-American Development Bank (IDB), and the United Nations.

Nevertheless, the decline in prices for many Latin American commodity exports since the end of 1974 combined with the OPEC policy of upward adjustment of oil prices has produced a latent source of conflict between regional oil-importing and oil-exporting countries, particularly Venezuela and Ecuador, which has already begun to surface. For example, in April 1975, the Colombian government criticized both the oil-exporting and the industrial countries for "victimizing" those states that must import oil and manufactured goods. The industrial oil-importing countries are able to compensate by raising

---

[b]Among the Andean countries, Peru is particularly concerned about Brazil's growing economic power. Peru's nonaligned military government remains suspicious of Brazil's pro-West, anti-Communist military government. Moreover, it has failed to match the Brazilian performance, as productivity steadily fell, while state ownership of the economy expanded.

the prices of their manufactured exports, but producers of primary products are caught between two price spirals not of their own making.

Since the mid-1970s, Mexico and Venezuela have pursued parallel foreign economic policies. Both countries are attempting to create a New International Economic Order that would include: the indexation of raw material prices, the creation of producer cartels, the recovery of national sovereignty over natural resources, the regulation of multinational companies, and the control of technology transfers. The New Order would thus result in a massive redistribution of world income from the developed to the less developed countries under the guise of improving Third World terms of trade.

Much of the New Economic Order has been criticized within Latin America as incoherent and contradictory. It is doubtful, for example, whether the ambitious proposals to cartelize international trade in mineral and tropical commodities will enjoy any lasting success. Venezuela's effort to support a Central American coffee producers' cartel, for example, has already failed because producer countries could not agree on any scheme that would keep coffee supplies off the market and thus force up prices.

Instead there is a better prospect for economic cooperation and integration through the creation of subregional political-economic groups such as the Andean Community (ANCOM), the Central American Common Market (CACM), and the Caribbean Common Market (CARICOM). Economic cooperation is more manageable among smaller groups of nations of similar economic strength. But even these partial, less ambitious steps toward integration must overcome serious political and economic conflicts among member states.

The 1969 war between El Salvador and Honduras has effectively paralyzed CACM and, despite repeated efforts by the community's other members, the two countries are still barely on speaking terms. The Andean Common Market has been divided over disputes concerning the foreign investment code (Chile versus Venezuela and Peru) and industrial sector programming (Colombia, in particular, versus the others). In addition, the Andean Community is rent by territorial disputes among its six members, and in each case a final settlement is still distant. Thus the central question for the future is whether these subregional political-economic groups will be able to create strong enough forces of attraction to overcome the centrifugal nationalism within each member state.

Relations with Japan

Most Latin American countries are now finding new markets for their products and they are looking for new suppliers. Many have enjoyed some success with Japan and Canada, and less so with the EEC, the Soviet bloc, and the Third World. Nevertheless, the changes in ten years are impressive and there is little evidence to suggest that current trends will reverse themselves.

Japan's economic relations with Latin America have expanded enormously in recent years with annual export growth rates of nearly 30 percent since 1968. In fifteen years, Japanese exports to Latin America have expanded from $303 million in 1960 to nearly $4.7 billion in 1975.c The Latin American market is still a marginal one for Japanese exporters, absorbing only 8.4 percent of Japan's total exports in 1975. From the Latin American vantage point, however, Japan has changed from an insignificant supplier of manufactured goods to an important alternative source to the United States and Western Europe. Evidence of this fact is that, in 1960, Japan provided only 3.5 percent of Latin America's imports, but in 1974 it was 10.7 percent.

The Japanese market has also become increasingly important to Latin America during the 1960s. Its exports to Japan have been expanding faster than total regional exports during the decade, rising from 2.0 percent in 1960 to 6.1 percent in 1970, but declining thereafter. The fall that occurred after 1972 resulted in large measure from the abrupt rise in the value of Japan's oil imports, induced by OPEC pricing policy and the revaluation of the yen.

Despite the recent slowdown in Japanese imports of Latin American goods (mainly metals, ores, crude materials, foodstuffs, and simple manufactures) the long-range potential for regional sales to Japan is still enormous. The main Latin American suppliers are Brazil (foodstuffs, ores), Cuba (foodstuffs), Mexico (textiles), Chile (ores), Peru (ores), and Argentina (foodstuffs).

Japanese direct investment in Latin America has risen dramatically from $380 million in 1967 to $1.8 billion in 1973 (see Table I-1). Compared to the magnitude of U.S. investment in Latin America—$18.5 billion in 1973—the level

Table I-1

Japanese Overseas Investment, by Region of the World, 1973

(millions of U.S. dollars)

	1967	Percent	1973	Percent
North America	406	28.0	2,462	24.0
Latin America	380	26.2	1,811	17.6
Asia	310	21.4	2,391	23.3
Middle East	240	16.5	1,496	14.5
Europe	58	4.0	1,217	11.9
Africa	18	1.2	254	2.5
Oceania	39	2.7	640	6.2
	1,451	100.0	10,271	100.0

Source: Ministry of International Trade and Industry, *1974 Report on Japanese Overseas Enterprises Activities*, Tokyo.

cIn 1973, 92 percent of Japan's exports ($2.5 billion) to Latin America were chemical and heavy industrial products.

of Japanese investment is still low, but it should be noted that it is growing far more rapidly than American or European investment (see Table I-2).

Japanese investors have emphasized Latin American manufacturing and have allocated nearly 60 percent of total investment resources to this sector; only 10 percent of investment has been devoted to mining. Japanese interest in resource development projects, however, is clearly on the rise—particularly in Brazil, Chile, Peru, and Venezuela. Japanese joint ventures and official economic aid will be directed to the development of Latin American mining and agriculture in the future.[2]

Over one-half of the total Japanese direct investment in the region has been received by Brazil. Japan has invested in the USMINAS steel works as well as large-scale projects in shipbuilding, automobiles, and textiles. The result is that Japanese capital provides an important share of total foreign capital in Brazil's shipbuilding (81 percent), steel (44 percent), and timber industries (31 percent), with significant amounts in textiles, machinery, and finance.

As a result of the rapid expansion of its overseas direct investments, Japan has become aware of the possibility of serious friction with recipient countries, particularly in Southeast Asia (Thailand and Indonesia), where nationalists strongly resent, among other things, aggressive Japanese business behavior. In contrast, Japanese investors have been accepted in Argentina, Brazil, Mexico, and Peru because of their low investment profile and still unobtrusive presence. Furthermore, the Japanese do not have a history of conflicting economic relations with Latin America. However, the continuation of good relations with Latin America may require much greater governmental efforts, particularly when Japan's investments in certain countries and economic sectors assume a larger dimension over the next decade.

Table I-2
Comparison of U.S. and Japanese Trade Turnover and Investment in Latin America, 1965-73
(millions of U.S. dollars)

	Trade Turnover[a]		Direct Investment	
	1965	1973	1965	1973
United States	7,494	19,595	10,900	18,452
Japan	1,065.6	4,716	380[b]	1,811
Japan as Percent of United States	14.2	24.1	3.5	9.8

[a]Trade turnover is equal to exports plus imports.
[b]1967.
Source: IMF, *Direction of Trade*, annual issues, 1962-66; U.S. Department of Commerce, *Survey of Current Business*, March 1975, and August 1974; and Ministry of International Trade and Industry, Tokyo.

Japan has the second largest development aid program in the world. Nevertheless, only 4.6 percent of Japanese official bilateral aid went to Latin America in 1973 (compared to 90 percent to Asia). But from a total in 1973 of $5.8 billion in Japanese resource flows abroad (bilateral and multilateral aid, export credits, direct investment, etc.) Latin America received $2.7 billion or 46 percent. Thus, measured in terms of total Japanese resource flows, Latin America is now beginning to rival Asia.

The Japanese government considers the Latin American countries too developed, in general, to receive large-scale bilateral aid, and prefers that private investment play the predominant role in Japanese-Latin American economic relations. Meanwhile, the Japanese did liberalize their 1971 preferential tariff scheme, and it has made a difference in Latin America's exports of manufactured goods.

Relations with Canada

Canada's interests in the Western Hemisphere (the United States apart) have been concentrated on the independent states and territories of the English-speaking Caribbean. At present, Canada has substantial trade and investment relations with Jamaica, Trinidad-Tobago, the Bahamas, Barbados, and to a declining extent Guyana. Investment is chiefly in banking, real estate, life insurance, manufacturing, and tourism.

Until recently, Canada's deep-seated mistrust of the expansion and power of the United States in the hemisphere has inhibited its involvement in Latin America and the inter-American system. Furthermore, it was thought that joining the OAS might bring Canada into direct conflict with the United States to the detriment of more important bilateral interests.

Nevertheless, Canada is beginning to move cautiously toward a deeper involvement in inter-American affairs. An important step was taken in May 1972 when Ottawa became a member of the Inter-American Development Bank. Canada has also appointed an official observer to the OAS, although still refraining from a full membership.

Despite these moves, however, public opinion in Canada still reflects a lack of identity with Spanish and Portuguese America, its problems and accomplishments, although Prime Minister Trudeau is attempting to overcome this by stressing his nation's hemispheric interests and downgrading its NATO military role.

In the 1970s, the Canadian private and public sectors have made a substantial effort to expand commercial relations with the Latin American countries as part of Trudeau's Third Option trade policy—i.e., the diversification of trade relations outside Canada's traditional American and British markets. In 1974 Canada's exports to the Western Hemisphere (excluding the United States) reached $1.2

billion, up sharply from $862 million the previous year. (In 1975, they leveled off to $1.1 billion.) In relation to Canada's 1974 exports to the United States of $20.6 billion, this is not a large volume of trade, but the Latin American market is no longer insignificant.

Canada's four major trading partners in Latin America are Brazil, Cuba, Mexico, and Venezuela. The Canadian government hopes to expand its trade with Brazil vastly over the next decade. Venezuela and Mexico, owing to considerable competition from the United States, present a more difficult problem for Canadian businessmen. Special opportunities do exist in those fields in which Canadians claim superiority, such as pulp and paper supply, hydro-power technology, and transport equipment. The Mexican State Railways, for example, recently purchased a $200 million package of railway cars, steel rails, and shop modernization from a consortium of Canadian firms.

Cuba is now emerging as one of Canada's more important trading partners. By 1980, the Canadian government expects exports to Cuba to rise to $400 million, up from $212 million in 1975. Cuba is not only viewed as an increasingly important outlet for its goods and services, but Canadian businessmen hope to be able to squeeze into the Cuban market before U.S.-Cuban commercial relations are reestablished. It is doubtful, however, that Canada will be able to sustain a special position in the Cuban market for very long except in specific products.

While Canadian investment is still largely concentrated in the English-speaking Caribbean, a process of diversification has been underway in recent years. Canada has a major investment in the Dominican Republic in Falconbridge Dominicana S.A. (nickel mining) and in Brazil in Brascan Limited (a diversified holding company). Brascan is Brazil's second largest foreign-owned corporation, and has expanded from public utility services into food processing, development banking, transport equipment, and real estate investment.

But the interest in Latin America has not been without problems. During the 1970s, Canadian-owned banks and industries became the target of the nationalist hostility customarily reserved for U.S. private enterprise in Latin America. In 1971, the Canadian-owned Demarara Bauxite Company (a subsidiary of the Aluminum Company of Canada-ALCAN), with assets valued at $150 million, was nationalized by Guyana. This substantially reduced total Canadian invest-ment in the Caribbean which currently amounts to about $500 million, according to Canadian government estimates. During 1974, ALCAN and several U.S. companies were required to pay a new levy on bauxite production which sharply increased Jamaica's total revenue from an annual rate of $30 million in 1973 to $165 million. But the worst reaction to "Canadian imperialism" occurred in Trinidad-Tobago in 1970 when anti-Canadian riots were organized by West Indian nationalists.

As a large net capital-importing country with attractive domestic investment opportunities, Canada has been more inward-looking and less interested in expanding overseas than the United States. But this is now changing. Trade expansion and development assistance have become important aspects of Canada's hemispheric policy. Although Canada's near-dominance in the financial sector in the English-speaking Caribbean has created problems, Canadian investments in the rest of Latin America are still well-received and prospects for closer Canadian-Latin American trade relations appear to be good.

Relations with Western Europe

With the exception of Spain, Western Europe still seems to be only dimly aware of Latin America. Western Europe's trade with Latin America, for example, is declining. In 1950, 8.5 percent of European exports went to Latin America, but by 1960 this ratio had fallen to 6 percent, and in 1974 it was only 3.0 percent. On the other hand, from the Latin American point of view, Western Europe is an important market, absorbing more than 30 percent of its exports and supplying about 30 percent of its imports, including much of the capital equipment essential to industrial growth. Thus, Latin American-Western European commercial relations are marked by a strong asymmetry.

The Western European countries continue to maintain an official optimism concerning trade with Latin America, but the traditional arrangement of providing raw materials in exchange for manufactures is no longer satisfactory to Latin America nor in conformity with recent trends in Latin American trade. The most dynamic sector of Latin American exports during the 1960s was manufactured products, and many of these manufactures and semi-manufactures are in direct competition with some European goods.

Europe shows little concern over the impact of its trade and agricultural policies on Latin American development. Under the European Economic Community's (EEC) Common Agricultural Policy (CAP), Latin American interests have not been given the consideration they merit. Argentina, Brazil, and Uruguay produce and export temperate agricultural products that are highly protected by the CAP. When European farms face difficulty, the CAP forces the adjustment burden to fall as much as possible on competing exporters, especially in Latin America.

The EEC's preferential trade agreements, established with its associate members in the early 1960s, have also hurt Latin American exports. In February 1975, the EEC signed the Lomé Agreement which discriminates seriously against the tropical exporting countries of the Caribbean (except Jamaica, Trinidad-Tobago, and Barbados), and Central and South America. The Lomé agreement provides duty-free access for a wide range of tropical exports, with the exception of sugar, from the 46 countries of Africa, the Caribbean, and the Pacific (the so-called ACP countries) although no reciprocity, in the form of reverse preferences, has been given to the EEC by the ACP members.

Meanwhile, the nonpreferential trade agreements signed between the EEC and Argentina, Brazil, and Uruguay have had little economic impact. Furthermore, the trade credits provided by Europe to facilitate trade with Latin America primarily benefit European exports and often carry burdensome terms for Latin American imports. These developments may well jeopardize what the Latins have so painfully gotten from the EEC.

But despite their disappointments with EEC policy, the Latin American countries look to Western Europe as a counterweight to the United States. They would, for example, like European support for the reorganization of the world economy leading to improved terms of trade for exports of raw materials, increased access to world markets for their manufactured exports, and expanded local ownership of the means of production. Thus far Europe has not given serious support to these initiatives, but there is hope that the current GATT negotiations could provide a mechanism for resolving some of these problems.

Western Europe can clearly do far more to assist Latin American development, but from the European viewpoint there is more to be gained from economic relations with Asia, Africa, and other developing regions. In light of this continuing imbalance it is not realistic to expect any fundamental change in Western Europe's calculated indifference towards Latin America.

Relations with the Soviet Union, Eastern Europe, and China

During the 1960s an increasing number of Caribbean and South American states established diplomatic and commercial relations with the Soviet Union, Eastern Europe, and China.[d] The major economic partners of the Socialist states are the larger Latin American states, Argentina and Brazil, and, to a lesser extent, Colombia and Peru. Mexico has no significant trade relations with the Socialist countries although economic missions were sent to Russia, China, and the Eastern European countries in the mid-1970s.

Various factors have contributed to Latin America's growing interest in economic relations with the Socialist states. They include the widespread desire to diversify export markets and to obtain new sources of capital and technology, partially as a result of the perceived protectionist trend in the United States as well as the difficulty of competing for EEC markets with Asian and African countries receiving preferential treatment. Moreover, balance of payments pressures which resulted from higher oil prices and an interest in relations with the Socialist states as a demonstration of "independence" from the United States have also contributed to this expansion of economic relations.

From the viewpoint of the Soviet Union and Eastern European countries,

---

[d]Cuba is a special case not included in the discussion of Latin America in this chapter because it is part of the Soviet bloc and a ward of the Soviet Union.

Latin America is a marginal trading area. Commercial interchange is growing in absolute terms but is declining in relative importance to the Soviet bloc. Nevertheless, some effort is being made by the Soviet Union and the Eastern European countries to broaden trade with Latin America and to create "mechanisms of cooperation" that will lend a more stable character to economic relations with the region. In the meantime, the Soviets have expressed support for the New Economic Order provided that order does harm only to Western interests.

Despite this mutual desire on both sides there are substantial difficulties that must be overcome. Trade expansion is inhibited by a persistently unfavorable trade balance maintained by the Soviet Union, China, and the Eastern European countries with Latin America. In general, Latin America exports its traditional primary commodities (sugar, coffee, cacao, hides, fruit, tin) to the Socialist countries, although sale of semi-manufactured and manufactured goods has occurred. The Soviet Union and Eastern European countries mainly export heavy industrial goods to Latin America.

Soviet imports from Latin America reached only $303.5 million in 1974. Nevertheless, they have been rising in absolute figures in recent years, and can be expected to expand slowly in the future. Soviet exports reached a peak of $66 million in 1966 and generally declined until 1974 when they jumped to $71.5 million.

The Eastern European Socialist countries have made independent efforts to establish trade relations with Latin America because they have a greater need for raw materials than the Soviet Union. Eastern European trade turnover with Latin America reached $434 million in 1972, compared with a Soviet trade turnover of $179 million (see Table I-3), with Brazil, Argentina, Peru, and Colombia accounting for about 90 percent of it. The Eastern Europeans have also begun to explore mixed state enterprises financed by local and Socialist state capital as a technique for generating additional exports to Latin America. In 1973, for example, the state mining companies of Romania (GEOMIN) and Peru (MINEROPERU) established a jointly-owned state mining enterprise to exploit the Atamina copper deposits.

Soviet economic aid to Latin America (again excluding Cuba) was negligible throughout the 1960s, but has been increasing in the 1970s as new opportunities arose. About two-thirds of all Soviet aid has gone to countries close to the Soviet borders, making Latin America last in priority among recipient regions of the world. Despite the rise in Soviet economic aid, it is still characterized by its smallness and erratic nature. During the 1966-73 period, Chile was the largest aid recipient and received $260.5 million during the Allende regime, which accounted for over half of total Soviet aid to Latin America. Brazil received a $85 million credit in 1966, making it the second most important aid recipient in the region. Since 1973, however, no Soviet aid has been authorized for any Latin American country.

Table I-3
Soviet Union, Eastern European and Chinese Trade with Latin America, 1968-72
(millions of U.S. dollars)

	1968			1970			1972		
	Exports	Imports	Turnover	Exports	Imports	Turnover	Exports	Imports	Turnover
Soviet Union	25.3	68.3	93.6	13.0	62.0	75.0	31.7	147.2	178.9
Eastern Europe	127.8	189.5	317.3	137.6	250.9	388.5	144.1	290.0	434.1
China	6.8	0.6	7.4	3.9	3.8	7.7	7.1	190.9	198.0
Total	159.9	258.4	418.3	154.5	316.7	471.2	182.9	628.1	811.0

Source: U.S. Department of State, Bureau of Intelligence and Research, *Communist States and Developing Countries: AID and Trade*, 1969, 1971, and 1973.

During the last ten years, East European countries have provided little economic aid to Latin America, and most of it has been delivered to two countries: Peru and Chile. By 1973, East European aid had fallen to $5 million from a high point in 1970 of $174 million.

Chinese economic activity in Latin America is still modest. Peking's exports are negligible, fluctuating within the narrow range of $4-8 million in the 1968-72 period. But Chinese imports from Latin America have risen rapidly, from less than $1 million in 1968 to $369 million in 1974. Argentina, Brazil, Chile, Mexico, and Peru are the main Chinese trading partners, accounting for about 95 percent of their trade with Latin America in 1974. Trading activity, however, despite its advances, is still highly unstable.

Peking's only economic aid to Latin America, a total of $133 million, was authorized in 1971 and 1972. In 1971, aid was given to Peru and Chile and in 1972 to Chile and Guyana. No aid per se has been authorized for Latin America since 1973.

Socialist bloc-Latin American trade will continue to be limited for some time to come by the sluggishness of the Communist state trading bureaucracies, the rigidity of their national five-year plans (which restrict the expansion of the foreign sector), the unsuitability of Socialist manufactured goods, their unfamil- iarity with the Latin American market, and their inefficiency in providing spare parts and components and after-sales servicing. Some of these obstacles are being overcome slowly, but a large-scale expansion of trade between the Soviet Union, Eastern Europe, China, and Latin America does not appear likely for the future.

Economic aid programs will remain an important element of Soviet and Chinese policy towards the Third World, but a large-scale commitment to Latin America, even to a friendly Socialist government (such as Allende's Communist- Socialist coalition in Chile) is unlikely. Both Moscow and Peking refused to provide the massive economic aid that the Allende government sought and needed to survive. Moscow will continue to provide economic aid to Latin American countries on a highly selective basis when the political situation warrants it. The Soviet economic (and military) aid program remains one of the few available instruments for expanding Russian influence in Latin America while at the same time weakening U.S.-Latin American ties and countering Chinese influence. In the meantime, Latin American interest in expanding trade ties with the Communist countries should continue unabated despite problems with their size and quality. This is so for several reasons. First, in economic terms, the Socialist camp is still perceived in Latin America as a vast untapped market. Second, the pursuit of good relations earns Latin American governments a certain amount of local popularity since it serves as a gesture of independence from the United States. Neither of these motivating factors is likely to change in the next decade.

Relations with the Third World

Historically, relations between Asia, Africa, the Middle East, and Latin America have been weak and sporadic. But over the past two decades, and particularly in recent years, this pattern has changed. Political and economic ties have been established where none existed before.

In the mid-1970s, for example, the impact of the oil crisis on Latin America and the rise of petrodollar surpluses have had an immediate effect on Latin American-Middle Eastern relations. Brazil has taken the lead in establishing ties with the oil-exporting nations of the Middle East. As the largest Latin American oil-importing state (new imports of $2.7 billion in 1974 compared to $588 million for Argentina), Brazil is understandably concerned about expanding and securing its overseas sources of supply. It has, therefore, established oil-exploration agreements with Egypt, Iraq, and Libya. It is planning to participate in a $500 million iron and steel complex in Saudi Arabia, exchanging Brazilian iron ore for Saudi oil. Trade agreements have also been signed with Kuwait under which Brazil will supply manufactured goods and rice for oil. In each case, Brazil's purpose has not been to obtain cheaper oil, but to get secure sources of supply.

Most of Argentina's trade and investment ties in the Middle East have been with Libya. The Qadhafi regime, which claimed to be a great admirer of Perón and Perón's Third Position, has entered into six commercial agreements with Argentina (sugar and cereals for oil) and extended a $200 million commercial credit payable in Argentine raw materials. In addition, Argentina has signed a nuclear research agreement with Libya, and has agreed to barter conventional weapons for Libyan oil and investments. But Argentina is largely self-sufficient in oil production, and therefore under less pressure than Brazil to establish diversified economic ties with the Middle East oil-exporting nations.

A growing number of Latin American republics consider themselves, in some respects at least, as part of the so-called nonaligned Third World, of which Moscow's Cuban client was a founding member. Third World efforts to alter the international economic system in its favor through confrontation tactics have attracted the support of some Latin American countries—notably Argentina, Guyana, Mexico, Peru, and Venezuela—in the recent past whose leaders believed they were enlarging their countries' role in the world.

In the economic sphere, new commodity arrangements among Latin American and other Third World producers have been established with mixed success for oil (OPEC), copper (CIPEC), and bauxite (IBA), and some other commodities. In addition, the Latin American countries have increasingly used the proliferating international organizations (the United Nations and UNCTAD, for example) and less formally organized groups such as the so-called nonaligned group to bring pressure on the industrial countries and to define their common Latin American interests.

Latin American exports to the Third World (excluding intra-Latin American trade) have been rising steadily in the post-World War II period. But their relative importance (measured as a share of total Latin American exports) has been declining and is now below 10 percent. For some countries, like Brazil, which is heavily dependent on oil imports from the Middle East and Africa, this general picture of the declining importance of Latin American-Third World trade may not be quite accurate.

The relative unimportance of Latin American trade with the other developing regions stems from the competitive nature of their economies. But as more Latin American countries shift from semi-industrial to industrial economies, the prospects for trade with Africa, Asia, and Middle East will tend to improve, as suggested by the Brazilian experience.

Meanwhile, there are areas of common interest between the Latin American and other Third World countries. This is especially true for such economic issues as the barriers to manufactured exports imposed by the industrial world and the treatment of multinational enterprises. On the other hand, serious differences exist among the Third World countries concerning trade preferences, negotiating strategy, regulation of foreign investment, and the unequal distribution of benefits from commodity cartels. With respect to trade preferences, the most common divisions are between EEC-associated developing countries and those nations, especially in Latin America, lying outside the preference area.

Therefore, while economic interactions between Latin America and the Third World have been on the rise, they are still far less important to Latin America than relations with the industrial countries of North America, Western Europe, and Japan.

Politically, there will always be some regimes (usually left-wing) attempting to align themselves with the aspirations of the Third World. The trend now, however, seems to be against Third Worldism in Latin America owing in large part to the serious internal difficulties of countries like Peru and Argentina, who once championed such a policy.

Latin America's Resources for the New Diplomacy

Can Latin America maintain the new diplomacy or is this simply a new illusion sustained by the ancient art of self-deception? That Latin America can now play a major role in world affairs completely independent of the United States is most assuredly an illusion. Maintaining its present position with prospects of something better in ten years depends, in large part, on Latin America's making full use of advantages lacking in most of the underdeveloped world.

Latin America is more cohesive than most geographical areas. It possesses a number of economies that can no longer be described as underdeveloped, and it has resources which will be in great demand over the next decade: food, minerals, and petroleum. Moreover, the region's republics have now begun to improve substantially their conventional arsenals, and two countries have the beginnings of an advanced nuclear industry. How well this potential will be exploited will, to a great degree, shape Latin America's future course in world politics.

Food Production

In 1939, Latin America was the major food exporting region (mainly grains and cereals) in the world. During the past quarter century, however, food production lagged behind local consumption, caused by a more than 2.7 percent growth in population, which has resulted in an inevitable decline in net food exports. In 1934-38, Latin America was exporting (net) 9 million metric tons of wheat (mainly from Argentina), but by 1973 the region was importing 5.5 million metric tons (see Table I-4). In 1973, Latin America was also a net importer of rice (400 thousand metric tons) and meat (1 million metric tons), as well as sugar, coffee, cocoa, bananas, and other fruits and vegetables.[3] Viewed in the context of world food production, Latin America is now barely self-sufficient as a food-producing region.

   Why has this situation come to pass in a region capable of feeding a population twice its present size? The slow growth of Latin America's agricultural production can be attributed largely to the postwar drive for industrializa-

Table I-4
Pattern of World Grain Trade
(millions of metric tons)

	1934-38	1948-52	1960	1969-71	1974-75
North America	+5	+23	+39	+54	+100
Latin America	+9	+1	0	+3	−3
Western Europe	−24	−22	−25	−22	−19
Eastern Europe and Russia	+5	−	0	−3	−9
Africa	+1	0	−2	−3	−3
Asia[a]	+2	−6	−17	−31	−40
Australia and New Zealand	+3	+3	+6	+11	+11

Note: Plus sign denotes net exports and minus sign denotes net imports. Grains include wheat and coarse grains.
[a]Includes Japan and Communist China.
Source: U.N. Food and Agriculture Organization and the U.S. Department of Agriculture.

tion which led most governments to discriminate against the farmer in favor of urban industry and labor. Low farm prices fixed by government fiat, heavy export taxes, discriminatory exchange rates, high priced locally produced inputs, marketing inefficiencies, credit scarcities, and inadequate extension services, including problem-oriented research, all played a part in reducing the incentive to produce and export agricultural products.

Latin America has more unused land available for crop production than the rest of the world combined. At present, only 16 percent of the region's available agricultural land is cultivated—leaving over 400 million hectares of land potentially available for cultivation. Over the next decade, Latin American agriculture should continue to expand at about the 3 percent per annum necessary to keep pace with population growth and provide a modest surplus, but a number of countries, particularly Argentina and Brazil, have the potential to increase greatly their agricultural production.

Argentina's long-term agricultural decline is attributable to price controls, production and export taxes, and other policies that have severely dampened incentives to produce and export foodstuffs. Argentine food prices are among the lowest in the world; grain farmers receive less than half the world price for their exports as a result of government price manipulation. On the other hand, Brazilian farmers have increased agricultural exports from $1.2 billion in 1963 to almost $2.7 billion in 1972, and modernization of the agricultural sector guarantees steady growth in the future.

Agrarian reform continues to be a key issue in many Latin American countries. Despite four decades of experimentation, the problems of raising agricultural productivity, and of improving the living standards of the campesino, persist even in countries like Bolivia, Chile, Mexico, and Peru where substantial land redistribution has taken place. The impact of agrarian reform on output and exports depends on the extent to which reform policy provides a framework of economic incentives for producers, coupled with the availability of credit and technical, marketing, and other assistance.

Despite Latin America's agricultural decline in the 1970s, there is a much greater awareness in the region of the importance of this sector for rapid and balanced economic growth. Latin America could again become a major exporter of food if its governments provide an adequate framework for economic incentives and assistance to the agricultural producer. Those regimes which are currently making this effort are Brazil and Chile. Meanwhile, Argentina's food potential remains great and, despite bad policy and political instability, that country had bumper crops in 1975.

Mineral Raw Materials Production

The production and export of raw materials have played a major part in incorporating Latin America into the world economy. Mineral exporting coun-

tries have become closely linked—financially, commercially, and technologi-
cally—to the major industrial consuming centers in North America and Western
Europe. Because of its huge capital requirements, mineral development has
attracted a large flow of foreign investment to Bolivia, Chile, Peru, and
Venezuela. While the pattern of ownership and control of the extractive sector
in Latin America is changing (with state-owned mining enterprise the predominantly emerging form), American, British, and other European firms continue
to play an important role in providing capital, technology, management
expertise, and world marketing facilities.

Before 1930, Latin America's dependence on raw material exports was
unchallenged. But during the 1960s, the acceleration of import-substituting
industrialization, the increased use of mineral raw materials in local production,
and the expansion of manufactured exports have reduced the share of the 15
leading raw materials (such as copper, iron ore, bauxite, tin, zinc) from 80
percent of regional exports in 1960-62 to 56 percent in 1970-72.

There is now new emphasis on mineral raw materials as a stimulus to further
industrialization. It is expected that the additional foreign exchange needed to
finance Latin American development will be generated through expanded
government participation and ownership of mining and related industries. Other
aims are increasing the number and quality of local technicians and adminis-
trators, and obtaining higher returns to local factors of production by reducing
the marketing power of the international oligopolies.

But with one or two exceptions (such as bauxite), the possibility of successful
cartelization of mineral raw materials along the lines of OPEC is extremely
remote, despite the best efforts of countries like Peru and Venezuela. The
conditions for successful cartels of the OPEC-type do not exist for most mineral
raw materials: mineral reserves are too widespread, and price elasticity of supply
is high enough to encourage new producers and the substitution of alternative
materials. The emergence of large suppliers like Australia and the introduction of
the Japanese formula for financing mineral expansion (repayment in mine
output) mitigate against successful cartel activity by Latin American metals
producers.

Copper increased as a proportion of Latin American exports from 4.7
percent in 1960 to 6.3 percent in 1970. Nevertheless, the Latin American
share of world copper exports fell from 40 percent to 25 percent over
the same period. After North America, Chile is the principal world producer,
followed by Zaire, Zambia, and Peru. Most Latin American copper was sold to
Europe and Japan in the 1960s, satisfying about one-third of Europe's requirements. Latin American mines are low cost producers because of a combination
of high grade ore and low cost transport. Therefore, the competitive outlook for
Latin America is good unless state mining enterprises permit productivity to
decline.

Iron ore slightly increased its share of Latin American exports from 2.8
percent in 1960-62 to 3.2 percent in 1970-72. In comparison with world iron
ore exports, Latin America's rose from 9 percent in the late 1940s to 25 percent

in the early 1970s. Brazil has become the largest producer, with Chile, Peru, and Venezuela providing significant exports as well. Between 1957 and 1971 iron ore prices declined, because new high grade ore deposits were opened up in Australia, Brazil, Canada, and Liberia, and the use of bulk carriers further reduced transportation costs. Since 1971 prices have risen but are still quite low in real terms. Supply seems to have outrun demand, as current production is some 20 percent below capacity. Furthermore, price elasticity of supply is high because nearly 90 percent of world production is from open pit mines, and these can be expanded significantly with a two and a half year lead time.

On the demand side, the expansion of the world iron ore market depends upon the growth of aggregate output in the industrialized countries. For the world as a whole, the responsiveness to price changes in iron ore by purchasers is small. Higher energy prices will make steel production more competitive compared with aluminum and plastics. On the other hand, owing to these high prices, transportation equipment (especially automobiles) will be lighter and more compact, utilizing less steel. The net impact is hard to gauge, but given the expanding availability of iron ore, a price rise in real terms does not appear to be likely during the 1970s. North America will decline as a steel importing area up to 1980, and Latin American exports will be primarily directed to Japan and Europe.

Mineral Resources and Law of the Sea. Controversy surrounding the proposed Law of the Sea (LOS) treaty is likely to continue in the near future. The debate has divided developed and underdeveloped, coastal and land-locked nations, and, more importantly for our inquiry, Latin America and the United States.

Two preliminary statements must be made, however. First, there are other issues regarding the LOS controversy besides mineral resources, but ultimately the last may prove the most important and difficult to resolve. Second, there is as yet no common Latin American position on all the issues involved in the LOS, but there is now a minimal consensus on issues that directly affect mineral resources.

Broadly speaking, this consensus involves the concepts of the patrimonial and territorial seas. By the 1970s most Latin American countries claimed some degree of sovereignty over living and mineral resources in an economic zone that extended up to 200 miles off their coasts. In addition to the patrimonial sea, many Latin American states also claimed territorial rights of up to 200 miles. Such rights usually included some control over navigation and overflight, among other things. But the claim to territorial sovereignty, especially in its extreme form (200 miles) has not been widely asserted in Latin America. Indeed, most states which claim a territorial sea, in fact, reserve only the first twelve miles under their strict control.

The United States has been embroiled in disputes with Latin America over these claims since the early 1950s, especially on the matter of the patrimonial sea in general, and fishing in coastal waters in particular. American fishing boats have been repeatedly seized and in response U.S. legislation was drawn up providing sanctions against the offending nations.

That policy did not work. Consequently the United States has altered its position in recent years. The United States would now, for example, accept a twelve-mile territorial sea, but continues to reject control of navigation and aviation rights beyond that point.

On the more complex matter of economic resources, the United States too has shifted its position. In regard to fish, it has adopted the "species approach" which would allow coastal states to regulate the exploitation of local stocks of fish, but would permit only international fisheries organizations to regulate migratory species like tuna.

On the more important issue of minerals, the United States now advocates a "Coastal Seabed Economic Area" in which coastal states can have exclusive rights to mineral resources. The United States has, however, not yet defined the territorial limit of a coastal nation's claim. But the United States has made significant concessions in recent years in regard to the patrimonial sea. Since mineral resources (including petroleum) are thought to be abundant, especially on South America's east coast, and since the United States has a decided lead in recovery technology, the United States and Latin America have much to discuss before those resources will be made available to this country on any terms. The prospects, however, have improved in recent years because of the shifts toward the Latin American position made by the United States.[4]

Latin America as World Oil Supplier

Latin America has been a major source of oil since the early part of the twentieth century and it may well continue to be through the end of the century. Production outpaced consumption in the region until the mid-1960s, when net exports reached a peak of 2.7 million barrels a day in 1964. Since that time, however, Latin America has become a declining net oil exporting region, as consumption rose faster than production, owing to the rapid industrialization of the region. However, large untapped reserves in Mexico and Argentina may reverse that trend.

For the purpose of analyzing the regional petroleum balance, Latin America can be divided into three categories: net oil exporters (Bolivia, Ecuador, Mexico, Trinidad-Tobago, and Venezuela); countries presently or potentially self-sufficient (Argentina, Colombia, Peru); and net oil importers (Brazil, Central America, Chile, Cuba, Dominican Republic, Haiti, Jamaica, Paraguay, Uruguay).

In 1975, Mexico became a net oil exporter, and Peru may achieve that status by the late 1970s or early 1980s, when its Amazon basin reserves are developed. Argentina, Ecuador, and Mexico are the only other countries that have a significant export potential in the near and medium term. It is unlikely that Colombia will become a significant oil exporting country or that the other net oil-importing countries will become self-sufficient in the near future. The balance of payments and economic growth performance of the net oil-importing countries have suffered considerably from the fourfold OPEC-induced rise in oil prices in 1972-74. This has been particularly true of Brazil where growth rates have dropped more than half in the last three years. These countries compete with the other oil-importing countries of the world, including the United States, for world oil supplies.

Venezuela can be expected to maintain its position as Latin America's most important oil exporting country, at least through the 1980s. It accounts for about 92 percent of the total value of regional exports (1974). Ecuador, Mexico, Trinidad-Tobago, and particularly Bolivia lag far behind, accounting for only 8 percent of total gross exports.

The United States is the major market for regional exports, taking about 50 percent of Venezuela's exports (1974) and about 70 percent of all Caribbean exports, which totaled 2,540,000 barrels a day in 1973. Over half of Latin American oil exports are refined petroleum products, much of which goes to the United States in the form of residual fuel oil.

Most of Latin America's petroleum has been discovered, pumped, and marketed by private foreign oil companies—for the most part, U.S.-owned. But the share of the region's oil produced by private firms has been declining sharply since the early 1960s, as state-owned oil enterprises have increasingly taken over private concessions and expanded production in new areas. Foreign oil companies have been expropriated in Peru (the International Petroleum Company has taken over in 1968), and Venezuela (oil company concessions expired in 1975) and state petroleum companies have a monopoly of production in Argentina, Bolivia, Brazil, Chile, and Mexico.

Traditional concession arrangements still exist in some countries (notably Bolivia, Ecuador, and Trinidad-Tobago), but government policy in Latin America is clearly shifting away from concessions and toward service contracts. Joint venture companies formed by state oil companies and private firms are also under consideration by many countries. The end result of this process will be to confine the private oil companies to being sellers of services, which does not necessarily imply the termination of private-sector oil exploration and development. The large number of firms working in Bolivia, Ecuador, and Peru confirm that service contracts can still be profitable for privately owned oil companies.

The total proved reserves of crude oil in Latin America are approximately 40 billion barrels with some 15 billion (37.0 percent) in Venezuela and 13.6 billion (33.5 percent) in Mexico and 2.5 billion (6.6 percent) in Ecuador, Peru, and Trinidad-Tobago, respectively. According to preliminary reports, Mexico has substantial newly-proven reserves, but no authoritative official estimates are yet available. Venezuela's share of regional reserves has declined steadily over the past decade, while Mexico and Ecuador have emerged with the region's second and third largest reserves (see Table I-5).

A word of warning: Far more oil may ultimately be recovered than is indicated in the figures of proved oil reserves. Venezuela's total oil resources alone are estimated at 150 billion barrels, ten times the proved reserves, *excluding* the heavy oil belt. Additional proved reserves are most likely to be found in the southern zone of Lake Maracaibo, the Gulf of Venezuela, and the Gulf of Vela. In addition, the so-called heavy oil belt along the Orinoco River is estimated to have 700-800 billion of barrels of oil, 10 percent of which is capable of recovery with present technology.

Another area likely to yield substantial new oil supplies in the near future is the Upper Amazon Basin of Brazil, Ecuador, and Peru, and the adjacent Beni area in Bolivia, which is now being actively explored by foreign oil companies.

Even more promising is Mexico, particularly its southeastern region, and Argentina's continental shelf. A recent official Mexican statement speculates that possible reserves amount between 30 to 60 billion barrels.[5] Argentina's new military government has announced a new policy of accepting foreign oil company assistance in the development of offshore deposits that may run to, according to a U.S. geological survey estimate, from 40 to 200 billion barrels of oil.[6]

Even if the minimum figures prove correct, the two countries alone would become major world producers of petroleum, and Latin America would once more become a major energy producer by the last decade of this century.

Table I-5
Latin American Proved Reserves of Oil, January 1975
(millions of barrels)

Country	Oil	Percent
Argentina	2,346	5.8
Barbados	25	a
Bolivia	250	.6
Brazil	775	1.9
Chile	200	.5
Colombia	900	2.2
Ecuador	2,500	6.2
Mexico	13,582	33.5
Peru	3,500	6.2
Trinidad-Tobago	2,500	6.2
Venezuela	15,000	36.9
Total	40,578	100.0

aLess than one percent.
Source: *Gas & Oil Journal*, Tulsa, Oklahoma, December 30, 1974. Reprinted with permission.

Conventional Arms Transfer

The transfer of conventional arms to Latin America over the past decade has been modest in comparison with other regions (see Table I-6) of the world. Latin American arms imports have never reached $500 million in any single year, but there has been a slight increase in their value in the 1970s. The major arms-importing countries over the past decade have been Argentina, Brazil, Cuba, Peru, and Venezuela.

Latin America's arms expenditures also have been comparatively modest, with their share of GNP remaining constant during the decade (about 2 percent or below)—the lowest of any geographic region. Latin America's per capita military expenditures have never exceeded $12 a year, and in 1973 were $8 a year, compared to the world average of $62 and the developed country average of $206. The average per capita cost of weapons purchases by the Latin American countries during the decade (subtracting known grant aid) was as follows: over $35—Cuba; $20—Peru and Venezuela; $10-$15—Chile and Argentina. All the other Latin American nations, including Brazil, spent less than $10 per capita on guns.

In the 1961-65 period, the United States was the major arms supplier to the Latin American nations with the exception of Cuba. By the 1970s, the situation has changed radically. France introduced *Mirage* supersonic fighters, after the

Table I-6
Military Expenditures, by Developing Region, 1973

	1973 Military Expenditures in Constant Dollars			
Region	Amount (billions U.S.$)	As % GNP	$ Per Capita	(1963-73) % Growth Rate
Africa	2.1	2.8[a]	7	6.5[b]
Latin America	2.9	1.3	8	3.9
Near East	10.1[c]	11.9[a]	56[a]	14.7[b]
East Asia	19.5	3.4	14	7.5
South Asia	2.4	3.5	3	2.9
OPEC	5.8[c]	5.7[a]	16[a]	11.9[b]
Developing Countries	32.9	5.6	11	7.2
Developed Countries	208.8	5.7	206	2.0
World	241.7	5.6	62	2.6

[a]1972.
[b]1963-72.
[c]Current dollars.
Source: Adapted from *World Military Expenditures and Arms Trade, 1963-73* (Washington, D.C.: U.S. Arms Control and Disarmament Agency, 1975), pp. 14-18.

U.S. Congress refused to permit the sale of its sophisticated warplanes to Peru. In the first half of the 1960s, the Soviet Union introduced massive amounts of military equipment into Cuba—more than twice the amount the rest of the world exported to Latin America. By 1975, Cuba had received over $2 billion in Soviet arms while smaller amounts went to Peru. The result is that Latin America has turned to Western Europe, Canada, and the Soviet Union for about 60 percent of its arms imports over the last decade.

France and Russia had been the primary suppliers of tanks; the British have provided naval vessels and aircraft, and West Germany has mainly supplied armored vehicles and naval vessels. Canada has increased its sales of subsonic aircraft while, recently, U.S. sales of F-5, A-37, and C-130 have surged, and the United States still dominates the helicopter market.

Meanwhile, Latin American indigenous arms production is expanding rapidly, with Argentina and Brazil in the lead followed by Peru and Colombia. Aside from light arms, such items as jet aircraft, helicopters, destroyers, submarines, tanks, and missiles are manufactured or assembled locally under coproduction or licensing agreements. The volume of intra-Latin American arms trade is still small, but it is also on the increase. Brazil is already beginning to export armored personnel carriers, and this may be followed soon by fighter aircraft.

The low level of Latin America's expenditures on military equipment reflects, in part, the lack of any credible external threat to the nations of the region. The near absence of any serious military conflict between the Latin American nations for three generations fortifies this perception, although military rivalries and revanchist claims continue. Latin American armies are primarily oriented toward internal threats, which explains the budgetary emphasis on manpower and the paucity of sophisticated equipment.

Cooperative regional efforts to limit and control the buildup of arms have a long and unhappy history. They have had little or no discernible impact on actual arms acquisitions. The Declaration of Ayacucho, signed in Lima in December 1974, is the latest effort to restrict the arms race in Latin America, but its value is vitiated by its restricted coverage to the six Andean countries, Argentina, and Panama,[e] while a major arms-purchaser, like Brazil, is not constrained by the declaration. Furthermore, it is clear that it is not even binding on the Andean countries, since none of them have interrupted their acquisition of new arms and military equipment overseas. Recent arms purchases by Chile, Peru, and other countries continue unabated.

Nuclear Technology Transfer

At present, no country in Latin America possesses nuclear weapons. But neither Argentina nor Brazil has disguised its intention to build and test nuclear

---

[e]The Declaration of Ayacucho signed in Lima, Peru, on December 9, 1974, included the signatures of the presidents of Peru, Bolivia, and Venezuela, representatives from Argentina, Colombia, Chile and Ecuador, and General Torrijos, listed as the Panamanian chief of government.

Table I-7
U.S. Military Sales Orders
(thousands of U.S. dollars)

	FY 1950-1965	FY 1966	FY 1967	FY 1968	FY 1969	FY 1970
Argentina	50,319	7,231	6,509	14,859	3,973	10,933
Brazil	42,902	223	26,451	4,265	11,413	2,458
Chile	18,314	1,058	2,560	4,043	1,675	7,569
Colombia	10,331	496	98	56	141	158
Mexico	10,466	101	802	96	399	12
Peru	25,089	2,664	3,338	1,220	980	2,200
Venezuela	81,163	11,687	9,769	1,138	1,168	777

U.S. Military Sales Credits
(thousands of U.S. dollars)

	FY 1955-1965	FY 1966	FY 1967	FY 1968	FY 1969	FY 1970
Argentina	5,773	12,955	9,250	9,595	11,000	–
Brazil	23,400	11,607	18,434	18,500	–	–
Chile	1,847	1,304	–	5,981	11,000	–
Colombia	–	–	–	–	–	–
Mexico	4,298	–	–	–	–	–
Peru	18,381	1,159	–	–	–	–
Venezuela	75,189	10,000	–	–	–	–

Source: U.S. Arms Control and Disarmament Agency.

explosives for peaceful purposes—most likely around the mid-1980s. The sole distinction between nuclear weapons and peaceful nuclear devices is, of course, the intent of the user.

Argentina and Brazil have the two most advanced and sophisticated civil nuclear energy programs, together with the greatest military potential in Latin America. Chile, Cuba, Mexico, and other countries trail far behind. The scope and depth of Argentina's nuclear energy and research program gives it an edge on Brazil, although this situation should change radically before 1985. Both countries have been acquiring the knowledge, the raw materials, and the infrastructure necessary for the production of nuclear explosives and weapons. They oppose international controls that would limit their programs for the peaceful use of atomic energy, including nuclear explosives for engineering purposes.

Argentina possesses the most advanced nuclear energy program and it has built five research reactors, one power reactor (Atucha 319 mw), with another (Rio Tercero-600 mw) under construction (see Table I-8). The five research

FY 1971	FY 1972	FY 1973	FY 1974	FY 1975	FY 1950-1975
12,808	15,932	16,481	8,618	14,100	161,763
17,845	33,801	16,766	69,059	27,025	252,207
2,889	6,260	14,975	75,104	29,038	163,485
2,168	5,397	1,197	1,090	965	22,098
437	175	893	411	153	13,944
1,511	900	24,811	46,989	23,599	133,300
1,643	43,496	24,124	4,884	33,540	213,389

FY 1971	FY 1972	FY 1973	FY 1974	FY 1975	FY 1955-1975
16,000	15,000	11,500	22,500	30,000	143,573
9,400	20,000	15,000	51,743	60,000	228,083
5,000	10,000	12,400	15,000	–	62,532
5,000	7,250	10,000	–	–	22,250
–	–	–	–	–	4,298
–	–	–	15,000	20,500	55,040
7,400	7,500	7,573	7,500	–	115,162

reactors are fueled by enriched uranium obtained from the United States and subject to International Atomic Energy Association (IAEA) safeguards. Argentina has far more uranium reserves than any other Latin American country, ample for its own needs plus a surplus for occasional export. It intends to develop a nuclear power program with a generating capacity of 30,000 mw (30 percent of the national total) by the year 2000. The historic and continuing rivalry between Argentina and Brazil is also a factor that contributes to Argentina's desire to gain international prestige as a member of the nuclear club.

Brazil's varied nuclear research program includes four operating research reactors fueled by enriched uranium supplied by the United States, and one power reactor (Angra dos Reis-626 mw) under construction.

In June 1975, West Germany signed a $4 billion nuclear technology agreement with Brazil that will provide a uranium enrichment facility, a fuel fabrication unit, nuclear reactors, and a facility for reprocessing spent fuel into plutonium which could be used to make nuclear weapons. This in effect would mean that Brazil would possibly acquire a complete fuel cycle by the mid-1980s.

Table I-8
Research and Power Reactors in Latin America

	Research	Power
Argentina	5	319 mw Atucha (I.O.)-natural uranium
		600 mw Rio Tercero (U.C.)-natural uranium
Brazil	4	626 mw Angra do Reis (U.C.)-enriched uranium
Mexico	4	660 mw Laguna Verde Ver I (U.C.)-enriched uranium
		660 mw Laguna Verde Ver II (U.C.)-enriched uranium
Cuba	1	
Chile	1	
Venezuela	1	
Colombia	1	
Uruguay	1	

Note: I.O.—In Operation. U.C.—Under Construction.

Brazil's agreement to submit to international controls for only part of the fuel cycle has aroused fears that West German technology may be used to build nuclear weapons and trigger nuclear proliferation in Latin America. In any event, there is every indication that Brazil is making a comprehensive effort to become preeminent in the nuclear energy field in Latin America. In the meantime, no other country in the hemisphere has taken so strong and public a stance regarding the validity of the peaceful applications of nuclear technology.[7]

At present Cuba has only one nuclear reactor, supplied by the Soviet Union. But at the end of 1974 Fidel Castro declared Cuba would install its first nuclear power reactor by 1980, and another before 1985. While Cuba is a member of the IAEA, it has refused to subject its research reactor to international safeguards. But there is a small possibility of Cuba's accepting its obligations as a cooperative member of the Latin American system when and if U.S.-Cuban détente proceeds. Cuba might then be persuaded by Mexico and others to sign the Treaty of Tlatelolco and assume a nonnuclear weapons status. If Cuba refuses (as well it might) the only safeguard against the development of at least crude weapons by Cuba are the expense and Soviet reluctance to part with military secrets.

The Latin American denuclearization movement has resulted in the 1967 Treaty for Prohibition of Nuclear Weapons (Treaty of Tlatelolco), and the Organization for the Prohibition of Nuclear Weapons (OPANAL). So far Mexico is the only Latin American nation with a nuclear weapons potential to have submitted its entire program to the safeguard procedures of the IAEA. Other Latin American countries (Chile, Colombia, Cuba, Peru, Uruguay, and Venezuela) have either acquired research reactors or have expressed interest in developing a nuclear research capability.

The Tlatelolco Treaty is a regional version of the Nuclear Non-Proliferation Treaty of 1968, but is more restrictive, since it also prohibits the establishment of nuclear weapons bases in Latin America. At present, twenty-two (out of twenty-four) Latin American states have signed the treaty, and it is in force in eighteen states that have ratified it. But OPANAL has been considerably weakened by the refusal of Argentina and Brazil to ratify the treaty and the inadequate financial support from the treaty signatories.

Apart from Latin American efforts to develop nuclear explosives, another grave danger to hemispheric security is the possibility of nuclear theft, extortion, and terrorism. Nuclear installations, particularly in less stable countries, are vulnerable to terrorist activity. Furthermore, unclassified information now exists to enable well-trained persons who are able to acquire fissionable material to construct a portable nuclear weapon, and the massive spread of fissionable materials increases the likelihood that some will fall into the hands of unscrupulous individuals or groups. There are more than fifty well-financed and armed international terrorist groups, five of them in Latin America. Thus, the rise of international terrorism accompanied by the proliferation of fissionable materials further increases the risks of criminal misuse of nuclear technology.

The theft of fissionable material is by no means a remote possibility. In Argentina, there has been at least one case of reported loss of fissionable materials, and an armed terrorist group attacked and briefly held part of the Atucha nuclear power plant in March 1973.

In brief, the spread of nuclear technology in Latin America could pose a serious threat in the years ahead. Argentina and Brazil have announced that they intend to develop nuclear explosives for peaceful purposes. Both countries will be capable of exploding a nuclear device before the mid-1980s. In view of their intense national rivalry, if one country exploded a nuclear device domestic pressures would compel the other country to follow suit. Only Mexico seems to be fully aware of the growing dangers of nuclear technology in Latin America.

Limits of Internationalism

The preceding sections have indicated some of the forces which are working to create Latin America's more balanced relationship with the world beyond the North Atlantic. It may be useful at this point to present a brief summary of them.

1. There is a widespread desire in Latin America to diversify markets and sources of supply of capital and technology in order to promote rapid economic development and reduction of vulnerability to external economic forces, especially those emanating from the United States.
2. The protectionist trend in the United States has adversely affected the

importing of some labor-intensive Latin American manufactured goods such
as textiles and footwear. Countries like Brazil, whose shoe exports were
subject to restrictions in U.S. markets, now seek markets elsewhere.

3. The preferential trading arrangements between the EEC and the less developed countries of Africa and Asia discriminate against Latin American
   exports of raw materials and tropical commodities. The result has been an
   intensified search for new markets outside Western Europe.
4. The success of OPEC in raising oil prices has also provided a powerful
   stimulus to establish producer associations in Latin America with other
   countries in Africa and Asia with the aim of regulating supply, raising export
   prices, and increasing foreign exchange earnings.
5. Owing to the balance of payments pressures of the net oil-importing countries
   in Latin America (whose primary commodity—sugar, cacao, coffee, copper,
   etc.—export prices entered a new period of decline in 1975), OPEC has also
   generated additional pressures on these countries to seek new markets and
   diversify exports.
6. The belief of some regional political leaders that Latin American and Third
   World unity can create irresistible pressures on the industrial world to meet
   their political and economic demands, and ultimately restructure the international economic system in their favor. Therefore, these leaders are making a
   considerable effort to establish close and regular political consultation and
   cooperation with various groups of developing countries.
7. The emergence of the Middle Eastern oil-exporting countries as major net
   exporters of capital has led to the establishment of completely new financial
   and economic relations on the part of some Latin American countries
   (notably Brazil and Argentina) during the past few years.
8. In some countries, such as Brazil and Guyana, new political and commercial
   relations have been created with Third World countries based on ethnic ties.
9. The revolution in global transportation and communications has made the
   remote areas of the world more accessible to the Latin American countries,
   thereby facilitating the interchange of goods, services, and people.

A review of Latin America's political and commercial opening up to Asia,
Africa, the Middle East, and the Socialist camp indicates that the intensified
political interaction has not been accompanied by any radical reorientation of
the region's international economic relations which are still concentrated on the
North Atlantic (United States, Canada, and Western Europe) trading area. The
only exception is Japan, which is rapidly emerging as a major new economic
partner for a growing number of Latin American countries.

There are, however, obvious limits to the process of diversification of Latin
America's political and economic relations. A crucial fact is that the North
Atlantic area plus Japan will dominate the world economy for the remainder of
this century. Presently accounting for about 70 percent of world trade and

about 60 percent of Gross World Product, the North Atlantic-Japanese trading area will account for an even larger share of world trade by 1980, and its share of GWP will not be much lower. This vast trading area will continue to offer the Latin American countries their major markets for their traditional mineral and agricultural exports—and, increasingly, for their manufactured goods—for the remainder of the century. Inevitably, it will be the dominant supplier of development finance, technology, management skills, and equipment essential for Latin America's further economic transformation.

Another crucial fact is that geography, climate, natural resources, demography, and levels of technology impose powerful constraints, as Castro's Cuba has discovered, on the extent to which the Latin American countries, particularly the smaller Caribbean republics, are able to establish significant economic relations with new regions outside of the Western Hemisphere and North Atlantic area. As the natural limits to effective diversification of relations are reached over the next decade, the superficiality of Latin American voluntarist orthodoxies (the belief that the Latin masses are infinitely malleable, that political will is all that is needed to transform societies and drastically alter old economic relationships),[f] will become manifest.

For some time it has been evident that the international system has entered a period of significant adjustment. In the forefront of these changes has been the insertion of Latin America into the world economy and its deeper involvement in the world political agenda—commodities, technology transfer, multinational corporations, and nuclear proliferation. This inexorable historical process clearly offers new opportunities for constructive cooperation between the Latin American countries and their traditional political and economic partners in North America and Western Europe. For these regions—whatever their differences and however imperfectly—share a common political tradition and a common cultural heritage that respects human rights.

Notes

1. Herbert Goldhamer, *The Foreign Power in Latin America* (Princeton, New Jersey: Princeton University Press, 1972), p. 33.
2. So far Latin America has received only a fraction of Japan's total aid program (4.6 percent in 1973). According to one expert: "The Japanese government seems to consider the Latin American economies to be 'mid-developing', and government policy is that 'economic cooperation to mid-developing countries should be extended through private resources rather than on an official

---

[f]This belief was most vigorously expounded by Che Guevara and Fidel Castro, and reached its logical limits in the campaign to harvest ten million tons of sugar in 1970. Others in Latin America, primarily the Peruvian generals, the Allende regime in Chile, and to a lesser extent General Perón's Argentina held similar views. In each case (including Cuba) the rhetoric as well as policy has been trimmed back.

basis'." "The 1974 White Paper on the Current State of Problems of Economic Cooperation" published by the Japanese Ministry of International Trade and Industry, and quoted in Hiroya Ichikawa, "Japan's Economic Relationship with Latin America" in Roger W. Fontaine and James D. Theberge, (eds.), *Latin America's New Internationalism: The End of Hemispheric Isolation* (New York: Praeger Publishers, 1976).

3. See U.S. Commission for Latin America Report: *El Desarrollo Latinoamericano y la Coyuntura Económica Internacional* (E/CEPAL/981 Vol. I, 1975).

4. For a comprehensive examination of the Law of the Sea question including the Latin American view see *Ocean Policy Project Conference*, Airlie House, October 21-24, 1974 and Karin Hjertonsson, *The New Law of the Sea: Influence of the Latin American States on Recent Developments of the Law of the Sea* (Stockholm: P.A. Norstedt and Soners Forlag, 1974). For the U.S. position on the Law of the Sea see Ann L. Hollick "What to Expect from a Sea Treaty" *Foreign Policy*, Spring 1975, and her "The Problem of Territorial Waters: Options" (unpublished manuscript: July 1974).

5. *Excelsior* (Mexico City), May 5, 1976.

6. Bernardo F. Grosslins, *Latin America's Petroleum Prospects in the Energy Crisis*, Geological Survey Bulletin No. 11 (Washington: U.S. Government Printing Office, 1975), p. 3.

7. Brazil's hopes for peaceful uses of nuclear explosions are outlined in Roger W. Fontaine's *Brazil & the United States* (Washington, D.C.: American Enterprise Institute, 1975), pp. 108-110, and the Brazilian weekly magazine *Manchete*, April 15, 1967, pp. 51-55.

II Latin America's Quest for Order and Progress

Latin America's quest for political stability, social justice and economic progress is one of the great dramas of the Western Hemisphere. As it unfolds, it will undoubtedly have a profound impact on United States relations with the region.

The following political and economic forecasts are obviously subject to considerable error, and they are made with a salutary respect for the volatile and unpredictable nature of Latin American politics. Nevertheless, they have been made in the belief that the analysis of political, economic and social trends in the region may provide insights into the special challenges and opportunities open to the United States for strengthening and recasting our traditional ties for friendship and cooperation.

The following comments are directed largely at Spanish America. Brazil will be treated separately since it is a special case of a continent size country that has been able to establish authoritarian political order and economic progress based upon an expanding mixed economy.

Prospects for Spanish America

General

In the next several years, Spanish America is not likely to face political and economic problems radically different from those its leaders have had to deal with in recent years. Most countries have achieved respectable, and in some cases impressive, economic growth. The classic problem of maldistribution of income and wealth continues to be a major one in most of Latin America, although efforts are being made in many countries to raise the level of income of the rural and urban poor, and correct the worst inequities. The prospects for sweeping social revolution (as in Cuba and Peru) appear to be poor but some of the military regimes that have emerged since the mid-sixties are likely to press forward with significant social reforms that benefit the rural and urban poor. The steady shift to military-authoritarian rule in most of Latin America over the past decade has ended comparatively liberal-democratic governments in Argentina, Chile, Peru, and Uruguay. The "new military" became disillusioned with liberal democracy because it seemed to provide a spawning ground for internal subversion carried out by radical groups espousing some form of Marxist ideology.

Nevertheless, a pendulum swing back towards civilian rule can be expected within the next five to ten years or even sooner. The reestablishment of political and economic order in countries like Argentina, Chile and Uruguay; the waning legitimacy of military rule as the internal crises become manageable; and, the rising popular pressures for the restitution of constitutional and civilian rule will tend to encourage the resurgence of new forms of representative government, perhaps better adapted to Latin conditions.

Since 1960, the Latin American countries (with the exception of Cuba, Haiti and Uruguay) have achieved steady and often impressive economic expansion. In varying degrees, most Latin American countries benefited from the economic boom of the industrial countries, and this was particularly evident in the early seventies as commodity prices rose dramatically. In many countries, a new middle class emerged during this period and the benefits of economic growth have come to be shared more widely. Nevertheless, serious social and economic problems still remain as a challenge to governments in nearly all countries.

Social and Economic Problems

Spanish America is living through the unsettling period of profound social modernization. Indeed, it is likely that the pace of modernization will be accelerated as the least developed countries (some of which are found in the Caribbean area) more fully adopt the social and economic institutions of the more economically advanced countries. By social modernization is meant a fundamental shift in beliefs, values, and institutions—from those associated with the traditional world (rural, religious, parochial) to those associated with the modern world (urban, secular, cosmopolitan)—as a result of the spread of literacy, communications (especially the expansion of the mass media), and urbanization.[1] But the transformation is still far from complete. Thus while old values have disintegrated, and new, commonly accepted ones, are not yet established, most Latin American countries will continue to suffer from social fragmentation.

Social modernization will resolve some problems but create additional ones. Furthermore, an adjunct phenomenon, rapid regional population growth (2.5 percent or more annually), will add to the difficulties involved in social modernization.[2] By the year 2000, for example, demographic densities generally will not be critical (El Salvador, Haiti, and perhaps Mexico are exceptions), but rapid demographic growth will put additional strains on available resources. More immediately worrisome than aggregate population growth is the rate of urbanization.

Large cities like Mexico City and Caracas are increasing their size from 6 to 8 percent a year—more than double the population growth rate.[3] This is significant because these large urban areas are the political nerve centers of the region. Riots, strikes, coups, and an occasional election are carried out in the megalopolitan capitals—Buenos Aires, Santiago, Lima—not the countryside. And as long as the City remains attractive and the rural areas are neglected by urban politicians (whose power is increasingly dependent on satisfying urban demands, such as low subsidized prices for food), this trend will continue.

The Latin American countries will continue to improve communications and increase literacy. In the urban areas at least, even the poor have access to television, and the transistor radio culture has spread to the remote rural areas. The absolute number of adult literates should increase, and in some cases, the literacy percentage will go up too.[4] The result of all of this will not be a "revolution of rising expectations," but there will be a modest increase in the number of demands made by more and more people.

Political decision-making will be more complicated in the coming two decades. Because the bulk of the resources allocated for improving communications and education will continue to be committed to the already developed urban areas, especially the capital cities, political leaders will be able to satisfy (though only barely) urban demands, but this will only help stimulate greater demands, particularly from well-organized groups. Furthermore, the improvement of city life and the consequent relative neglect of the rural areas will only further encourage continued migration. The cumulative effect of all of this in the 1980s might well be the kind of social unrest that had been predicted for the 1960s.

Social modernization, therefore, may not have the positive effects it is supposed to have, but on balance may be profoundly destabilizing in the coming decades.[5] What should make this problem particularly acute by 1985 is the likelihood that social modernization will not be matched by the ability of the state to satisfy the growing demands of an urban society. Rapid economic growth will not be adequate to ameliorate the social problems and tensions. In the past decade in many countries import-substitution possibilities have been exhausted, agriculture was neglected, foreign investment was treated badly, and a large public enterprise and social service sector was built up, which led to spectacularly unbalanced budgets and runaway inflation.

This trend can be seen most clearly in the relatively advanced countries in Spanish America: Argentina, Chile, and Uruguay. With their European populations and rich natural resources, they attracted foreign capital and technology in the nineteenth century and as a consequence developed rapidly. But their growth had slowed by the 1930s, and since World War II the growth performance of these countries has not lived up to earlier expectations and at present there appears to be small hope that this will change in the near future.

Some of the smaller, less developed countries—Bolivia, Paraguay, Ecuador, and the Central American countries (except Costa Rica)—may experience slower rates of social modernization than the others but that will be accompanied by varying rates of economic growth. By 1985, therefore, and through the subsequent decade, dramatic changes will not be apparent in the smaller countries. But the bulk of Spanish America's population will be experiencing the social tensions and demands of the modernization process and relatively slow growth performance. Budgets will remain unbalanced and low food and public utility prices will be maintained, which will keep relative peace in the cities but discourage increased production on the farms.

Political Problems

At the root of the problems faced by Spanish American governments is the political process itself. Government has steadily assumed more and more responsibility for running society; it has set wage scales for private industry as well as for the governmental bureaucracy, for example, and fixed the price of food, public utilities, transportation, and even luxury goods. But while the responsibilities of government have grown, administrative efficiency and sound management have not. The political process remains highly personalistic. If a group has a grievance, it does not work through organized political parties (even when they exist) to get candidates elected.

Nor do groups bother lobbying the legislature, the courts, or even the bureaucracy, since these often possess little independent power themselves. Instead, groups aim their demands or protests directly at the powerful chief executive, civilian or military, and they often do so in the streets. A president who has been elected with the help of a political party often finds the party too divided or too poorly organized to muster effective support for his programs. The result is a surrender to one group's claims which often stimulates other groups to press theirs either in counterprotest or merely to duplicate the success of the first group. This process can be kept at a tolerable level until excessive demands are placed on the scarce resources of the economy, leaving organized groups such as labor unions, students, shopkeepers, and junior officers even more dissatisfied and thus more willing to resort to violence.

The result of this demand overload will continue to be endemic, and accompanied normally by small-scale, internal violence. Strikes, riots, terrorism, and coups will continue, though widespread rural insurgency shows little likelihood of revival in the foreseeable future. But several countries where class hatred has increased, possibly Argentina, Chile, Colombia, or the Dominican Republic, could suffer from violent civil wars.

All this violence, however, is unlikely to produce a major social and political revolution in Spanish America in which the old regime is completely destroyed and a new, more stable order is imposed. The basic reason is that no group, no matter how well organized and bent on violence, will be able to marshal the broad support required for such an undertaking. The political leaders prone to such a course are middle class in origin, but they cannot lead an already badly divided middle class, and they are unable to make successful appeals to the unorganized poor. Moreover, in many countries the rural areas (often populated by Indians who live in a world unto themselves) are difficult to communicate with, much less politicize, and thus will offer no greater opportunities for Castro-style guerrilla insurgencies than they did in the 1960's.

The inability to bring off a revolution, however, will not lessen the turmoil. Furthermore, new actors may add to the confusion. Radical priests may become increasingly important as organizers and promoters of popular protest movements. During the next decade, however, the Church's hierarchy may well become disillusioned with the lack of positive results and, consequently, alarmed over the divisions that clerical political radicalism will cause within the Church—at least alarmed enough to crack down on rebel clergy. Whether it succeeds in imposing discipline, however, is quite another matter.

The traditional method of halting political violence has been a military takeover. Until now, the military's first reason for seizing control has been to preserve, and sometimes extend, its institutional interests. The armed forces have been most likely to move when threatened by large budget cuts, the organization of armed labor militias, civilian-encouraged noncommissioned officer insubordination or uncontrolled revolutionary violence. Internal disorder and the corruption of civilian politicians have been somewhat less compelling reasons for military takeover as has the need to modernize the country.[6]

Now the temptation for many military rulers is to remove themselves from power in order to protect the institutional integrity of the armed forces. Spanish American societies are increasingly complex politically and, therefore, more difficult to govern. A ruling junta soon finds itself divided on a large range of questions and in order to stay reasonably united the officers often are under some pressure to return control to the civilians. This tendency will be reinforced as officers increasingly realize that they have no special skills or formulas for transforming countries. The result by the 1980's is likely to be a return of power to civilian leadership, less military rule and fewer coups.

A possibly significant variation occurs when the military provides the radical leadership needed for an attempt at imposing revolution from above. Generals

Velasco in Peru and Torres in Bolivia are examples of this phenomenon. No doubt others will try to imitate their examples in the future, but to carry out such a revolution it is first necessary to keep the officer corps united, and this has so far proved impossible to do.

Political disorder and economic stagnation have not occurred to the extent predicted for Latin America only a few years ago. That disaster scenario rested on the alleged existence of "the revolution of rising expectations." This "revolution," as a description of empirical reality, is of dubious validity and therefore an inadequate rationale for policymakers. It begs precise definition and rests on a simplistic formula for human action—that the poor are quickly learning about the good life; therefore that they have come to expect rapid improvement in their lives, and failing that, they will rebel.

There is a growing body of evidence that dismisses this model as too simple. In the first place, the groups historically involved in most Latin American violence—students, organized labor, and junior officers—belong to the relatively privileged strata. Second, the poor, including the urban poor, seem to have a different view of the world than earlier hypothesized. Recent migrants from the countryside to the city have reported feeling that their lives have improved and they were optimistic about further improvements, especially for their children. There is little evidence to support the notion that profound frustration of expectations among the poor is occurring now on a large scale. Long-time city residents or even second generation urban poor are not frustrated to any great degree, either. Their expectations are not much out of line with actual possibilities ("reality trims expectations"), and indeed a majority of them have better jobs than their fathers.[7]

Radical groups, furthermore, have not been able to exploit the misery that does exist. Those who are genuinely frustrated are far more likely to resort to apathy, alcohol, or religion than to political action. Such political activity as exists is extremely sporadic and tends to support conservative-authoritarian politicians (and ex-dictators) like Rojas Pinilla of Colombia, Juan Perón of Argentina, and Pérez Jiménez of Venezuela. Short of extreme economic reversal, the trend of passive support for the system among Latin America's urban poor will probably continue through the next decade.[a]

Violence should then be endemic in the coming decade in those societies that are the most fragmented socially, the most economically stagnant and ruled by corrupt and repressive political leaders. Since instigators of violence (ranging from urban guerrilla assassins to shopkeepers who go on one-day strikes) usually come from the middle class and are from relatively advanced economies, countries such as Argentina, Uruguay, Chile, Colombia and Peru, may be the most turbulent in the coming decade.

---

[a]Actual violence may occasionally be employed by the poor. But its most important form will be in defense of their possessions; for example, urban squatters have been known to resist police attempts to evict them from land they do not own legally, but very much possess.

On the other hand, the turmoil, while destructive, will not be great enough or sufficiently focused to push any society out of the seemingly endless round of strikes, coups, and acts of terrorism that will plague Spanish America in the coming decades. Radical change resulting from sweeping social revolution is unlikely anywhere in Spanish America but economic and demographic growth will inexorably lead to fundamental socio-economic structural change in the long run.

It is against this background that the human rights question must be considered. Abuses of human rights by Latin American and other governments (in the sense of physical abuses of prisoners or detainees) are nothing new and have a long history. As long as Latin American governments face violent attacks on their authority, grave violations of human rights will occur as official efforts are made to destroy insurgent groups and reestablish domestic peace. In general, human rights flourish only when the basic political order is accepted by nearly all; for without that consensus, non-violent political competition is extraordinarily difficult to maintain.

The culprits will not simply be the right-wing military dictators, however. Human rights have already been violated by left-wing, essentially civilian, regimes (Perón's Argentina, Allende's Chile, and Castro's Cuba) as well as by the highly personalistic regimes of Rafael Trujillo in the Dominican republic and François Duvalier in Haiti. There is no reason to expect that future regimes, of whatever political make-up will be any great respecters of human rights, particularly when any of them are under violent attack. Therefore, there is no end in sight for human rights abuses, even though Latin governments are becoming more aware of the domestic and international political reactions created by gross violations of human rights.

Prospects for Three Major Countries

The political and economic prospects of Latin America are neither uniformly good or bad, but better described as mixed. Some countries obviously will do much better than others in coping with the management of social change and pressures, maintaining rapid economic growth and ensuring political stability. Three countries have been chosen for closer examination in the sections that follow because of their special importance to the United States: Brazil because of its size and potential; Mexico because of its social problems and proximity; and, Venezuela because of its oil and other natural resources.

Brazil

Brazil will not necessarily be immune to the great stresses that the Spanish American societies will be undergoing in the coming two decades. Until 1964,

Brazil experienced nearly all the demographic, economic, and political difficulties that characterize the rest of the region. There is no guarantee that Brazil has escaped them permanently. Again, it must be stressed that the country will have problems, but it should be able to escape the economic and political troubles that continually plague its neighbors. Brazil's economic boom of the late 1960s, and early 1970s is likely to have been a special interlude but it is still a reasonable expectation that the country's growth performance, while slower, will exceed that of most countries in the hemisphere over the next decade.

Why is Brazil different? First, there are Brazil's obvious geographic and resource advantages. With an area of 3.3 million square miles, it is the world's fifth largest country. Moreover, much of that continental land mass is usable even with today's technology (in contrast with that of China, the Soviet Union, and Canada). In addition, Brazil is bordered by weak neighbors and also possesses enormous material resources, although little petroleum.[8] Thus, for example, it has the fourth largest hydroelectric potential in the world.[b] It has the largest amount of yet uncultivated arable land in the world, and that already under cultivation has not reached its potential output; and it contains large quantities of nearly all minerals (including uranium and thorium) necessary for extensive industrialization through the time period under consideration.

Demographically, Brazil has a population of 107 million (1975 estimated), and it is believed that it could reach 215 million by 2000.[9] Brazil has the room for this growth in population, but whether all those new Brazilians will act as a drag or a stimulus to development is not certain. Until very recently no Brazilian leader showed any interest in slowing the population increase. Now, however, in light of the economic downturn, second thoughts on population are being expressed in studies that are circulating among top government officials.[10] Nevertheless, even if the new arguments prove persuasive, no effective national birth control program can be expected for at least five years. The government feels more people are needed to fill the empty spaces (like the Amazon Basin) that overcrowded nations, they assume, will begin to envy. In the meantime, Brazil, unlike its immediate neighbors, has many points of urban growth rather than only one (for example, Argentina's Buenos Aires) and thus can spread the effects of urbanization.[c]

Brazil now has a Gross National Product of nearly $100 billion, and with an 8 percent growth rate it would, in twenty years, have a GNP comparable to that of Japan in the early 1970s.[d]

[b]Brazil does possess enormous deposits of oil-bearing shale that stretch from southern São Paulo to Rio Grande do Sul. By 1985 the Brazilians could, with U.S. help, possess the technology to make the deposits economically worthwhile.

[c]Brazil has five cities with more than one million people, plus others, like Brasilia, which could absorb much of the pressure involved in the will to urbanize.

[d]Brazil has been affected by the world economic recession and growth rates have been low for 1974 and 1975. Our assumption, however, is Brazil will recover in the latter part of 1976.

But landmass, natural resources, and economic vitality are not sufficient explanations for Brazil's distinctiveness. Argentina possesses many of these attributes, though on a smaller scale, but it has experienced slower economic growth due to poor economic management and political instability since World War II. Brazil's success is largely due to the military and civilian elite that took power in April 1964. More precisely, the particular faction of the army that made the major decisions in the critical years after President Goulart's overthrow was qualified to carry out a program of effective reform. Unlike other Latin American officers, many of them had fought in World War II and had thus been able to receive foreign training without developing an inferiority complex. Their experiences had led them to believe in strong government and private enterprise as the two keys to economic development. They were not the simple statists that most Latin American officers are—they did not believe that economic development took place by government fiat.

The Brazilian officers also remained in contact with civilian experts and were willing to use them after they seized power. Their combined efforts proved successful and investor confidence was restored at home and abroad. Unlike other military regimes that have toyed with austerity programs, they stuck to theirs through the necessary lean years until success was achieved.[11] Moreover, the military officers, unlike their Argentine counterparts, were not confronted with well entrenched, highly organized labor and student groups who would have strongly opposed their austerity measures. Brazil, although probably no more cohesive socially than Argentina, was on the other hand less politicized and therefore easier to rule.

The military will remain pretty much in control over the next decade and the top officers will select the chief executives. After the next succession, that is, after 1982, the civilians may well demand a larger voice in such key decisions, and presidential selection then may well resemble the Mexican electoral process in which a small group of perhaps a dozen men (military and civilian, including the incumbent) are consulted before the final choice is made and then ratified by the electorate. By 1986, a civilian may be chosen for the presidency, though he would be following the path Mexico took after 1946 when that country's first civilian took power—twenty-five years after the revolution had been more or less concluded. Much of this will depend on Brazil's economic performance, and to a lesser extent on its ability to win acceptance as a major power.

How smooth the transition to civilian rule will be depends on the military. The sharing of power has not been easy for the officers since they took command. And in Brazil today there is a significant bloc of officers who would oppose any wholesale return to civilian rule and who could hinder even a small or gradual transfer of responsibility despite the fact that most Brazilian officers believe the military is above politics or at least the moderating power—a role it self-consciously assumed after the emperor was overthrown and the republic established in 1889.

Despite differences on succession policy, the basic political system will continue to be supported by a mixed military-civilian elite, although disagreements will arise. (The government's serious dispute with some of the Roman Catholic hierarchy is an example and the amount of electoral success permitted the opposition party, the *Movimento Democrático Brasileiro* [MDB] is another.) This elite will possibly become even more nationalistic by 1985, and its determination to make Brazil a first-class power will be unabated. Thus, its penchant for grand scale projects (such as Brasilia, the Trans-Amazon Highway, nuclear development) will continue, though some of these efforts will prove costly and even court failure and disillusionment. But their accumulated successes should preserve their self-confidence for an intensified effort in the last two decades of this century.

Mexico

Mexico is the most politically stable country in Latin America. Since 1934, it has had a succession of elections and an orderly transfer of power from one government-party presidential candidate to another. The opposition parties in the meantime have been relatively free to operate although largely ineffective. Mexico has also largely avoided internal violence since the 1930s. Serious outbreaks (usually student-led) have occurred only twice in recent years; in 1958 and in 1968. Guerrilla activity, minimal during the 1960s, has increased in the 1970s in both rural and urban areas. The Mexican government, however, has reacted with great force, and by mid-1976 violent opposition was limited to occasional acts of terrorism. The Mexican authorities have been aided in their struggle by the still widely held belief that it is they who represent the Mexican revolution and not the guerrillas.

The economy has grown impressively in the last two decades, and although the rate of growth has dropped slightly in the last few years (from 8 to 9 percent between roughly 1958 and 1965, to 6 to 7 percent between 1966 and 1972), Mexico still possesses some advantages unique in Latin America: the nearby U.S. market, a large tourist industry, a long-term rational foreign investment policy, and political stability.

By 1985 Mexico should continue on its present economic and political course although its institutions, especially the government party, the *Partido Revolucionario Institucional* (PRI), will have to go through periodic renovation. Opposition parties will continue to function, but will not achieve power. Any sign of growing strength on their part will be a spur to government reform or repression.[12] The military will continue to work behind the scenes and there is no reason to believe that its corporate interest will be sufficiently threatened for it to seize control from the civilians.

Mexico has one serious problem, however, which may have serious implications in a decade, and that is its rapid increase in population. At present rates of growth, Mexico's population could be 85 million people, and Mexico, unlike other Latin American countries, does not have the resources to accommodate that many people.

Venezuela

Venezuela has succeeded in recent years in an unlikely enterprise, that is, it has reversed the political and economic trends of its first 140 years of independent existence. Politically, it has had uninterrupted legal rule since 1959, and in 1969 it accomplished a feat unique in Venezuelan history: the party in power surrendered the presidency to the opposition party after a peaceful election. In 1973 that same phenomenon repeated itself when the moderate *Acción Democrática* (AD) candidate defeated the *Comité Organización Política Electoral Independiente* (COPEI) candidate by 400,000 votes.

Economically, the country is strong by average Latin American standards. GNP growth (6.6 percent in 1975) and current per capita income are high (nearly $1,300 in 1970 prices), natural resources are plentiful (especially oil and iron ore), and its foreign trade position is good. There is enough room for a growing population through the rest of the century and the Venezuelans have taken their agricultural problems seriously for over a decade. Problems, of course, exist: until recently, the Venezuelan economy depended on oil while its manufacturing sector (even by Latin American standards) remained a high cost, inefficient one. Moreover, the government's recent nationalization of the oil industry and its strict interpretation of the Andean investment code will greatly discourage new foreign investment. Yet Venezuelan officials believe that their greatly expanded returns from petroleum will give them the resources needed to establish a balanced modern economy by the 1980s. Their optimism is probably exaggerated because the professional and technical managerial manpower required to effectively utilize the oil revenues for development purposes is in scarce supply.

Despite the fact that the pattern of political stability and democracy is recently established, Venezuela has the best chance, after Mexico and Costa Rica, to maintain moderate stable civilian rule. Poor political and economic management leading to widespread disillusionment with constitutional government, could threaten Venezuela's stability.

However, if the country maintains its pace of development and there is no political deterioration, violent opposition to the government (such as rural or urban insurgency) is unlikely to be a major problem.

Some Possible Trends

A number of political trends of consequence to the United States could become apparent in the coming decade.

First, while there is almost no chance that a rural-based guerrilla army could seize power anywhere in Latin America, there is some possibility that a regime could unexpectedly swing quickly to the left. The most likely possibility would be the seizure of power by a junta of junior officers. Most Latin American military academies have curricula that include social science courses taught by civilian and Marxist-oriented professors. Future officers might well be more consistently leftist (and anti-American) then General Omar Torrijos and more successful than General Torres of Bolivia.

The rise of a radical leftist military regime could pose serious problems for United States policymakers. Foreign property might be nationalized without adequate compensation, and foreign policy might shift toward alignment with the so-called non-aligned movement, close ties with Cuba and possibly the Soviet Union, and undisguised hostility for the United States.

A second possibility is the legal election of a Marxist regime. It might take the form, for example, of the return to power of a Marxist regime in Chile. The Chilean military, like their Argentine counterparts, are unlikely to eradicate Marxism completely. In Argentina, it took eighteen years for the Peronists to return to power. In Chile, it may take less time. Within a decade, and in a relatively open election, the old leftist coalition might be revived and appeal to a new generation of Chilean voters.

Another possibility is the emergence of authoritarian but populist parties, possibly even led by retired military officers. The latter would be similar to Perón of Argentina and Rojas Pinilla of Colombia (who nearly won the 1970 presidential election). These parties' candidates would be elected with the support of the lower middle and lower urban classes. Although popular, it is not likely that these parties would be able to solve their countries' economic and social problems and judging from past performance their economic mismanagement would probably exacerbate them. Relations with the United States might become strained. Their penchant for expropriation, for example, is as great as anyone's.[e]

A direct clash between the United States and Spanish America may occur over Puerto Rican independence. If Puerto Rican nationalism were to revive in the next decade, the island's independence could become an issue and a cause to be embraced by other Latin American countries besides Cuba. Since nationalism (with its attendant political, economic, and cultural elements) now seems stronger than ever in the world, this problem might well arise in the next decade.

A disturbing trend in the Caribbean is the radicalization and anti-imperialist

---

[e]Expropriations will continue no matter what type of regime is in power in any Latin American country. Although the U.S. investor will be chiefly affected by this, European and Japanese corporations may also be taken over. Some sort of international settlement procedure is not likely to be worked out in the future, however, as Latin American practice since the late nineteenth century is to keep all investment disputes within its own boundaries, and to resist all attempts at international arbitration.

(anti-U.S.) orientation of politics in Jamaica, Guyana and to a lesser extent Trinidad and Tobago. Radical political experiments may increase in a desperate effort by governments in the Black Caribbean to alleviate intractable poverty and social inequalities. The facility with which revolutionary governments turn to anti-Americanism as a source of internal cohesion and the United States as a scapegoat for their failures would tend to undermine our traditionally friendly ties.

Conclusions and Implications for the United States

Most of Latin America will continue to be politically turbulent in the coming decades as a result of continuing change in social and economic structures. In short, Latin America's chances for political stability and representative democracy should continue to be problematical, although there is likely to be a return to civilian and constitutional governments in a number of countries now under military rule during the remainder of the 1970s and early 1980s.

Some countries, like Brazil, Mexico, and Venezuela, have a reasonably good chance of maintaining political stability and economic progress. Middle-sized countries like Peru and Bolivia, will continue to advance economically but the expansion of the state sector and economic management based on ideology rather than pragmatism soon tends to lead to crisis. The smaller Central American and Caribbean states, vulnerable to external political and economic changes, can also be expected to progress economically and struggle with social change and the incorporation of the popular masses into the political-economic system.

Brazil deserves close attention because of its aspirations to major power status, which it may approach by 1985, and its long tradition of good relations with the United States. Such relations are likely to continue, which might make Brazil by the end of the period the major partner for the United States in the region. Outside of Brazil, the disappointed material expectations of leading elites, even though economic progress is considerable, may well exacerbate anti-Americanism. The United States will be the scapegoat for regimes uncertain of their legitimacy and eager to seek internal cohesion at the expense of the United States.

While Latin America is not nearly so important to the United States as Europe or the Middle East, there is a lingering public perception in the United States that the area is within the United States sphere of influence (as well as responsibility), which will provide the basis for continued difficulties for United States foreign policy.[f] Latin America's failures will be interpreted as United States

---

[f]Latin America could become more important to this country if the Soviet Union greatly increased its influence in the region. So far with the notable exception of Cuba it has not done so. On the other hand, some regimes might find playing one superpower off against the other rather tempting. It has been tried on occasions before (Quadros in Brazil, Perón in Argentina), and could happen again.

failures. Latin American hostility toward the United States will be accepted as a defeat for the United States.

Intensive nationalism will probably result in more expropriation of United States firms (especially in the extractive and manufacturing sector),[g] more Latin American cooperation against the United States on aid and trade matters, and selected bilateral problems that affect United States-Latin relations such as the Panama Canal and Puerto Rican independence. It could include an attempt to dismantle the OAS and establish a Latin organization that excluded the United States, but many countries will probably oppose this and the necessary unity of action would remain extremely difficult to obtain.

The U.S. government will be criticized in Latin America no matter what it does but in the coming decade and probably beyond, the principal criticism should revolve around alleged neglect of their interests by the United States. The decline in United States bilateral economic and military cooperation will lead to charges of abandonment and the inability of the United States to meet the trade preference demands of the Latin countries will be criticized as economic aggression or lack of consideration. More diversified political and economic relations with the rest of the world may lead to an increase in Latin realism and pragmatism in its relations with the United States, although the sense of rejection by the United States could also increase hostility and tensions.

It might be added that relations between very powerful and very weak neighboring nations are never satisfactory. The latters' condition can only change if the weak acquire powerful, extra-regional allies and benefactors or if the weak themselves become stronger through successful regional cooperation on issues of common concern. Neither is an immediate possibility in Latin America.

In conclusion, the internal problems and evolution of the Latin American republics will obviously profoundly affect the kind of relations that they develop with the United States. It is also true that the United States can do relatively little to shape the course of events within each country. Nevertheless, understanding the nature of Latin America's political and economic ills should help prevent mistaken diagnoses and inappropriate prescriptions.

Notes

1. Samuel P. Huntington, *Political Order in Changing Societies* (New Haven: Yale University Press, 1968), pp. 32-34.

2. Whether population increases match economic growth and thus produce equilibrium or whether economic stagnation depresses population growth rates, the result is the same—small, if any gains for each country as a whole. In Spanish America, Argentina and Uruguay are exceptions. It is not clear why they should be different from the others, although a variation of J.D. Duesenberry's

[g]There is still some $16 billion in U.S. direct investment in Latin America.

"fundamental psychological postulate" may help to explain it. Duesenberry's postulate is that once people achieve a modicum of comfort they will strongly resist any sudden lowering in living standard. That would include going without children, or, more often, without too many children. Both Argentina and Uruguay developed fast, then stagnated, and birthrates declined. (The same phenomenon may be at work in Czechoslovakia, which has experienced no significant economic growth since 1938.) By the 1990s a number of countries in Latin America, like Peru and Colombia, may develop a large enough middle class willing to limit family size in order to preserve their life-style, but there is no sign of it yet. The optimum combination of modest but stimulating population increase plus rapid economic growth has not occurred in Latin America. See Albert O. Hirschman for another version of the Duesenberry principle in *Strategy of Economic Development* (New Haven: Yale University Press, 1958), pp. 175-82. For the original, see J.S. Duesenberry, *Income, Saving and the Theory of Consumer Behavior* (Cambridge, Mass.: Harvard University Press, 1949), p. 84.

3. Joan Nelson, "The Urban Poor," *World Politics*, April 1970, p. 393. The cities are attractive because despite their problems they provide more amenities and opportunities for the migrants than the small towns and rural areas they have fled.

4. In a sample of migrants to Mexico City up to 70 percent had some education and 68 percent possessed some work skills. See Wayne A. Cornelius, "Urbanization as an Agent in Latin American Political Instability: The Case of Mexico," *American Political Science Review*, September 1969, pp. 839-40.

5. For a fuller account of the effects of social modernization, see Huntington, *Political Order in Changing Societies*, pp. 1-92.

6. Eric Nordlinger, "Soldiers in Mufti: The Impact of Military Rule upon Economic and Social Change in the Non-Western States," *American Political Science Review*, December 1970, pp. 1131-48.

7. Two recent and independent reviews of the literature confirm this analysis and include surveys of attitudes and opinions held by the urban poor. See Nelson, "The Urban Poor," pp. 393-414, and Cornelius, "Urbanization as an Agent in Latin American Political Instability," pp. 833-57.

8. It is exceeded only by Zaire, China, and the Soviet Union, and its potential is more accessible than that of Zaire. Brazil's lack of large petroleum reserves makes this source of energy of critical importance. See Frances Foland, "Whither Brazil?" *Inter-American Economic Affairs*, Winter 1970, pp. 43-44.

9. *Boletín Demográfico*, Santiago, Chile, July 1972, Table 1, pp. 4-7.

10. *Latin America* (London) June 18, 1976, p. 190.

11. The best account of Brazil's military in politics during the 1960s is Alfred Stepan, *The Military in Politics: Changing Patterns in Brazil* (Princeton, New Jersey: Princeton University Press, 1972).

12. See Susan Kaufman Purcell, "Decision-Making in an Authoritarian

Regime," *World Politics*, October 1973, pp. 28-54; Barry Ames, "Bases for Support for Mexico's Dominant Party," *The American Political Science Review*, March 1970, pp. 153-67; and Cornelius, "Urbanization as an Agent in Latin American Political Instability," for recent evaluations of the Mexican political system that present empirical evidence supporting the general hypothesis of on-going Mexican political stability.

III Latin America: Critical Choices for Regional Issues

Few today would argue that Latin America was the sole responsibility of the United States. In fact, the United States is no longer a patron and not yet an equal partner, but occupies an ambiguous middle ground. Nevertheless, as the dominant political and economic force in the Western Hemisphere, the United States still has special responsibilities, dictated by its ideals and enlightened self-interest, for assisting the development of our Latin American neighbors.

An attempt is made in this section to select those issues in U.S.-Latin American relations that seem likely to be important, enduring and intractable. The list is not meant to be exhaustive but does cover some of the major political, economic and security problems facing the United States in the hemisphere for the foreseeable future.

In setting forth the critical choices, the historical background is first sketched out and is followed by a listing of U.S. objectives and an analysis of U.S. policy. Finally those options that are considered reasonable are presented along with comments on the likely consequences of their adoption.

The policy sections fall into two broad categories: those dealing with problems affecting the entire region and those involving relations with key countries. United States regional and bilateral policies, which are treated here, together have the greatest impact on United States relations with its neighbors. But it is also important to note that United States global policies, though not discussed in this volume, will have an increasingly important role in shaping our regional and bilateral relations.

The following sections concentrate on economic issues that will likely play a major role in United States-Latin American relations. The specific topics cover regional economic integration and OAS reform. In addition, United States trade and investment problems in Latin America will be examined, and finally the special issues of Latin America as a producer of minerals and food will be considered.

Regional Blocs in Latin America

Background

Since the early days of the American Republic, men have dreamed of a free, republican, and united South America as a natural partner and perhaps ally of North America. But that vision has rarely gotten in the way of sober and practical policymaking. Therefore it should come as no surprise that until the late 1950s the United States consistently opposed any Latin American regional economic integration scheme which did not include the United States. (The counter-proposals of Henry Clay, James Blaine, and Cordell Hull for a *hemispheric* customs union were similarly rebuffed by the Latins.)

This long-standing divergence of interests should be kept in mind since it will probably continue in the future. The conventional idea that simple promotion of Latin American economic unity by the United States is a cost-free policy runs against the historic grain.

American opposition in the nineteenth century rested on the assumption and fear that an exclusively Latin common market would look inward and would thus deprive the United States of legitimate outlets for its goods, while at the same time providing a very dubious gain for Latin America. And to be sure, the early attempts promoted by Simón Bolívar all failed, usually at their very inception. Later U.S. resistance was rooted in the conviction that America's own policy of promoting universal free trade would be undercut by the acceptance of permanent regional trading blocs.

Despite these beliefs, the United States dropped its opposition to such schemes in the late 1950s. By then, American leaders were faced with a slowdown of Latin American economic growth, frequent complaints from south of the border about U.S. neglect, and the growing truculence of the Cuban revolutionaries. Thus by 1961 in the Punta del Este Charter, American spokesmen were willing to endorse "the integration of Latin America so as to stimulate the economic and social development of the continent."[1]

Six years later at the Meeting of the Presidents, held again in Uruguay, President Lyndon B. Johnson made economic integration a leading object of the Alliance. By that time, American policymakers believed that Latin American economic union would provide a significant stimulus to economic development, which in turn would promote social peace and political decency. They also saw it as a step toward rather than away from eventual world free trade. Furthermore, since the U.S. aid program by the mid-1960s seemed unable to alter radically the Latin American economies, common markets became fashionable, since supporting them seemed both cheap and consistent with new aid doctrines stressing self-help. Supporting Latin American integration was now consistent with the overall American interest in global stability and growing prosperity, since the new economic trading bloc in Latin America was viewed only as temporary. That is to say, it would last long enough to make Latin America economically strong which in turn would let the region participate more fully in the world economy.

Critical Problems

The question of economic integration leads to the heart of the matter: how best to stimulate rapid economic development in the area over the next decade? Latin America's problems in a sense are unique: it is advanced beyond most of the Third World but still far behind the First. Moreover, the old policy of promoting industrialization through import substitution has lost its appeal for even its most enthusiastic supporters.

But economic well-being is not all that is at stake. Latin Americans have increasingly felt that the region has declined in importance politically. It possesses little leverage vis-à-vis the developed world and, as a collection of small and medium-sized states, has shown even less capacity for leadership of the underdeveloped nations.

Economic union seems to be a way out. First, it would expand domestic markets which in turn would rationalize industry by providing true economies of scale. Not only would the production of current manufactures rise but an enlarged market would permit even more ambitious industrial projects, especially in heavy industry. That in turn would promote more rapid growth and at the same time save on foreign exchange. With a more streamlined economy, the region would be far more competitive in manufactured goods in world markets, and it could finally shift away from dependency on a short list of primary products.[a]

Integration would also, oddly enough, spring from a growing nationalism since there are political as well as economic motives for bloc formation. But besides reducing their economic vulnerability, integration would provide these

[a]Has this, in fact, happened? The answer is a qualified no. It is qualified because no integration scheme has been fully tested. LAFTA and CACM are moribund. CARICOM, though very much alive, has a total population approximately equal to Ecuador's. Only the Andean experiment has any chance of fulfilling these objectives although it is too early to say. Nevertheless, at the moment intra-Andean trade is only a fraction (about 4 percent) of the total trade for these countries. And the reasons that little trade occurred between them are still largely valid: their economies are competitive rather than complementary. Moreover, intra-Andean transportation is still primitive. Finally, the region is still rent by political quarrels which undermine the mutual trust needed to make economic integration schemes work.

countries with the kind of leverage they need in negotiations with the developed West on subjects ranging from .trade to territorial sea limits. This kind of nationalism can also cause problems; economic integration schemes (as in the case of the Andean Common Market) can promote policies that are harmful to the United States. For example, ANCOM's common foreign investment code (Decision 24) strictly regulates outside capital. ANCOM also provides nearly limitless opportunities to coordinate positions prior to world economic conferences—positions which often are at variance with Western views on trade and aid.

Complementing the Latin American trend toward regionalism is the United States' own disillusionment with bilateral aid programs. The latter appear less and less likely to be the critical ingredient for economic takeoff. The times (as well as Congress) demand something cheap and effective, and economic integration schemes seem to be the answer. They also fit conveniently within the new thinking which stresses the importance of self-esteem through self-help. Moreover, the demand in Latin America for large sums of government bilateral assistance has also dwindled since such aid programs have not produced the positive outcome once expected in the 1960s.

Despite the apparent promise of economic integration projects, however, serious problems have developed. At the end of the 1960s, the Latin American Free Trade Association (LAFTA), embracing all of South America and Mexico, was moribund. The Central American Common Market (CACM), paralyzed by a hopelessly tangled conflict between Honduras and El Salvador, seemed hardly better off. The newly formed Caribbean Community (CARICOM) which included all the ex-British Commonwealth territories and had a total population of only five million, appeared likely to exhaust its economic potential in the not too distant future. The Andean Common Market (actually a subregional organization within LAFTA) alone seemed to be succeeding, but it had become increasingly anti-American in tone. So, despite the great interest in economic integration throughout the hemisphere, fifteen years of effort have not yet produced lasting results. The objective of a common market embracing all of Latin America appears remote—well beyond the target date of 1985 set at the 1967 summit meeting.

U.S. Objectives

The United States should not be an uncritical booster of regional economic blocs within Latin America. Indeed, it is important that this country only support those schemes that more or less meet the following tests:

1. that they provide rapid economic growth through free market economies;
2. that they be outward looking, and not unsympathetic to foreign private investment;

3. that they not be used to promote overt anti-American alliances and policies such as cartel formation, investment confiscation, and so on.

Current Policy

American ardor for economic integration has waned a bit since Lyndon Johnson's 1967 pledge to help construct a full Latin American common market by 1985. For one thing, that grand design no longer seems achievable. Second, the United States, while still favoring economic union, has made it clear in recent years that "decisions on how far and how fast this process of integration goes, of course, are not ours to make."[2] That dictum has generally meant a scrupulous refusal to interfere in the way the various regional blocs conduct their business. For example, American policymakers have conspicuously refrained from making any judgment on ANCOM's controversial Decision 24—the highly restrictive foreign-investment code that has directly affected the fortunes of American firms in the area.

Meanwhile, U.S. financial aid has been given principally to three common markets: ANCOM, CACM, and CARICOM. Although the aid has not been insubstantial (as some critics charge), the most interesting fact is the variation in the sums given to each (see Table III-1). Since 1961, the United States government has loaned CACM's Central American Bank for Integration $182.5 million, and has given another $19.9 million to other Central American institutions. CARICOM's Caribbean Development Bank has received $32.3 million since June 1970, but ANCOM, the largest of the functioning economic blocs, has so far gotten only $15 million from the United States, with another $200 thousand for technical assistance, since June 1972. That amount, however, was supplemented by IDB loans of $5.4 million and another $750 thousand in technical assistance.

At the OAS General Assembly in Santiago (June 1976), Secretary of State Kissinger reaffirmed United States support of regional and subregional integra-

Table III-1

U.S. Bilateral and Multilateral Aid to Latin American Regional Economic Blocs[a]
(millions of dollars)

	ANCOM	CACM	CARICOM
U.S. Government	$15.2	$202.4	$32.3
Inter-American Development Bank	6.15	—	—

[a]Total Loans as of December 31, 1973.
Source: U.S. Department of State; *Andean Times*, November 2, 1973, p. 7.

tion including, apparently, ANCOM's industrial development programs. He also suggested changes in the administration of trade laws to encourage further integration, but announced no new financial support.[3]

In general, United States support of these schemes continues, and there are even signs of renewed interest. But the initiative remains with the Latin Americans.

Policy Options

There are two clear choices for the United States regarding economic integration. The first means active United States support, the second takes a far more cautious approach.

More Active U.S. Support for Integration. Recognizing the value for Latin America of economic cooperation and integration which promotes growth, stability, self-respect and increased trade, under this option the United States would support sub-regional economic communities far more vigorously than it has in recent years. The following policy guidelines might be considered:

1. increased United States capital contributions to the Caribbean, Central American and Andean development banks.
2. encouragement of Central American political cooperation.
3. maintenance or expansion of the capital and technical assistance programs of the Regional Office for Central America and Panama (U.S. Agency for International Development) in support of the Central American common market.
4. encouragement of Caribbean-wide trade (including Puerto Rico) and investment in related transport and communications infrastructure.

Consequences. An increase in the flow of United States resources to the common market banks would accomplish little in the short run. Most, if not all, of the Andean countries, for example, lack well designed integration projects. Furthermore, it is the absence of political will (especially evident in the unresolved Honduras-El Salvador border conflict) that is the decisive obstacle to more rapid movement towards closer political Andean and Central American communities. Nevertheless, increased United States support for regional economic integration would tend to strengthen United States political and economic relations with the countries of these sub-regional communities.

Limited U.S. Support for Integration. This would mean:

1. selective support for economic blocs, depending on their friendliness and cooperation.
2. selective credits that aim at increasing sub-regional cooperation such as projects jointly financed and administered by two or more countries in the sub-region.

3. encouragement of the OECD countries to increase their financial and technical contribution.
4. support for efforts to increase both intra-regional and extra-regional trade of the sub-regional blocs.

Consequences. The more successful the bloc, the more restrictive its policies toward the United States tend to become. Historically, Latin American integration has been driven by the desire to provide protection against the great powers which in the twentieth century has meant the United States.

But the United States is no longer the only hemispheric power that causes concern amongst its neighbors. ANCOM was created, at least in part, by the medium-sized Pacific coast republics of South America as a defense against economic competition from their larger neighbors, especially Argentina, and Brazil. Because Brazil has vastly increased its economic strength since the mid-1960s, there is particular concern among some ANCOM members that they will fall under the political and economic influence of the South American giant.

Moreover, there are other special factors that may well make the Andean bloc difficult to get along with. Despite the overthrow of the Allende regime, the political tenor of the pact has slipped leftward in recent years, as a result of the emergence of new leadership in some of the countries that are keen on promoting a so-called New Economic Order, which implies a substantial shift in economic resources and advantages to the less developed countries.

Unlike CACM whose members are relatively similar in level of economic development, ANCOM includes three relatively large and sophisticated economics which are capable of providing some support to the weaker ones of Ecuador and Bolivia. While inter-ANCOM trade has expanded substantially, it is doubtful that it can develop some form of political union in the next decade. The latter notion has so far played little part in ANCOM deliberations but it is very much a part of the old Bolivarian dream.

It should be noted that a successful experiment in regional integration could create more immediate difficulties and tensions in member country relations with the United States than if the members had remained separate and dealt with the United States on a bilateral basis. Over the longer run, it is impossible to say how successful integration would affect United States relations with the Latin countries. In any event, American experience with Western Europe before and after the formation of the EEC might well be borne in mind by policymakers over the next decade.

The Reform of the OAS

Background

The world's oldest regional organization, the inter-American system, has been evolving since 1890. Today that system is institutionalized in an intricate international body known as the Organization of American States (OAS).

The evolution of the institutions that now comprise the OAS did not proceed smoothly. In theory, any organization composed of a single superpower and a score of middle and small states would have to be racked with controversy. In fact, seldom in the history of the inter-American system has there been anything but uneasy last-minute compromise at best, and open rancor at worst.

The existence of such divisiveness within an institutional framework raises an important question: why has the organization even survived? With no guarantee for the future, it can be said that the OAS is alive because it has served the interests, often conflicting though they are, of both Latin America and the United States.

Latin America's interest in the OAS is much clearer cut than ours. The organization provides a regular forum in which it can press overriding concerns on the region's principal source of hope: the United States. First, Latin America has lobbied vigorously for an American commitment to nonintervention. Second, and especially recently, Latin America has used the OAS to secure U.S. pledges to support economic development through, among other things, the provision of cheap capital with as few strings attached as possible.

The U.S. interest in the OAS is much less focused. At times, we seem to support the OAS because it is there; at others the United States has believed that a well-developed inter-American system would provide machinery for hemispheric defense and the peaceful settlement of disputes. And, although it was formerly opposed to such schemes, the United States has also come to believe that the OAS can play a role in regional economic development and social welfare schemes.[4]

The OAS, pulled in different directions by conflicting interests, may change again. A new drive to reform the organization has been led by a handful of Latin American countries: Peru, Mexico, and Panama. Their dissatisfaction is rooted in the belief that the OAS serves only the interests of the United States.[b] At the moment, they are particularly interested in making the OAS a useful instrument for advancing their economic interests, primarily in the area of better or at least stable prices for their exports. Meanwhile, any country with any grievance (Panama and the Canal, Guatemala and Belize) remains free to turn bilateral problems into a multilateral concern. This, of course, is hardly fair to this country. Neither is the ongoing complaint about our leadership being needed and resented at the same time. But that is precisely what the United States can and must expect in a regional organization that contains such a heterogeneous collection of states.

---

[b]The most frequently cited case in point is the lengthy American campaign to legitimize the 1965 intervention in the Dominican Republic. There is a certain justice to this complaint, and it may be prudent policy for the United States not to use the OAS when in fact we are confronted with a bilateral problem. Our use of the OAS does not legitimize U.S. actions in Latin American eyes. On the contrary, it merely involves us in embarrassments that could have been avoided in the first place.

In fact, most of the reforms are simply old proposals that have been resurrected once more for debate. For example, the recent arguments advanced by Peru in favor of including an article on economic aggression in the Rio Treaty are basically the same ones made by the Guatemalan delegation to the Rio Conference in 1947.[5] While they are not new, these proposals will always need careful study. Moreover, the U.S. commitment to regionalism itself should be examined. Does membership in this organization serve American interests, either in the short or the long haul? Or are we simply maintaining the status quo because it seems the easiest thing to do in a policy area not deemed especially vital? If we are to remain active in the OAS, what useful purposes can it serve without additional commitments of resources on our part? Moreover, what do those Latin American countries who are not our fixed enemies want from the organization?

Critical Problems

In recent years there has been a trend toward restructuring the OAS. The substance of these reforms would give Latin American regimes, especially the more radical ones, additional leverage over the United States. The last wave of reform talk has been led by Peru's left-wing generals, and they have received support from the self-styled revolutionary governments of Mexico and Panama.

Peru's efforts, so far, have not met with any great success. Its firm ally, Chile's President Salvador Allende, was overthrown in September 1973 and other regimes have remained noncommital or even critical of the reforms. Consequently, since June 1974, Peru has trimmed its more extreme proposals although it has not yet ended its efforts.

Complete complacency on this matter, therefore, would be a mistake. If a longer view is taken, a major drive for "reform" could be revived at any opportune moment. For example, if Cuba were again admitted to the OAS (which is a dim possibility by 1985), it could mount a very serious effort at remodeling the OAS along more "revolutionary" lines.

One aspect of the reform campaign will undoubtedly attract more support than most of the others. This is the call for ideological pluralism which was meant to ease Cuba's reincorporation into the OAS. After Angola, this particular slogan has lost a few adherents but it has not disappeared altogether and may have a revival in a few years. For the United States, the widespread acceptance of ideological pluralism means the end of the OAS Charter's commitment to preserving and pursuing representative democracy in the hemisphere.

In any case, the United States must be prepared to face the possibility of periodic calls for revision of the OAS, spearheaded by those regimes, military or civilian, which have taken on a hard left-wing and ultra-nationalist coloration. What must be kept firmly in mind is that North and South American perceptions of reform and restructuring are quite different. To the North American, these terms imply a pragmatic adjustment of old institutions and procedures to fit new situations. For Latin Americans, this is not the case. Restructuring does not just mean tinkering with the machinery but rather it implies a reworking of the much broader and more fundamental framework of U.S.-Latin American relations.

Current U.S. Policy

The United States, until recently, has played a small role in the debate over OAS reforms which is supposed to culminate in an extraordinary OAS General Assembly in Lima in March 1977. It did not initiate the movement and only lately has it contributed any major proposals.

In general, the United States has not opposed small-scale changes in the OAS Charter or the Inter-American Treaty for Reciprocal Assistance. In regard to the latter, for example, it has supported the inclusion of the recently adopted United Nations definition of aggression as well as changes in wording that would make the treaty more consistent internally.

The principal American role has been to oppose those changes that would be in conflict with U.S. interests or, for that matter, would threaten the existence of the OAS.

U.S. officials have always considered the Rio Treaty a valuable device for maintaining peace in the hemisphere. They have steadfastly denied the common assertion that the treaty had its origins in the cold war and that it subsequently has served the cold war policies of the United States.

Furthermore, the United States has opposed adding an article on economic aggression to the Rio Treaty. For one thing, American officials have stressed that economic aggression is an extremely difficult concept to define, and second, that it is quite alien to the spirit and meaning of the treaty itself. The United States has also stressed that amicable solutions to economic matters are better arrived at bilaterally than in the very public arena of OAS debate.

The question of OAS reform was met head on by the United States at the Santiago OAS meeting held in June 1976. First, U.S. officials made it emphatically clear that the reforms proposed by Peru and the others would not be signed nor recommended to the Senate for ratification. Second, the U.S. delegation advanced three major reform proposals of its own: first, the annual meeting of the OAS foreign ministers should be upgraded in importance with the financial and economic ministers in attendance. Second, the three OAS Councils, the Permanent Council, the Inter-American Economic and Social Council, and the Inter-American Council for Education, Science, and Culture, should be downgraded, meeting less frequently, and perhaps eventually being eliminated. Third, the Charter should be changed so that the United States cut its financial support of the Organization—a contribution that now amounts to two-thirds of the OAS budget.

It must be said these proposals have enjoyed little support in Latin America, and it seems now that at least a number of the changes the United States has objected to will be passed by the extraordinary assembly scheduled for Lima in March 1977.

U.S. Goals

American goals within the OAS continue to be those espoused in the OAS Charter:

1. strengthen the peace and security of the continent and provide the means for peaceful settlement of disputes;
2. seek the solution of political, juridical, and economic problems that may arise among the hemispheric nations;
3. promote, through cooperative action, the social, economic, and cultural development of the organization's members.

But, in addition, the United States must:

4. prevent the OAS from becoming an anti-American alliance, failing which it may consider withdrawal from the OAS and the establishment of close bilateral relations with our remaining friends in the hemisphere. U.S. policy has been reluctant to do this in the past but it may be forced to in the future. Those countries which are important to us and likely to respond are: Brazil, Chile, Venezuela, and perhaps Mexico.

Policy Options

In the coming years the United States will probably encounter repeated calls from some Latin American countries to reform the OAS. How great and persistent these pressures become will in large part determine which option the United States must choose over the next decade. There are three major options available to the United States:
   1. *Support the OAS as Currently Organized.*
      a. If the U.S. encounters only scattered and sporadic pressures for reform, it may then openly oppose the reopening of reform talks. The organization, it may well argue, is better off if it is not repeatedly subjected to review which results in greater division within the hemisphere as countries see opportunities to further their national interests in the guise of reforming the OAS. Furthermore, there is little profit to the United States since "reform" can easily be used as a stick to beat the bogy of "American imperialism."

2. *Sponsor Reform of the OAS.*

a. If the pressures become strong and persistent, then the United States must initiate its own review of the problem, and subsequently submit detailed plans for reform which naturally are consistent with its own self-interest and the goals espoused in the OAS Charter;

b. The core concept of U.S.-sponsored reform would be the restructuring of the OAS to make it a more purely technical assistance and economic development agency. Its political function would be taken over by ad hoc meetings of the hemisphere's foreign ministers.

3. *Withdraw from the OAS.*

a. If the United States is defeated on major questions of OAS reform and is confronted with what amounts to a radical challenge to U.S.-Latin American relations inimical to this country, we may consider withdrawal from the OAS;

b. This naturally would be a radical action and its consequences must be weighed fully. Leaving the organization would itself have negative effects. It would create a vacuum for rivals and enemies within and without the hemisphere to exploit. Furthermore, withdrawal would be considered a defeat for the United States—at least a temporary one. Finally, American withdrawal from the OAS would lead to a decreasing U.S. concern for and attention to the area—to our detriment;

c. Nevertheless, if the OAS becomes a vehicle for anti-Americanism, there is compelling reason for the United States to end its support for that organization. A variety of circumstances might force the United States to withdraw, but one specific possibility suggests itself. If an economic aggression article were attached to the Rio Treaty, the U.S. could expect to be harassed by every anti-American regime at will. Among those likely to take such action within the decade would be Cuba, a self-proclaimed expert on American "economic aggression."

d. Withdrawal from the OAS may also spark a reconsideration of the Rio Treaty. The Treaty itself is an entangling alliance which commits us to peace-keeping and collective security with countries that are no conceivable threat to us. Furthermore, use of the treaty as a cold war weapon is no longer feasible, and in addition, any attempt to multilateralize a bilateral dispute adds, at best, only the smallest of increments to our own position.

Future of the OAS

Dire predictions about the future of the OAS may not be borne out by events. But the following trend, aside from the reform question, seems irreversible: namely, that Latin America is reaching out for closer political and economic relations beyond the Western Hemisphere. Japan, Western Europe, the Soviet bloc, and the Middle East are its current favorites (although, for the present,

Latin American demands on the United States have not decreased). Consequently, the "special relationship" between the United States and Latin America (which really developed only after World War I) may continue to erode. Therefore, either the OAS will be adapted to Latin America's growing global interests by bringing the world into the OAS, or the OAS itself will cease to dominate Latin America's diplomatic world, instead limiting its focus to very specific issues that affect only the United States and Latin America. It should be stressed that over the next decade and beyond the list of those issues will continue to grow shorter.

United States Trade Relations with Latin America

Background

The United States has long had a special interest in expanding trade relations with our "near neighbors" in Latin America. In the nineteenth century, commerce was principally an exchange of temperate and tropical primary products. But the United States' share of Latin American imports was relatively small compared to that of major European powers (primarily England and France) which often won preferential tariff treatment from Latin Americans eager to purchase European consumer goods.

The United States only became the major trading partner of Latin America with the outbreak of World War I and the subsequent disruption of traditional patterns of trade. It has retained this position until the present.

Recently, however, the Latin American nations have begun seriously looking outside the hemisphere for new trade partners. Japan, the Communist countries, and Western Europe, have increased their purchase of Latin American products and have secured Latin American markets for their own goods, especially the products of their heavy industry. While United States exports to Latin America grew by only 10.2 percent between 1956-58 and 1967-69, Canadian exports went up 82.5 percent, Japan's 272.3 percent, and Western Europe's 55.9 percent. In the same period, Latin American exports to the United States grew by only 4.7 percent, while exports to Canada increased 192.0 percent; to Japan, 167.3 percent; and to Western Europe, 57.9 percent.[6]

In the past, when faced with extra-hemispheric competition, American leaders have urged a Western Hemisphere trade preference area but have received little or no positive response from Latin America. Recently this proposal was revived by the 1969 Rockefeller Report on Latin America, with the stipulation that such a preference arrangement be made only in the event that the EEC failed to extend its system of special preferences beyond Africa and the Mediterranean. The EEC, through the new Lomé Agreement, has extended its system of preferences only to the former British possessions in the Caribbean:

Barbados, Guyana, Jamaica, and Trinidad-Tobago. In the meantime, the United States has not seriously attempted to revive the hemisphere trade area scheme since it has been opposed by Latin Americans.

Today, Latin American trade issues will play a major part in the current multilateral trade negotiations in Geneva. Latin American countries, for example, have pressed for the removal of all trade barriers affecting tropical product imports—a grievance largely aimed at the EEC. Moreover, they have also sought an end to meat quotas—again imposed by the Europeans. Furthermore, they may still use Geneva as an opportunity to improve relations with other Third World primary producers. Beyond Geneva, it is quite likely that in the next decade trade issues will increasingly set the tone of the United States-Latin American relations as the region's leaders accept the proposition that promotion of exports is inextricably linked with promotion of growth. Whether these issues will be settled amicably or acrimoniously or even settled at all depends, in part, on the kind of trade strategy the United States adopts over the next ten years.

The United States will also continue to depend on Latin America for a wide variety of raw materials for at least the next decade.[7] For all of these reasons, trade issues, along with the resolution of the Cuba question, should strongly affect inter-American relations for the foreseeable future.

Critical Problems

What are the key trade issues facing Latin America and the United States over the next decade? Answering this question is itself part of the problem, because perceptions of the issues vary greatly north and south of the Rio Grande. Latin Americans tend to express alarm over the fact that their share of world trade has been cut in half, dropping from 11 percent in the early 1950s to 5.5 percent in the late 1960s as other areas of the world (North America, Western Europe, Japan, even Taiwan, Hong Kong, and South Korea) have proven far more dynamic in promoting exports. In addition, they claim that there has been a long-term deterioration in the terms of trade for their principal products, while primary-product prices have been extraordinarily unstable over the short term. Thus, prices for sugar have climbed rapidly to record highs, only to plunge again steeply in just a few months.

Latin Americans also consider it likely that protectionism will increase in the United States and Western Europe and that this will make the retention (much less the expansion) of their old markets all the more difficult. Recent moves, like the U.S. imposition of an (albeit temporary) across-the-board surcharge on imports in August 1971 and the EEC ban on meat imports, are taken as signs of a shift away from the relatively free trade world of the 1960s. But despite the friction with the European Community, antagonism has been aimed mostly at the United States. There is criticism, for example, of this country's use of countervailing duties against selected Latin American exports. There has been a much greater outcry against the new U.S. trade law. The provision for special preferences is not generous enough, it is argued, and denial of Generalized Special Preferences (GSPs) to OPEC members (meaning Ecuador and Venezuela) has been widely denounced as economic aggression. Most importantly, the Latin Americans desire better and more stable prices for their products, and they want to acquire U.S. goods and technology on more advantageous terms. How they propose to do this is not clear to them but they are meeting on an ongoing basis to devise such a strategy. The future course of Latin American-U.S. trade will also be affected by the kind of regional economic integration that will take place over the next decade. The most viable scheme, the Andean Common Market, will most certainly be a model that others might follow. ANCOM's character will be determined in the next few years as its members negotiate a common external tariff. If that tariff wall is high, and ANCOM becomes increasingly autarkic, then trade relations will hardly improve, and the two sides will drift even further apart.

In the United States, however, there is increasing concern about the formation of producer cartels controlling a wide variety of products ranging from bananas to tin. Cartels, of course, generally seek higher prices through restricting production. In an era when the U.S. demand for raw materials is increasing, our concern seems justified. In addition, there is growing worry that the whole international trade and monetary system that has worked well since World War II is under severe strain and may collapse if new rules under the GATT, for example, are not agreed upon. The fact that a number of Latin American countries still do not belong to the GATT only adds to the problem as it is viewed by the United States.

Some of the difficulty in deciding what is important may well be rooted in the fact that neither the United States nor much of Latin America has a well-focused trade strategy. The United States has simply not needed one, since foreign trade has played a relatively small role in the accumulation of its great wealth. While this is not the case with Latin America, the region has not developed a trade strategy either, with the exception of Brazil since 1964. According to one Latin American economist, these countries lack "any systematic, integrated, and coherent foreign trade policy responding to rationally defined objectives . . . " Moreover, their trade policies such as they are tend to be "short-term, consisting of isolated measures adopted in response to short-term considerations and to the usually powerful vested interests of the export sector."[8] Thus, effort is devoted not to finding new markets but to defending traditional markets without bothering to adapt products and marketing practices to such changed conditions as the appearance of synthetics.

Instead of adopting an export-oriented growth model, Latin America in the past has used import substitution and is now relying on regional economic integration as the primary stimuli for economic development. But import substitution meant the establishment of inefficient industries unable to satisfy either local demand or world markets at competitive prices. These overprotected infants did not even improve their trade accounts since manufactured goods, as imports, were soon replaced by the capital goods, raw materials, and technology needed to make those manufactured goods. Regional integration has not yet gone far enough to make much of a difference. Intra-Andean trade, for example, was little more than 4 percent of these countries' total trade, and ANCOM is the most advanced of all of the Latin American integration schemes.

If, on the other hand, Spanish America adopts and adapts the Brazilian model, the United States may still face special problems if recent relations with Brazil are any indication. The fact is that a number of acrimonious disputes have arisen between Brazil and the United States (traditionally good friends) over trade issues like soluble coffee and countervailing duties on Brazilian shoes. The same or worse could be expected from the rest of Latin America if growth by export is considered vital for Latin America's future. This is not to say that the United States is or will be at fault in most of these disputes but it must expect more trouble on the issue simply because it is, for most Latin American countries, their export market par excellence. This problem will be only compounded if the United States becomes more protectionist over the next decade.

In the meantime, although the United States has granted Generalized Special Preferences to Latin American manufactured goods, it is still likely that the restrictions on the GSPs will become further points of controversy with the Latin nations. Those which have already aroused heated comment are the trade law's section 501 which excludes OPEC members (Ecuador and Venezuela) and section 504 which limits any exporting country's share of each article's U.S. market to $25 million and "50 percent of the appraised value of the total imports of such article into the United States during any calendar year."[9]

On the multilateral front, Latin America will certainly press the EEC to lower its barriers on tropical products. In the meantime, the United States has quite rightly shown a willingness to cooperate with Latin America in removing European restrictions on Latin American tropical products and meats. If success is limited, Latin America is likely to bring heavy pressure to bear on the few remaining American barriers, especially on items such as rum and meat. In any case, all the hard bargaining lies ahead, and it is likely that United States-Latin American relations in general will be judged on how well these economic issues are settled.

U.S. Goals

A principal American objective in the coming decade is to encourage Latin American countries to adopt export-oriented economies. The region can no longer afford development by import substitution which has only resulted in the creation of a wide assortment of inefficient, high-cost plants producing goods which do not even satisfy domestic demand. Nor can Latin America afford development by industrial promotion schemes which have been drawn up for the Andean Common Market.[10] The soundest approach is the promotion of those activities which will result in products competitive in world markets. That means emphasizing the processing of local agricultural and raw materials along with the production of carefully selected manufactured goods.

None of this is likely to happen, however, unless the United States keeps its own trade barriers from going up. By so doing the United States would avoid placing itself in the questionable position of preaching free enterprise and practicing something else. Within this overall goal of fostering balanced development, the United States should also achieve the following:

1. the preservation of U.S. markets in Latin America, which have provided us a trade surplus on current account;
2. the preservation of U.S. access to Latin American raw materials at fair prices;
3. the encouragement of commodity agreements that eliminate wide fluctuations in price but do not fundamentally interfere with the market mechanism;
4. the encouragement of membership in the GATT for the Latin American countries that have still not joined.

Current U.S. Policy

The United States is now placing great emphasis on reaching "concrete solutions to specific problems in the trade field" with Latin America. As part of the new look, the State Department sent the President's special trade representative on a swing through Latin America in April 1974 in order to test Latin opinion and shape U.S. policy accordingly.

Since then the United States has adopted a two-pronged approach. First, direct appeals to Latin America have been made, particularly during Secretary of State Kissinger's visit to the region. Secondly, fresh approaches toward trade matters have been tried at international meetings like the Nairobi UNCTAD Conference held in May 1976.

In Santiago, Chile, the United States made three pledges aimed specifically at Latin America. First, the U.S. government would try (Congress willing) to make Ecuador and Venezuela, despite their membership in OPEC, eligible for GSPs. Second, the United States would in Geneva lobby for an agreement that would relax the rules on countervailing duties for underdeveloped countries. Third, a hemisphere information sharing scheme on commodities was proposed. The purpose of this exchange, according to the secretary of state, would be the establishment of an early warning system which would "identify problems in advance and enable us to take appropriate corrective action nationally, region-ally, or through worldwide organizations."[11]

In Nairobi, the secretary of state accepted the much discussed problem of widely fluctuating prices for raw materials whose earnings are critical to the LDCs. He endorsed, in principle, buffer stock schemes to help alleviate that problem, and urged "producer-consumer forums" for a wide range of products, iron ore and bauxite in particular. In the sensitive area of compensatory financing he underlined the value of the IMF trust fund which now provides concessional financing for the poorest, and noted that the United States might help in the fund's expansion.[12]

The United States is not likely to see export-oriented economies springing up in Latin America in the near future even if it resists the protectionist temptation. But the United States can encourage the process by several methods. First, it can cultivate particularly good relations with those countries disposed to accept an export growth strategy. Brazil, of course, Chile, and Colombia are currently the best bets. Second, the United States can reorient its aid and credit policy to stimulate those activities which would be most competitive in world markets as well as radically improving those countries' research and development facilities. That, in turn, would lay the basis for a second generation of manufactures which would also be available for export.

Policy Options

Within a general framework of advocating export-oriented economies in Latin America, the United States should not merely wait for Latin American proposals on trade issues. The following options will not be easy to adopt, owing to internal pressures. Moreover, resistance to lowering trade barriers will increase if the recovery of the U.S. economy proves to be a drawn-out process. Neverthe-less, without this bold approach, relations with much of Latin America will increase in difficulty, and this country will have done nothing to promote rapid economic development. And thus, while Latin American prosperity does not guarantee political stability, much less democracy, without it neither will prove possible at all. Therefore, despite the obvious difficulties in adopting such a strategy, the following are recommended:

1. The United States should encourage the rest of Latin America to join the GATT on the general principle that those nations unwilling to make commit-ments should not expect to receive the benefits from the agreements of others. Such a course of action would also help propel Latin America into the First World.

2. As part of its export strategy, the United States might encourage Latin American nations to build labor-intensive manufacturing plants through the extension of Generalized Special Preferences.

3. The United States should encourage the refining of raw materials in Latin America by reversing our tariff structure on raw materials and semiprocessed goods.

4. The United States should avoid pushing a Western Hemisphere trade preference system although it should not be ruled out if there is future broad Latin American support.

5. The United States should head off producer cartels by working out practical commodity agreements that all can live with. Indeed, over the next year, now that commodity prices have fallen (and before raw material prices rise rapidly, which they may, as the world economy recovers), the United States has an opportunity to advance practical and acceptable commodity arrangements that will eliminate the extreme fluctuations in prices that Latin American countries have experienced in the last few years. But it must be emphasized that the initiative must come from the United States. This country should not wait for "Latin American" proposals which may never come forth or if they do, may be too extreme in nature.

U.S. Private Direct Investment in Latin America

Background

Foreign private investment has played an important role in Latin American economic development throughout the nineteenth and twentieth centuries. Foreign firms have generated income, employment, and export earnings for the host countries. They have also helped transfer technology, trained managerial and technical labor, and forged backward and forward linkages, thereby helping to create more integrated, broadly-based and self-sufficient national industries.

It is highly unlikely that, in the absence of foreign investment, local entrepreneurs, skilled managers and technicians, or sizable amounts of capital and technology would have been forthcoming to produce an efficient pattern and rate of industrial development.

Even in the case of extractive industries, where linkages with the rest of the economy were initially weak or nonexistent, it is highly questionable whether the Latin American mineral-exporting countries like Chile, Peru, and Venezuela would be better off today if no foreign investment had been made in this sector. A distinction, however, must be made. First, it is true that the *direct* impact of foreign investment in mining on the course of economic development has been small. Nevertheless, the *indirect* impact on the rate and pattern of economic development has been enormous, depending on government policies in obtaining revenues or "scarcity rents" from the foreign-owned mineral sector, and the ability of the Latin American governments, and society, to use these revenues productively.

It is no secret that despite its favorable impact, foreign investment has been under attack in Latin America, particularly among intellectuals and local entrepreneurs, for some time. Despite the lessons of the past, when severe economic dislocation followed the rapid nationalization of foreign firms and local economies subsequently were wrecked (Bolivia 1952, Cuba 1959, Chile 1971), the myth of the rapacious foreigner persists.

Today, the takeover of large foreign firms is still announced in some countries as a "blow in favor of national liberation" and is the occasion for patriotic celebration.[c] Peru, for example, observes the anniversary of the takeover of the International Petroleum Company (IPC) as the "Day of National Dignity" and other countries are following suit. The substantial and visible U.S. investment in Latin America is the principal target of nationalist attack. Again, less consideration is given to the economic consequences of the takeover of American firms than to the satisfaction of very real political and psychological needs of Latin American governments and peoples. National control and ownership of major industrial sectors is increasingly a top priority of national policy, and this current wave of economic xenophobia will continue in many parts of Latin America until severe economic problems occur—a stage already reached by Argentina and Peru.

Critical Problems

Slow Growth of U.S. Investment Since 1960. U.S. direct investment has been growing more slowly in Latin America during the post-World War II period than in Canada, Western Europe, Oceania, Africa, and Asia. An examination of the worldwide distribution of U.S. private investment since 1929 shows that until 1950 the Latin American region was by far the largest recipient ($4.4 billion) outstripping Canada ($3.6 billion) and Western Europe ($1.7 billion). By 1960, however, Latin America had already fallen behind Canada ($8.4 billion versus $11.2 billion). In 1965 Western Europe slipped past Latin America (nearly $14 billion compared to $9.4 billion) as a target for American investment. In 1974, with a total of 19.6 billion (book value) of U.S. private investment, Latin America still ranked third in importance but American investment in Asia (including the Middle East) now seems likely to overtake Latin America in importance around 1980, assuming the continuation of present trends.

As for sectoral distribution over the past two decades, U.S. investment in Latin America has exhibited slowest growth in petroleum and mining and smelting, and has declined absolutely in public utilities. Nationalization of oil

---

[c]The Latin American businessmen's complaints are, in part, justified. They have, for example, great difficulty in competing with the multinationals. They cannot hope to match them in technology and marketing skills for example. Furthermore, foreign corporations have a far easier time raising capital locally (and at lower rates of interest) than the native entrepreneur does.

and other mineral production in Venezuela over the next few years will further reduce the importance of U.S. investment in these sectors. On the other hand, U.S. investment has expanded rapidly since 1945 in manufacturing and "other" sectors ("other" includes agriculture, transportation, commercial and financial services). As a result, U.S. investment in public utilities, mining and smelting, and petroleum sectors now only account for about 28 percent of total investment compared with 65 percent in 1950. Today, manufacturing ($7.5 billion in 1974) is the single most important sector for U.S. investment and accounts for nearly 40 percent of total American investment in the region.

Anti-foreign capitalist sentiment has existed in Latin America since the beginning of the nineteenth century. Foreign merchants, bankers, and companies with superior contacts abroad and access to cheaper credit, enjoyed obvious advantages over native Latin Americans in foreign trade. This created strong suspicion and resentment. The history of foreign-owned public utilities in Latin America, for example, is predominately one of friction between the companies and host countries. As foreign investment took hold in mining, petroleum, manufacturing, and other sectors in the late nineteenth and early part of the twentieth centuries, conflicts and frictions between foreign-owned enterprises and local governments emerged there as well.

It is often charged that Latin American countries have been exploited by foreign "imperialism" since colonial times, which accounts for the relative backwardness of the region compared to North America and Europe. It must be remembered, however, that throughout the nineteenth and much of the present century, many Latin American governments were unstable, inefficient, and corrupt. This was not the ideal condition for promoting economic development nor for establishing effective control over foreign enterprise. Nevertheless, the sovereign political power of Latin American governments was seldom disputed by the foreign business community. The fact, however, that foreign business provided essential capital and expertise not available locally placed severe limits on the bargaining power of Latin American governments. Therefore, by today's standards, foreign companies did wring out highly favorable advantages, particularly in Argentina, Chile, and Mexico.

The ambiance changed radically in the twentieth century, particularly after World War II, as a result of the spread of education, the expansion of the professions, massive immigration of skilled labor, and the increasing availability of local savings to finance domestic capital formation. This newly acquired capacity made it increasingly possible for Latin America to dispense with the capital and technology previously provided by outsiders and to alter the forms of foreign participation in Latin America's industrial development. And Latin American governments continue to do so despite the advantages of such investment, since politically the presence of foreign capital is proving increasingly unacceptable.

Current U.S. Policy

Despite this climate, the United States government has long encouraged American investment in Latin America. Even during the early years of the Alliance for Progress private capital was supposed to play an important part in developing the region. The U.S. government has backed its rhetoric with investment guarantee programs administered first by AID and then, since 1969, by the Overseas Private Investment Corporation (OPIC). Despite the strong possibility of heavy losses in Chile, the program continues, primarily in Brazil and Mexico.[d]

But encouragement is one thing, protection is another. Legislative and executive attempts have been made (the Hickenlooper amendment in particular) to impose sanctions on governments that did not provide prompt and adequate compensation for expropriated American property. But they, in fact, have been seldom used, particularly after 1962. Occasionally, as in the case of IPC in Peru, American officials have acted as mediators, but more often U.S. corporations have been left to their own devices.

The latest major policy initiative by the United States in foreign investment was launched at UNCTAD IV in Nairobi. There, Secretary Kissinger proposed an International Resources Bank. Its mission would be to promote rational investment in the uncertain world of raw materials production. The bank's relation to the foreign investor is the same as its relation to the host country. As a middle man the IRB would work out with both sides project agreements "specifying the conditions of the investment on a basis acceptable to all parties."[13] The bank would also provide guarantees which in effect would lessen the risks run by private investment. Finally, both host country and investor would from the beginning receive a fixed share of the raw materials.

The proposal was narrowly voted down (33-31) in the last few hours of the conference. Therefore, it is likely the United States will continue promoting this scheme. Its reception (if established) by both governments and private enterprise, however, is still to be determined.

Future of U.S. Investment in Latin America. The prospect for U.S. investment in Latin America over the next decade is for a continuation of the slow growth that set in during the 1960s. It is, however, quite possible that U.S. investment

[d]OPIC has virtually ended writing insurance in Andean countries. OPIC took this step because of reduced investor interest and because Article 51 of the investment code cast doubt on subrogation and arbitration rights which the U.S. government has traditionally obtained in its agreements with countries initiating OPIC programs. OPIC officials have recently indicated that it would do limited business within the Andean Common Market on a bilateral basis. That is to say, it will insure U.S. investment in countries like Bolivia which are eager for capital for projects that do not involve intra-Andean trade, and thus are exempt from the common code's regulations.

will decline and stagnate at $15-18 billion in the 1980s.[e] Nevertheless, there will always be countries with particular problems that will need to attract foreign investment. Furthermore, U.S. capital may also flow increasingly to those few countries with broad domestic markets where private enterprise is fostered, and the rule of law is maintained. In any event, U.S. investment will probably continue to be concentrated in the manufacturing sector, particularly in those subsectors that the Latin American governments want to promote but lack the foreign capital and technology to do so. Meanwhile, U.S. investors will have to develop new investment strategies, including fade-out formulas which would turn control of the enterprise to the host country over a specified period of time. Joint ventures whereby repayment of the investment plus a reasonable profit might take the form of a share of production, and the right to market the product overseas, are also possibilities. Moreover, foreign investors should find that service contracts and other styles of operation may be more secure legally, and just as profitable, as concessions which have aroused nationalist hostility in the past.

Policy Options

The options facing U.S. policy are:

1. continuation of present support of U.S. investment overseas through OPIC insurance, Ex-Im Bank credits and guarantees, and tax advantages;
2. prevention of increased hostility toward foreign investment by requiring all U.S. firms benefitting from government support and incentives to engage in joint ventures (with U.S. investors taking a minority position) and to accept fade-out formulas;
3. creation of a new institution, within the IDB or World Bank, which would assist foreign investors to divest themselves of their interest in Latin America when they are no longer welcome.

U.S. Access to Latin America and Third World Mineral Raw Materials

Background

Until recently, the United States was widely perceived as a rich and self-sufficient nation. In fact, its dependence on imported mineral raw materials and oil

[e]The now five member Andean Common Market has a common investment code which lays down strict rules governing foreign capital. There is no doubt that it has discouraged outsiders although several members (Chile and Bolivia) have attempted to "interpret" the rules in a more liberal fashion in the past.

has been growing for the last twenty years. That in itself is no great cause for alarm since most nations have always lived in need of imports: self-sufficiency is the great historical exception, not the rule.

Nevertheless, increasing United States' dependence on foreign supplies comes at a time when world trade in metals, minerals, and oil is undergoing rapid change, and international competition for mineral resources has become severe only in the recent past.

How great then is the danger? Or has it become exaggerated after the shock of rapidly increased oil prices set in?

For particular minerals such as iron ore, manganese, zinc, and aluminum, imports already constitute a significant and growing proportion of U.S. domestic consumption.[f] Theoretically, the impact of a sharp price increase or a sudden disruption of supply could be substantial in the short run. In the longer run, the scope and severity of any disruption to the U.S. economy would also increase if U.S. requirements continue to be filled by foreign sources.

Future U.S. supply will have to be met to an increasing extent from Latin America, the Third World, and Communist countries. In order to insure an uninterrupted flow of vital supplies from these areas, new approaches and working relations may have to be introduced in our dealings with mineral-exporting countries, and with other consumer nations as well.

In 1970 nearly 90 percent of U.S. petroleum-product imports, 80 percent of crude petroleum imports, and over 90 percent of nearly all bulk metallic minerals and scrap originated in South America, the Caribbean area, and Canada. Of the 40 major minerals imported by the United States in 1972, 23 of them were supplied by Caribbean and South American countries.

In the past, proximity to the U.S. market, American ownership and control of much of Latin America's mineral production and marketing, and the existence of friendly governments resulted in lower production costs and general reliability of supply. The United States thus enjoyed considerable advantages over other industrial nations in the competition for Western Hemisphere mineral raw materials. That happy circumstance, however, will not hold for the future. The rapid growth of manufacturing industries, particularly in Argentina, Brazil, Mexico, and Venezuela, will claim an increasing share of their mineral raw material output. The establishment of processing facilities in the mineral-rich Latin American countries will also continue over the next few decades.[g]

Therefore, the United States will have to find other suppliers in Africa, Asia,

---

[f]The United States imported 20 percent of its iron ore, 98 percent of its manganese, 63 percent of its zinc, and 86 percent of its aluminum (ore and metal) requirements in 1973. Latin America was our leading supplier of manganese (33.1 percent of import requirements) and aluminum (65.9 percent), and third supplier in iron ore (28.5 percent) and zinc (8.3 percent). (Department of State figures.)

[g]In the case of iron ore, Venezuela, our chief supplier from Latin America (35 percent of our import requirements in 1973), will cease exporting ore in 1985 in order to provide for its own rapidly growing steel industry.

Australia, and possibly some Communist countries. Minerals from these areas should be more expensive because of higher shipping costs, and they will be less secure—with the exception of Australia.

Critical Problems

The recent rapid rise in prices (on the average over 50 percent in 1970-74) and the emergence of shortages of many mineral raw materials has raised questions about the U.S. mineral supply system. The short-term factors that explain these twin phenomena are:

1. speculation in minerals as a hedge against inflation import prices;
2. exchange rate realignment which raised U.S. mineral import prices.

Over the longer term (to 1985) the adequacy and price of U.S. mineral supply will also be affected by:

1. the severe strains placed on our finite resources due to the rapid growth of mineral usage;
2. growing U.S. vulnerability and dependence on mineral imports to meet domestic requirements;
3. the revolution of producer-foreign investor relations which is transferring control of important mineral resources from reliable western companies to weak and unstable governments in Latin America and the rest of the Third World;
4. efforts by such mineral-rich Latin American countries as Peru, Mexico, Chile, Venezuela, Jamaica, and Guyana to establish producer alliances and cartels to regulate supply and raise prices (or at least to guarantee prices at the highest possible level);
5. the prospects for effective Third World producer cartels would be enhanced if the developed countries like Australia cooperated fully;
6. the emergence of effective cross-cartel price coordination and financial support (especially between OPEC, CIPEC, and IBA)[h] is possible over the next few years, and efforts are being made toward that objective by the more nationalistic Third World countries such as Peru and Algeria.

It seems, then, the United States' growing dependency on mineral imports should make this country more vulnerable than in the past. And our recent experience with petroleum imports makes the problem appear even more acute. But appearances can be deceiving, especially when other factors have not been considered.

[h]OPEC (Organization of Petroleum Exporting Countries); CIPEC (Counseil Intergouvernemental des Pays Exportateurs de Cuivre); IBA (International Bauxite Association).

Only copper, bauxite, and perhaps a few other minerals, for example, are candidates for effective cartelization, and the prospects of radical action to restrict supplies of these minerals are small at present. Producing countries now have neither the power nor in most cases the motivation to do so. For one thing, disruption would encourage consumer nations to seek substitutes. Moreover, producer nations, for the most part, are still dependent on their leading customers for capital and technology. Finally, of course, producer nations must sell their products, and their generally precarious economies could not sustain a lengthy embargo of their principal exports.

However, over the next several years the American economy could be confronted with some supply dislocations and monopolistic pricing from one or two of the cartel candidates. While the U.S. economy may not be seriously threatened, the cumulative actions of mineral producers can be costly with higher prices and persistent shortages in the short run.

Leaving out the threat to prices posed by cartels, what are the chances for another 1973-74 style price surge in mineral raw materials? That question has two answers. First, price rises will be moderate over the next few years for three reasons. Western economies are recovering at a slow rate resulting in no great spurts in mineral demand. Second, metal stocks are still abundant, particularly in copper, tin, lead, zinc, and silver. Third, there is considerable spare capacity owing to the recession among mineral producers, particularly in copper, tin, and aluminum.

The long run, however, is not so bright. New investment needed now for production in five to ten years is not being made, and therefore, if the world economy moves into a boom in three to five years, prices may again soar and shortages develop. Guaranteeing an adequate supply in minerals over the long term thus presents an important challenge to U.S. policymakers.

Current U.S. Policy

The U.S. government believes that no serious threat to the American economy exists at present as a result of efforts of raw material suppliers to establish producer alliances and cartels. Consumer and producer countries, it is felt, have a common interest in avoiding excessively high prices that will result in new investment in high cost alternative supplies and the loss of traditional markets on the part of raw material suppliers.

Therefore, the U.S. government is attempting to establish new international rules for managing commodity supply problems that take into account the interests of both suppliers and consuming nations.

The U.S. government admits that a more active commodity policy is needed and will consider the following actions.

1. through multilateral trade negotiations the United States will explore the possibility of establishing: (a) joint producer-consumer consultative groups to exchange information on investment and pricing decisions and (b) developing commodity codes, specifying investor rights and obligations and assured access to markets;
2. negotiation of the financing of buffer stock schemes on a product-by-product basis although tin is now the only mineral raw material the United States has accepted as ripe for a commodity agreement;
3. adjustment of the legal and environmental restrictions on raw material investment in the United States. Tariff protection and subsidies for domestic investment does not appear to be desirable at present;
4. support of U.S. raw material investment overseas through OPIC and Ex-Im Bank credits;
5. establishment of an economic stockpile for some commodities as a measure of self-defense against supplier actions;
6. retaliation against arbitrary behavior of foreign suppliers is considered only as a last resort in reaction to hostile actions against U.S. interests.

In general, the U.S. government considers that it is not in its interest, nor in the interest of supplier countries, to reduce U.S. dependence on raw materials, for example, by restricting imports. However, it is rightly concerned with long-term supply problems, and has already proposed an International Resource Bank that will provide both guarantees for investor and host government alike to make otherwise risky investment in minerals productions. As noted earlier, the IRB proposal was voted down at Nairobi although the United States is likely to continue pressing for its creation.

U.S. Goals

The main objectives of U.S. mineral raw materials policy over the next decade for which there seems to be a considerable domestic consensus are:

1. assuring reliability of minerals supply from domestic and overseas sources;
2. achieving the lowest cost to society for mineral raw materials;
3. safeguarding the quality of the environment.

These objectives for a minerals policy are often in conflict. Insuring adequate supply, for example, could conflict with a clean environment. Any policy involves making choices which trade off objectives against each other.

The major objective of U.S. policy toward Latin America and the Third World will be to assure reliable access to vital mineral raw materials at reasonable prices with the minimum of conflict in our relations. Agreements will have to be reached with the Latin American mineral exporting countries and their Third World partners over what constitutes a "fair" price, and arrangements must be made to assure access.

Policy Options

Securing access to Latin American mineral raw materials must be viewed in the broader framework of maintaining adequate supply from both domestic and all foreign sources. This is a global issue which cannot be dealt with on an isolated basis in the context of U.S.-Latin American relations. Therefore, the following broad options are open to U.S. policymakers.

Feasible Independence. Under this option the United States would move to reduce its dependence on distant, unstable sources of supply in Latin America and the Third World by limiting domestic demand and increasing domestic production of those minerals (or substitutes) available in the United States. In the trade-off between the higher cost of relative self-sufficiency and our growing dependence on mineral imports, the United States should rely on imports of minerals to the minimum extent feasible.

Increased self-sufficiency will lead to higher mineral prices for American industrial consumers and could provoke retaliation and hostility against the United States on the part of the producing countries. Higher prices could also adversely affect our international competitive position if our economic rivals established access to cheaper sources of mineral supply. On the other hand, this option would tend to enhance the U.S. bargaining position with foreign mineral exporting countries.

As U.S. productive capacity expanded and mineral imports declined, the export earnings of the Latin American countries would suffer. Pressure would build up for mineral exporting countries to lower their export prices and U.S. producers would demand increased protection to offset the lower import prices.

In view of the growing world competition for Latin American and Third World minerals and the future uncertainties concerning overseas mineral supply, the United States should provide specific economic incentives to expand domestic production and restrict imports in the direction required by an expanding American economy and national security.

Continued Foreign Dependence. Essentially this option envisages a continuation of the policy of reliance on foreign suppliers for an increasing share of domestic mineral requirements over the next decade or so. It is designed to avoid or minimize restrictive actions on the part of both consumer and producing nations in the interest of insuring access to overseas supply by maintaining an open international trading system.

Insuring access on the basis of continued dependence on foreign supplies has variants:

1. *"Do Nothing."* Under this alternative, the United States assumes a passive role and allows market forces to bring an end to high prices and scarcities. High prices make mining investments more attractive and induce multinational corporations and foreign governments to expand their productive capacity. The resulting expansion of mineral supply exerts a downward pressure on prices and shortages disappear. This option assumes that cartelization of the mineral trade will not be successful and thus poses no threat to the United States.[i]

2. *Producer-Consumer Collaboration.* This option recognizes the interdependence and mutuality of interests of mineral producing and consuming nations: their need for our capital and technology is balanced by our need for their mineral raw materials. The United States still retains a strong lead in technology and remains the major world source of capital needed for mineral resources development. These could be exchanged on a new basis for the needed supplies of mineral raw materials. The alternative aims at avoiding conflict, supply dislocations, and excessive prices through mutual accommodation and collaborative efforts.

These efforts could range from establishing informal machinery for regular consultation on market conditions and investment for specific commodities, to creating producer-consumer commodity arrangements, like the International Tin Council, which has intervened in the world market to reduce excessive fluctuations of supply and price.[14]

3. *Expand World Mineral Production.* The United States could influence the expansion of foreign mineral supply by providing incentives to U.S. mining corporations and giving the Export-Import Bank and AID a much larger role in financing and insuring mining, mining infrastructure, and mineral-processing projects in Latin America and the Third World. The U.S. government could also encourage the World Bank Group, the Inter-American Development Bank, the Asian Development Bank, and the proposed International Resources Bank to allocate a larger share of their loan portfolios to mineral sector development, particularly in the lesser developed countries. In the meantime, if the IRB continues to be rejected by Third World countries, it might be tried as an experiment in this hemisphere alone.

Mining expansion can be an important factor in the economic development of some countries, particularly those with few alternative investments from which revenues and foreign exchange can be derived. Both suppliers and consuming countries have an interest in expanding the mineral production capacity of the developing countries.

Private mining companies with the capital and expertise to develop the mineral resources of the developing countries are increasingly reluctant to

---

[i]This has not worked in the case of OPEC because the principal oil supplier, Saudi Arabia, could afford to cut back production and survive. Option (a) assumes that Saudi Arabia is unique, that is, no other single exporter of any other mineral is in this kind of position.

undertake the substantial costs of exploration and development with the large investment requirements ($100-400 million is not uncommon) and considerable political risks involved in most of Latin America and the Third World.

For their part, the developing countries are dissatisfied with the traditional concession and enclave arrangements of the past but lack the financial resources and expertise in both public and private sectors to engage in large-scale exploration and development on their own.

An expansion and diversification of foreign mineral supply would tend to exert a downward pressure on mineral prices and make effective cartelization of the mineral trade difficult. Producer countries with heavy investment in fixed assets and large debt amortization payments are reluctant to restrict mining output and exports.

4. *Defensive Counter-Action.* The United States could prepare for defensive counter-action when confronted with a case of politically or economically motivated restriction of essential mineral exports by producer countries. This would require that the U.S. government take appropriate steps to enhance our bargaining leverage with foreign mineral suppliers and producer alliances such as:

a. establishing an early-warning minerals information system which would provide continuous and comprehensive analysis of supplies and shortages in the American economy stemming from domestic and overseas supply problems;

b. in addition to maintaining an organized strategic mineral reserve, which is now under review by the National Security Council, an economic stockpile could be created that could be used to avoid costly dislocations in foreign supply and moderate international prices of critical minerals;

c. close consultation and coordination of our actions with other consumer countries should be undertaken whenever feasible and in preference to independent and competitive action. But the United States must be prepared to take prompt defensive measures (including retaliation) alone, if necessary, to protect its economic well-being and national security;

d. creating legislative authority on a standby basis (as a deterrence) so that the government is in a position to control imports and exports, subrogate the rights of confiscated U.S. investors, cut off economic and military credits, and restrict tourism.

Latin America as a Declining Food Surplus Region

Background

World Food Situation. World food production has grown steadily over the past two decades with growth in the developed countries roughly paralleling that in the less developed countries, including Communist Asia.

Population growth has been more rapid in the less developed countries than in the developed. One consequence has been that most less developed countries in Asia, Africa, and Latin America have become net food importers. By the early 1970s only Latin America as a whole was a net food exporting region, largely as a result of Argentine cereal and meat exports. In the developed countries, production has increased much faster than population, providing for a substantial gain in production per capita, and permitting increasing net food exports from North America, Australia, and New Zealand.

The steepest increase in production occurred in Eastern Europe and the Soviet Union. Least growth has been in the United States and Canada where food production until 1974 was restricted by public policy. Wide year-to-year fluctuations in several regions (the USSR, Canada, and Oceania) reflect the effects of weather but generally do not obscure the upward trends. In the developing countries, on the other hand, population gains have absorbed nearly all of the production increase; here production per capita has registered only a slight improvement.

The much higher total value of food production in the developed regions reflects mainly the consumption of higher value commodities such as livestock products. For the world as a whole, however, cereals continue to play a dominant role, both for direct consumption as a food and also as a feed for expanding livestock economies. The developed countries in 1966-70 accounted for almost two-thirds of world grain production on an area slightly less than that in the less developed regions.

Despite high prices and temporary recent shortages, the fundamental conditions of the world food economy have changed very little. Patterns of food consumption are largely determined by habits, tastes, and taboos which alter little from year to year, and patterns of production are likewise remarkably stable. The developed regions on the average consume considerably more total calories and calories from sugar, vegetables, fruits, fats, and animal products than the less developed countries, where consumption per capita is high for cereals, starchy root crops and plantains, and the pulses-and-nuts groups of food.

For the world as a whole, cereals supply just over half of the calories derived from food consumption and they also supply foodstuffs in the production of meat, milk, and eggs. Meat consumption is increasing in nearly all countries with rising incomes. The rising affluence of upper-income consumers around the world is leading to increased domestic meat consumption supplied by either domestic production or imports or both. To meet this rising demand for meat—including poultry—producers must use increasing quantities of concentrated feed since there is not enough grassland and roughage. Concentrated feed includes protein-rich commodities like oilcake and fishmeal but consists predominantly of grain.

Cereals have long been used in the United States for livestock feed. Since the 1950s, the use of cereals for feed in other developed countries has increased. Output of grain has fluctuated with weather and government policies in the major producing countries, but has tended to increase faster than population on a world basis. Use of grain has fluctuated less than production and has shown practically the same upward trend per capita as output.

In the United States the food use of grain per capita has been declining since 1909. Other developed countries exhibit similar long-term downward trends. Among poor countries the opposite trend is evident: grains are substituted for potatoes or other root crops and the total caloric intake per capita increases with rising incomes.

In recent years the depletion of world grain stocks has significantly increased grain prices. Wheat stocks on July 1, 1973 in the four major exporting countries were at the lowest level in two decades, and coarse grain stocks were the lowest since 1967. Recent crop estimates indicate record harvests in many countries, including the United States and Argentina. But until stocks are rebuilt, world grain supplies will be dependent on current and upcoming harvests. This could present a precarious situation if there are serious early crop failures in a few key countries.

The outlook for world food production has been affected by the energy crisis, particularly as reflected in the prospects for nitrogen fertilizer supplies. The impact of the current fertilizer shortage may be more severe in some of the less developed regions than in developed countries because fertilizer imports account for a major portion of the fertilizer supply in the less developed

Table III-2
Cereal Production
(1,000 metric tons)

	1961-1965	1972	1973	1974
Developed				
North America	197,288	263,722	274,291	235,958
West Europe	109,328	148,098	150,639	158,603
Oceania	11,350	11,514	17,930	17,552
Developing				
Africa	36,918	44,985	38,664	43,923
Latin America	53,051	67,798	73,922	76,840
Near East	36,565	47,755	41,179	45,485
Far East	171,388	208,015	233,791	220,681
Centrally Planned				
Asian	174,255	222,944	235,015	241,478
Europe, USSR	172,115	235,286	287,613	263,093

Source: *FAO Production Yearbook*, 1974, Volume 28-1, table 12.

countries (LDCs). Also, world market equilibrium is being reached at higher price levels which will strain already depleted foreign exchange reserves in some LDCs. The wheat and rice varieties that characterize the Green Revolution generally produce little more than traditional varieties unless well fertilized and irrigated.

Grain Projections to 1985. Trade in food grains and coarse grains are projected to 1985 in Table III-3 and are derived from U.S. Department of Agriculture estimates. The inputs to this analysis were growth rates for population and income, demand and supply price elasticities, and assumptions about basic underlying economic trends and policy constraints. The medium variant of the UN population projections is used while the world economy is assumed to continue to grow at the rapid rate of recent decades. Normal weather (i.e., average conditions which cancel out both unusually poor or good years) is assumed. An attempt is made to take into account trends in tastes and preferences in consumption, such as increasing desire for livestock products, and changes in yields thanks to such phenomena as the Green Revolution. Unless otherwise specified, an essential continuity in present policies guiding domestic production, consumption, and international trade is assumed.

1985 World Grain Trade projections attempt to anticipate what would happen should world demand grow more rapidly than suggested under a more conservative hypothesis and incorporate the following assumptions:

1. the USSR and Eastern Europe attempt to increase livestock production and consumption at a faster rate of growth even if it means importing grain and high overall levels of trade with the western world;

Table III-3
Pattern of World Grain Trade: Long-Term Trends, 1934-1985
(millions of metric tons)

	1934-38	1948-52	1960	1969-71	1974-75	1985
North America	+5	+23	+39	+54	+100	+101
Latin America	+9	+1	0	+3	−3	−2
Western Europe	−24	−22	−25	−22	−19	−15
Western Europe & USSR	+5	−	0	−3	−9	−14
Africa	+1	0	−2	−3	−3	−12
Asia	+2	−6	−17	−31	−40	−73
Australia & New Zealand	+3	+3	+6	+11	+11	+15

Note: Plus sign denotes net exports; minus sign denotes net imports. Grains include wheat, coarse grains.

Source: FAO and USDA. Projections based on USDA estimates which assume high demand for livestock products in developing countries.

2. the People's Republic of China becomes more trade oriented and imports more grain to improve city diets;
3. the enlarged European community finds it advantageous not to pursue as strongly its self-sufficiency policy by setting lower price targets for production, thus permitting continued imports of grain;
4. the livestock economies, particularly poultry, of the developing world grow faster, either in countries with enhanced petroleum revenues, or in countries with unexpectedly higher rates of economic growth; and
5. fishmeal production stagnates at the 1969-71 level.

The higher demand for livestock products under these assumptions should substantially increase the demand for coarse grains and oilseed meal with some impact on the demand for wheat. Higher feed prices would encourage more feeding of wheat in the developed countries, particularly Western Europe where wheat competes well with barley for feed use. The projections suggest that the United States could meet nearly all the increased world import demand for coarse grains—with net U.S. export of feed grains reaching about 100 million tons by 1985.

The consumption and trade of wheat and rice should grow less rapidly than coarse grains because of the increasing need of feed for expanding livestock and poultry production. Countries in the developed and centrally planned parts of the world will continue to be the major producers and consumers of wheat and coarse grains. The developed exporting countries will continue to supply the less developed importing countries with grain, and the Latin American region seems likely for the immediate future to become a net grain importing region. The developed importing countries will increase their grain imports in order to promote livestock production.

Most of the less developed countries, because of limited foreign exchange resources, will give food grain imports priority over feed grains. However, some with abundant foreign exchange could show a rapid growth in imports of feed grains.

Projected production in trade in the less developed countries should permit their per capita consumption of grains to increase slightly over the base period. But any larger increase will most likely have to come from greater domestic production rather than from larger imports. Korea and Taiwan, however, are examples of areas where little grain is grown but where significant growth in imports of wheat and feed is projected. The wheat will be needed for direct food consumption. Coarse grains and protein feeds will be needed as these populations move toward more animal protein in their diets.

These projections assume adequate supplies of fertilizer, chemicals, and fuels. Obviously, if producers cannot obtain these, the ability to reach the projected yield levels could be impaired. These projections also assume price relationships between commodity prices and input costs will be favorable for increased production and that there will be no serious environmental problems. The extent to which the 1973-74 surge in world grain trade represented a reaction to monetary changes and a desire by some of the importers to acquire stocks, and the extent it represented a basic rise in world demand for food still is not known—all of which tends to cloud the 1985 projections.

As can be observed in Table III-4, North America has become the world's major grain exporting region, with the United States dominating the world grain trade. Dependency on North American food exports leaves the world in a precarious position in the event of adverse crop years coinciding with the exceptionally large expansion of imports elsewhere.

Latin American Grain Trade. Before World War II, Latin America (mainly Argentina) was exporting about 9 million metric tons a year of grain, an amount substantially above North America's (Canada and the United States). Shortly

Table III-4
Pattern of World Grain Trade: 1985 Projections
(millions of metric tons)

	1969-71	1985	
		L	H
North America	+54.0	+73.6	+100.7
Latin America	+2.7	−1.2	−1.7
Mexico and Central America	−1.8	−4.9	−5.9
Brazil	−.7	−2.0	−2.0
Argentina	+8.3	+12.6	+13.7
Other South America	−3.1	−6.9	−7.5
Western Europe	−21.6	−7.9	−15.1
Eastern Europe	−7.3	−1.2	−5.2
USSR	+4.0	−.3	−8.3
Africa	−3.1	−10.6	−11.9
South Africa	+1.2	+4.1	+4.3
Asia	−31.4	−66.3	−73.2
Southeast Asia	+3.6	+6.1	+6.1
China	−3.1	−4.2	−5.2
Japan	−14.4	−35.1	−37.1
Australia and New Zealand	+10.8	+14.1	−14.9

Note: Plus sign denotes net exports; minus sign denotes net imports. Grains include wheat, coarse grains and milled rice.

L = Low Estimate   H = High Estimate
Source: United States Department of Agriculture.

after World War II, North America's net exports to world markets left Latin America far behind. Rapid population growth and a strong government bias in favor of industrial growth at the expense of agriculture threatens Latin America's status as a net food exporter. The slowness of most Latin American governments to reform agriculture and provide adequate investment incentives to farmers has already sharply reduced Latin America's net grain exports. (1973 was an exceptionally poor year for food production in Argentina, Mexico, and Chile.) With a few exceptions, Latin American countries are now net food importers.

In the future, unless a much greater effort is made to become more self-sufficient in food production, the Latin American region will become a regular net food importing region. This shift from a net food exporting to net food importing region could occur by 1980. On current trends Latin America will be importing (net) several million metric tons of grain by 1985. High demographic growth rates, the progress of industrialization, and rapid urbanization will place new burdens on the Latin American agriculture to provide the cereals and meat needed to meet regional food consumption requirements.

Latin America's food production and export potential is, of course, much greater than current trends would suggest. This is particularly true in countries like Argentina, Chile, Colombia, Brazil, Uruguay, and Bolivia where conditions are favorable. By 1985, Latin American grain production could be doubled (from the 1973 level of about 68 million tons to about 120 million tons) under reasonably optimistic conditions of weather, institutional reforms, and government incentives. This would enable Latin America to become once again a major net food export region, with grain exports reaching 15-20 million tons by 1985.

Land Availability. Pessimism concerning the availability of land to produce more food has existed since Malthus but new sources of land and new ways of increasing food production have materialized after each successive wave of anxiety. Uneasiness and concern persist, however.

According to the FAO, large amounts of land physically suited for crop production still exist in the world. In the developing world, *Latin America has the largest reserve of potentially productive cropland, with 77 percent of its suitable land (440 million hectares) unused in 1962.* While there has been an increase in land used for crop production in Latin America over the past decade, the general picture remains unchanged, with Latin America today the major food reserve area in the Third World.

Despite the fact that the world is not, according to FAO, running out of land, serious problems persist in Latin America and other developing regions of raising agricultural output and productivity due to the policy bias against agriculture.

Latin America is overall a food privileged region, yet it should be noted that considerable disparities in food production and dependency on imports exist from country to country. The densely populated Caribbean islands (such as Jamaica, Barbados, Haiti), for example, do not have the relatively large surplus

Table III-5
Land Use for Crops and Potential Use, Developing Regions
(millions of hectares)

Region (1)	Land Suitable for Crops (2)	Land Used for Crops[a] (3)	Land Potentially Available (4)	(2) (3) (5)
Africa (south of Sahara)	304	152	152	50%
Asia & Far East	252	211	41	84%
Latin America	570	130	440	23%
N.W. Africa	19	19	–0–	100%
Total or Average	1,145	512	633	45%

[a]1962.
Source: Food and Agriculture Organization of United Nations, *Indicative World Plan*, vol. 1, August 1967, p. 49.

croplands available for food production that many South American countries do such as Argentina, Bolivia, and Brazil. However, even in the densely populated Caribbean islands, there is still some scope for expanding food production and reducing inputs by raising yields.

A key problem resides in overcoming the resistance of Latin American governments to shift scarce resources to the food producing sector, and to provide adequate economic incentives in order to raise yields and expand production. The political and institutional factors that account for Latin America's sluggish agricultural production and export performances since World War II have been analyzed in great detail by the IBRD, the IDB, and the United Nations. Fundamentally, what is required is a major commitment on the part of the Latin American governments to give a much higher priority to agriculture than has been the case over the past two decades.

Latin America is so closely integrated into the world economy already that adverse developments abroad, including the rising price of farm machinery, fertilizers, and energy plus widespread protection of agriculture in the industrial and developing countries affect its agricultural production and exports.

Over the past few years renewed efforts have been undertaken in Latin America to improve the terms of trade of agricultural commodities by establishing agricultural commodity cartels.

Policy Options

U.S. interest in world peace and progress is served by encouraging adequate production of food supplies in the Third World. With respect to Latin America the following policy options should be considered:

1. encourage Latin American countries to formulate plans for food production through agricultural and fisheries development;
2. channel a large share of existing bilateral U.S. development assistance to Latin American food production, shift resources to the food production sector, and provide stronger economic incentives for food production and exports;
3. encourage the international and regional lending agencies (World Bank group, Inter-American Development Bank, Andean Development Corporation and Caribbean Development Bank) to allocate a large share of their lending portfolios to food production and rural development, especially in the low-income farm sector;
4. encourage Latin American governments to develop food and nutrition programs and improve related facilities such as nutrition education, family planning services, pure water supplies, special feeding programs for children and other vulnerable groups;
5. encourage international agencies (FAO, World Meteorological Organization) and Latin American governments to improve scientific water management, including irrigation, drainage flood control, the development of better use of ground water, and brackish water for food production;
6. encourage research and studies by international organizations such as the United Nations to examine the interrelationship between population growth, food supplies, and depletable energy and mineral resources;
7. encourage the UN Conference on Trade and Development to examine new approaches to commodity stabilization problems for consideration by the importing and exporting countries.

Notes

1. Quoted in Joseph Grunwald, Miguel S. Wionczek, and Martin Carnoy, *Latin American Economic Integration and U.S. Policy* (Washington, D.C.: The Brookings Institution, 1972), p. 76.

2. Richard M. Nixon, speech to the Inter-American Press Association, October 31, 1969.

3. Henry Kissinger's speech, June 9, 1976 (Department of State, Bureau of Public Affairs, Washington, D.C.).

4. See, for example, John C. Dreier's *The Organization of American States and the Hemisphere Crisis* (New York: Harper & Row, 1962) for a concise summary of the United States hopes and expectations regarding the OAS over the years. Mr. Dreier was a long-time American ambassador to the OAS. The best Latin American critique of Pan Americanism (and by extention, the OAS) is Antonio Gómez Robledo's *Idea y Experencia de América* (Mexico City: Fondo de Cultura Económica, 1958).

5. Roger W. Fontaine, "Politics and the Inter-American Conference for the Maintenance of Continental Peace and Security," unpublished paper.

6. Clark W. Reynolds, "Relations with Latin America: An American View," pp. 242-243, in Victor L. Urquidi and Rosemary Thorp (eds.), *Latin America in the International Economy*, (New York: John Wiley and Sons, 1973).

7. See Chapter III of this study, "U.S. Access to Latin America and Third World Mineral Raw Materials."

8. Santiago P. Macario, "The Role of World Trade Policy: A Latin American Viewpoint," p. 68 in Victor L. Urquidi and Rosemary Thorp (eds.), *Latin America in the World Economy*, (New York: John Wiley and Sons, 1973).

9. U.S. Public Law 93-618, 93rd Congress, January 3, 1975, p. 90 and p. 93.

10. See Chapter III of this study, "Regional Blocs in Latin America."

11. Henry Kissinger's speech, June 9, 1976 (Department of State, Bureau of Public Affairs).

12. Henry Kissinger's speech, May 6, 1976, (Department of State, Bureau of Public Affairs).

13. Henry Kissinger's speech, May 6, 1976, (Department of State, Bureau of Public Affairs).

14. The latest attempt of the Tin Council was in December 1975 when it declared the first quarter of 1976 "an export control period" with a total export amount of 32,000 metric tons permitted by its seven members. *Tin News* (Malayan Tin Bureau, Washington, D.C.) January 15, 1976, p. 1.

IV Latin America: Critical Choices in Key Countries

Latin America is something more than a geographical expression, but one can exaggerate its unity and commonality. Below (or perhaps above) the rhetorical level, the United States has nearly always cultivated (and counted on) as many good bilateral relations as it could get in the region. The Latin Americans may be angry at us, so the argument runs, but the Brazilians, Chileans, and Mexicans still like us. That attitude still prevails, primarily at the State Department, and while the wisdom is a bit shopworn, it does have considerable merit.

Historically, the United States has given priority to countries in two areas: the Caribbean and the Southern Cone. That order should continue. In the Caribbean three countries are of special importance: Cuba, Mexico, and Venezuela. The second group consists of Argentina and Brazil.

We begin, however, with an examination of the Caribbean as a security concern for this country. Although strictly speaking it is of a subregional nature, our practical problems in the area usually revolve around the sensitive and difficult relations we maintain with a number of highly individualistic countries, Cuba and Panama in particular.

U.S. Security in the Caribbean

Background

American leaders have always viewed the Caribbean with great concern and high hopes. They feared foreign intrusion, but the proximity and tropical climate of the Caribbean also prompted the expectation of profitable trade.

89

Spain's hold on the area was already seriously weakened by 1800, and Americans worried about the possible Caribbean adventures of any major European power. Their fears were crystalized in the Monroe Doctrine, which was a unilateral warning against further European colonization in the hemisphere. Later, when it was apparent how fragile and debt-ridden the newly independent Caribbean regimes were, the United States repeatedly intervened in order to deny European creditors control of any Caribbean state. Slowly, the United States acquired the role of protector and guarantor of these republics—a role which it has only gradually, and partially, given up since the 1930s.

Traditionally, the United States has maintained a physical presence in the Caribbean, either through military bases[a] or through prolonged intervention (for example, in the Dominican Republic, 1916-1924). The building of the Panama Canal further heightened the need for U.S. power in the Caribbean.

With the increase of American military might and the development of nuclear weapons, do these long-standing security concerns make sense today or for the future? Is the Caribbean, in short, still strategically vital to the United States? Or is it a relatively minor area littered with bits and pieces of half-formed, often impoverished nation-states with little commercial value and seemingly endless and insoluble political problems?

Before the critical problems facing the United States are examined, it should be made clear what states comprise the Caribbean region. The lists vary, but the following have been included for both geographic and historical reasons: the island states of the Greater Antilles including Cuba, Jamaica, Haiti, the Dominican Republic, Puerto Rico plus the Leeward and Windward Islands and Trinidad-Tobago; on the northern South American littoral, Venezuela, Guyana, and Surinam; finally, the five Central American countries plus Panama.

Critical Problems

What are the current and emerging critical problems that will continue to affect the United States in the coming decade? First, under the general heading of nationalism, the following difficult problem areas can be listed:

1. Black power movements, largely confined to the ex-British commonwealth states like Trinidad-Tobago and Jamaica, have helped undermine otherwise friendly governments by their sharply anti-American tone.

2. Fervent Panamanian nationalism demanding the return of the Zone and the Canal to exclusively Panamanian jurisdiction is making orderly negotiations difficult, and a mutually satisfactory treaty unlikely.

[a]Major U.S. military bases currently operating in the Caribbean are Guantanamo (Cuba), Roosevelt Roads (Puerto Rico), the Canal Zone, and Andros Island in the Grand Bahamas. Minor naval and air facilities are on Eleuthera (Bahamas), Grand Bahama, Turk Islands and Caicos.

3. The growing economic nationalism of some Caribbean states has led to the expropriation of U.S. investments, and more important, to attempts to form commodity cartels (in bananas and bauxite, for example) in order to raise prices and restrict production.

4. Subregional ambitions, such as Cuba's and Venezuela's clear desires for leading roles in Caribbean affairs, may have destabilizing results.

5. Cuba in particular raises some serious questions. Its new adventurist policy in Africa may in the future be tried out closer to home. At the moment, however, the Castro regime has not altered its rather cautious course in the Caribbean. Nevertheless, a number of problems could arise in the near future. Puerto Rican independence has recently become a Castro cause. Until now, the Cubans have stopped short of heavy support for armed insurrection but the possibility cannot be ruled out in the future. In both Guyana and Jamaica the Cubans have warmly supported increasingly radical regimes. In the case of Guyana that country has assisted in the Cuban bridge to Africa by providing refueling facilities. Both countries will drift further to the left, and will be Cuba's firmest supporters in the region.

In addition, the region presents serious indigenous political and economic problems:

1. Most Caribbean states are faced with the interrelated problems of poverty, limited resources (especially land), and growing populations. The poverty trap could well cause these countries endless social and political turmoil.

2. It will probably also ensure the continued vulnerability of small and weak states to Soviet penetration if and when the USSR chooses to do so.

3. With or without political subversion, there will continue to be, barring American action, a growing Soviet maritime presence in the Caribbean. At the present rate of escalation, it could easily reach strategic proportions within a decade.

Current U.S. Policy

Present American policy in the Caribbean has both strategic and economic elements. The United States clearly wishes to prevent any further violations of the Monroe Doctrine (witness the Dominican Republic intervention). It still suspects Cuba, with good reason, of promoting subversion and being a potential site for a substrategic Soviet military base. At the same time, it will not tolerate any strategic threat in the form of missiles, bombers, or nuclear submarine bases on the island. The result has been more than a decade of embargo which the United States has only recently, i.e., before Angola, indicated it might change.

Meanwhile, American policy has shifted on the Panama Canal question and is now committed to renegotiation of the 1903 treaty. How far we will go to accommodate Panamanian demands is not clear at this date.

American economic policy has been much less focused than security policy. We have favored economic integration and provided some capital but we have refrained from heavy involvement. No trade policy has been specifically tailored for the region, although the sugar quota ended in 1974.

Alternative U.S. Objectives and Options

There are three sets of American goals for the Caribbean, which can tentatively be called: limited intervention, strategic disengagement, and positive activism.

Limited Intervention. This course implies:

1. removal of the Soviet presence from the Caribbean;
2. preservation of U.S. military bases in the Caribbean or, at most, their gradual phasing out on a quid pro quo basis;
3. reincorporation of Cuba into the Caribbean community as a result of a careful bargain between the United States and Cuba;
4. maintenance of American de facto control of the Panama Canal.

The option of limited intervention is based on the assumption that the United States has limited but important interests in the Caribbean, and that these interests are unlikely to vanish in the coming decade.

Furthermore, whether we like it or not, the Caribbean has been considered by Americans and others as especially important to the United States. Wholesale removal from the area, even on narrowly rational political, legal, and military grounds, would have a considerable negative impact on the American public, and would encourage our enemies in the belief the United States is a declining power, unable to protect its interests on its own doorstep.

1. The Panama Canal must remain efficiently managed for the sake of our commerce and naval strategy. In addition, as a great power we have a responsibility to preserve the commercial interests of other users of the Canal. Exclusive management of the Canal by Panama would probably not be efficient or protect those interests, and its multilateral operation seems unfeasible.

2. A modus vivendi may be worked out with Cuba, but only a strictly quid pro quo basis.

3. The United States is very eager to secure continued access to important raw materials that can be obtained in the region, including oil and bauxite, at reasonable prices.

4. The United States will act decisively to prevent any regime in the area from making available strategic military facilities to the Soviet Union.

5. While military bases in Cuba and the Canal Zone are not vital to the defense of the United States, they do facilitate the defense of the Canal and the

surveillance of the Caribbean, and provide training and logistical facilities for the Navy. Any curtailment of such bases should be part of a reciprocal benefit package. Strict guarantees that Guantanamo will not be handed over to the Soviets must be obtained.

Consequences. There would be some lessening of the U.S. presence in the Caribbean, but it would not be dramatic in scope or in swiftness. Furthermore, it would have to be clearly linked with a scaled-down Soviet presence in the area.

Strategic Disengagement. This course involves:

1. gradual withdrawal of all U.S. military bases from foreign soil;
2. limitation of Soviet military presence in the area to nonstrategic activities;
3. rapprochement with Cuba on generous terms;
4. an end to U.S. unilateral responsibility for the operation and defense of the Panama Canal.

The policy of strategic disengagement is based on the assumption that there are no immutable, vital U.S. interests per se in the Caribbean. Indeed, it could be argued that within the coming decade, the United States should stand down in the area. Paring down our Caribbean commitments would involve four specific policies.

1. All military bases and residual rights to such bases not located on U.S. territory will be abandoned, including those in the Canal Zone, Cuba, and Trinidad-Tobago.

2. The United States will not intervene militarily in the affairs of any Caribbean country unless that country has clearly committed itself to the establishment of a Soviet military base on its soil.

3. The United States will make arrangements to give up any rights to the Canal Zone, along with its military facilities, and attempt instead to broaden participation in the efficient running of the Canal. The unilateral operation of the Panama Canal is a thankless and burdensome task that the United States will not perform in perpetuity.

4. The United States will seek at the earliest possible moment a modus vivendi with Cuba. The expectation is not friendship or even normal diplomatic relations (at least not at first) but rather an end to the island's cold war isolation. It should be made clear that under strategic disengagement the United States is still committed to securing its sea lanes by conventional arms, and will not tolerate their interdiction. In addition, strategic disengagement manifestly repudiates any sphere-of-influence doctrine in the Caribbean. The regimes in the area are free to do what they will in the way of political and economic experimentation. The United States also takes the opportunity of refusing to recognize spheres of influence claimed by other countries elsewhere in the world.

Consequences. Strategic disengagement would have the following results:

1. The United States is freed from the tangle of endless negotiations with nationalistic regimes over questions of sovereign rights in which there is never any certainty of satisfying compromise.
2. The United States avoids the trauma of intervention, which often accomplishes little and inflicts increasingly costly consequences.
3. Strategic disengagement lays the basis of genuine rapprochement with Cuba, and strengthens the long-term possibility of reincorporating Cuba into the Western Hemisphere's family of nations.
4. On the other hand, the adjustments and accommodations demanded by strategic disengagement are psychologically painful and economically costly (for example, the relocation of military facilities). It would therefore be imperative that the whole process be spread over at least a decade. Furthermore, once disengagement is completed it would be difficult to get those bases back (or prevent someone else from using them). The latter is particularly the case with Guantanamo. Moreover, the future shape of military strategy is not clear enough to assume these bases are forever obsolete.
5. In addition, while intervention is never easy, the consequences of not intervening when American security is actually threatened would, of course, be even costlier. The Cuban missile crisis provides a salutary example of this observation.
6. Finally, it is extremely important for the United States to avoid the appearance of weakness or surrender in such actions. If it is not to appear weak, these measures must be its own initiatives, not someone else's. But the time for independent action is short, and the first steps would have to be taken now.

Positive Activism. This means:

1. promotion of at least the beginning of a Caribbean-wide economic community;
2. sustained economic growth in much if not most of the area;
3. increased and mutually beneficial trade relations.

In the case of positive activism the assumption is that the United States has some interests in the region as outlined above, and in addition to dealing with the military questions, it will also protect those interests by more active participation in the economic and social development of the region. Since most of these countries lack the resources to make it on their own, the United States would carry out the following program:

    1. The promotion of economic integration schemes in the area, including

CACM and CARICOM. Such encouragement could take the form of heavier funding of regional banks like CABEI and the Caribbean Bank. (It is assumed that strong support of these organizations will dilute their incipient anti-Americanism.)

2. The encouragement of cooperation between the already established customs unions—cooperation which could evolve into a Carribean-wide common market.

3. The encouragement of participation in the financial support of such institutions by other countries, especially Venezuela.

4. The granting of Generalized Special Preferences to Caribbean products, including manufactured and semi-manufactured goods.

Consequences. It cannot be simply assumed that such measures will succeed in solving the Caribbean's economic problems, or, even if they are successful, that they will guarantee good relations with the United States. But without them the potential for embarrassment is high and trouble in the Caribbean would prompt the adoption of hastily drawn up, ill-conceived, and costly bailout economic development schemes.

The Very Special Problem of Panama

The Panama Canal could well be this country's most intractable problem in Latin America. The issue may be resolved over the next year with the writing and ratification of a new treaty but there are forces at work which may prevent that from happening. Moreover, a ratified treaty may not end the matter while security questions may go unanswered.

The first problem, of course, is the negotiations themselves. They have been proceeding, off and on, for the last twelve years, although the end of the negotiating phase is apparently in sight. While the exact content of the draft treaty is not yet fixed, Panama's objectives are clear enough. It wants control of the Canal and the Canal Zone within twenty years. That means the United States will play no role in the management or defense of the Canal after 1995. Until then, the United States must pay a much larger amount to Panama for the use of the Canal based on a percentage of income derived per ton moved through the Canal in place of the present fixed annuity of $2 million. In addition, any construction of a sea level canal or improvement of the present Canal will be financed solely by the United States and will revert to Panama by December 31, 1995 at no cost to that country.

The United States, on the other hand, advocates a less stringent timetable. For example, U.S. negotiators want this country to manage the Canal for another 25 years and to defend it for 50. In addition, the United States wishes to retain authority over some 85 percent of the present Canal Zone until the end of the century, and it also wants the sole right to improve and expand the present Canal.

These issues have proven difficult to find agreement on but even if they (and others) were solved there will be more difficult problems to overcome. Because the question is so sensitive in the United States, opposition to any treaty will be great—a matter which is already reflected in the United States Senate. Moreover, the likely mood of the country after Vietnam and Angola will be to view such a treaty as another surrender to men who wish the United States no good. The fact that General Omar Torrijos has cultivated a close relationship with Fidel Castro will only fuel that suspicion.

How the matter will be resolved (and it may well not be within the next decade) is also very unclear. Nevertheless, the following scenarios are offered as the most likely. In the first, the Senate would ratify in 1977 a treaty that returns the Canal and the Canal Zone to Panama after a fixed period of continued U.S. management and defense. The immediate consequences in Panama would be a defusing of the issue, with Torrijos given credit for a victory over American imperialism. However, Torrijos would be criticized for not immediately obtaining sole Panamanian jurisdiction over the Canal. Within ten years that criticism should mount, especially if the United States is perceived as not surrendering control fast enough. That, in turn, might mean that Torrijos, or his successor, would be strongly tempted to renegotiate the treaty in order to shorten its duration and exact other concessions. That campaign would very likely be punctuated with low level violence in Panama directed at the United States. Since the United States has already accepted the principle of American withdrawal, it could well be tempted to shorten the time period and thus spare itself additional trouble in Panama and the rest of Latin America.

The more likely chain of events, however, would begin with the Senate rejection of the treaty. The first likely consequence will be the overthrow of Torrijos, who has risked his prestige on getting a favorable treaty. This would not damage American interests but it would add another element of uncertainty to an already uncertain situation. Predictions of what would happen next have varied from low level violence to guerrilla warfare. The former is certain to occur because it is part of the Panamanian political way of life. Demands, of course, will be made for renewed negotiations with the United States, but the atmosphere would hardly be conducive to orderly negotiations. Conceivably, after a prolonged period of trouble, a new treaty would be offered to the Senate whose terms would be no better and possibly worse than the earlier version.

The worst possible outcome would be a prolonged campaign of terrorism and outright guerrilla warfare. In such a case, U.S. military forces would be employed to protect the Canal as well as American lives and property. But the effectiveness of our counterinsurgency would be limited because of the sanctuary that Panama proper would offer to the guerrillas.

The prospect is an unhappy one, but at the moment it remains an unlikely occurrence. No group in Panama recommends that course of action. More importantly, no group is now capable of conducting such a campaign. If it were to do so in the near future it would require outside help. That help could only come from Castro's Cuba. In such a case, the United States should certainly take the measures necessary to protect itself from outside intervention. However, it is important to note that Castro, on the occasion of General Torrijos' visit to Cuba (January 1976), did not advise the use of force. Instead Castro proposed that Panama continue to engage in a long-term struggle in order to line up support in Latin America and throughout the world, and thus to isolate the United States. Although one must not make the mistake of assuming Castro was offering a moderate (rather than prudent) view of the situation, it is clear that the Cuban dictator still believes the United States will meet force with force in an area it considers vital and where its military strength is already deployed.

Thus, without foreign or official Panamanian support, guerrilla warfare would not resemble Vietnam's but the urban terrorism that once flourished in countries like Brazil and Uruguay. Robberies, kidnappings, bombings, and assaults on police and civilian functionaries in the Zone and Panama proper may well occur. This, in turn, would be exacerbated by a hot pursuit problem. That is, U.S. military and police units would find it tempting to chase terrorist groups into Panamanian territory, thus provoking nationalist outcries in Panama.

On a lower scale of violence there is the danger of sabotage of Canal facilities. This is more plausible because the Canal is vulnerable. A small group reasonably proficient in explosives could do serious damage. A number of circumstances, however, reduce the possibility of this happening. First, an act of sabotage has never happened despite the long and frequently bitter U.S.-Panamanian relationship. More importantly, such an act would be quite properly labeled self-destructive since Panama needs a functioning canal for its own well-being. Nevertheless, sabotage cannot be ruled out in the aftermath of a treaty rejection. The possibility would place a heavy strain on the police and military forces within the Canal Zone.

Although the exact nature of the possible violence is not clear, the official Panamanian reaction is. Panama's government will double its efforts to solicit worldwide support, particularly in Latin America. Therefore, at a minimum, the United States can expect heavy criticism in the OAS, the United Nations, and indeed wherever Panama meets with other countries. But such attacks are not likely to create a favorable climate of opinion, for a new treaty—a development that will make the work of the next administration even more difficult.

But despite the bleakness of the prospect, it should, nevertheless, be turned into an opportunity. Since 1964, American officials have painted themselves into a corner on the Canal question. A rejected treaty would give them the chance to review our policy. How important is it for us in economic, military, and political terms, now and in the future?

In economic terms are we prepared to accept a Panamanian imposed increase in toll rates that will just fall short of shipping costs around Cape Horn? In an increasingly economically interdependent world are we prepared to accept a closing of the Canal by the Panamanians for whatever reason? Do we as a superpower have a special role in protecting the economic interests of other major users of the Canal?

How important is the Canal in military terms for the next quarter-century? The answer to that depends on the size and type of navy the United States intends to have in the coming decades. Since the debate has not yet ended, it may well be by 1977 that the United States would find a canal of greater importance than many had previously assumed. A navy, for example, that relied on smaller but faster vessels would find the Canal of great value when rapid deployment was required.

In political terms, would the eventual return of the Canal to Panama without any restrictions create a precedent for other American facilities in the Caribbean? Would it merely reinforce the image of America-in-decline? And politically is it possible to build an alternate canal in some other country?

None of these questions can be answered easily, and they may not have to be asked. But if no treaty is signed and ratified, the opportunity to ask them will present itself. That opportunity should not be wasted.

Cuba

Background

The Caribbean has always been a particularly sensitive area for Americans, and within that area Cuba has been perceived for nearly two centuries as the most vital spot. For nearly as long, the island has held great economic promise for the United States: until roughly 1850, Cuba was our leading trade partner in Latin America, and by the 1920s it had become a major target of American private investment.

But national security was more important than profits to American leaders. Cuba has always been seen as a potential threat if controlled by an unfriendly major power. Thomas Jefferson, for one, was quick to recognize this fact. Writing to President Monroe in 1823, he confessed:

. . . I have ever looked on Cuba as the most interesting addition which could ever be made to our system of states. The control which . . . this island would give us over the Gulf of Mexico, and the countries and isthmus bordering on it . . . would fill up the measure of our political well-being.[1]

But Jefferson was sensitive to the fact that annexation would mean war with England, and this he refused to consider. Cuban independence and even, if necessary, continued Spanish control were preferable. But under no circumstances would Spain be permitted to transfer control of Cuba to another more powerful nation.

These security concerns, however, led, among other things, to a good many unofficial attempts to assist the Cubans in breaking free from Spain. Throughout the nineteenth century, a good many American lives and dollars were spent on such quixotic adventures. After our war with Spain in 1898, the United States established a virtual protectorate over the island for a generation—a benign protectorate for the most part, but one that was highly resented by the Cubans.

Nevertheless, by midcentury our relations with Cuba seemed to be problem free and friendly. The United States had renounced its role as protector, and no outside power seemed able to challenge the American position in the Caribbean. Thus, with all sense of possible danger forgotten, the United States became strategically complacent, which helps explain why it reacted too late and too weakly to Castro's alliance with the Soviet Union. The strategic problem posed by Cuba, well understood in 1820, was not fully comprehended again until October 1962.

Since that time, the United States has attempted to isolate Cuba and increase the cost of the revolution for both the Cubans and the Soviets. Strategically, it has attempted to keep Cuba free of Soviet offensive weapons. Within the limited range of these objectives, American policy has succeeded.

But can it do more? Is the best course of action some sort of rapprochement? Or does Cuban intervention in Angola, and its support of Puerto Rican independence, make that impossible? On the other hand, should the United States do more to combat Cuban activity abroad? Are there any realistic measures that would help break the links between Cuba and the Soviet Union? Finally, is there any possibility, in the distant future, in ending the poisonous relationship that has existed since 1960?

Critical Problems

Until recently, the United States has been under increasing pressure to review its policy toward Cuba. This pressure came from various sources:

1. More and more governments in Latin America ignored the 1964 OAS-imposed sanctions by making preparations to resume commercial and diplomatic relations with Cuba. Even previously hostile regimes like Honduras were changing policy. This new trend in Latin America, at least in part, came from a fear of being left behind, as the Latin Americans detected rising domestic pressures in the United States for a shift in official attitudes. All of these factors culminated in a vote of the OAS foreign ministers in July 1975, permitting each country to pursue its own policy vis-à-vis Cuba—in effect, removing the decade-old sanctions.

2. The American response to Latin American rapprochement with Cuba has

been low-key, and this, of course, has only encouraged their efforts. It is unlikely that this trend will be reversed, although some countries may have occasional second thoughts.

3. The real danger in all of this was the serious undermining of OAS prestige (which was not too high to begin with) by member states who openly flouted the general sanctions. The alleged isolation of the United States (rather than Cuba) on this issue, however, was not that serious for this country, although it may have bolstered Fidel Castro's confidence for future bilateral negotiations with the United States.

4. The Soviet Union too has called for the resumption of Cuban-American relations. Moreover, there were signs of Cuban interest in negotiations (before Angola) since Castro has reluctantly accepted the Soviet policy of peaceful coexistence and the need to normalize relations with Latin America and the United States.

5. Within the United States, there has been growing pressure, especially within the liberal bloc of the Congress, to review our Cuban policy. This is, in part, a natural outcome of détente. It is also an aspect of the American tendency to change any policy or program after a certain number of years.

This pressure from within the Congress has all but disappeared in 1976 because of Cuban intervention in Angola. But other factors also affected the course of U.S.-Cuban relations. First, the Cuban regime in 1975 began a well-publicized campaign to promote Puerto Rican independence. Second, Cuba's first Communist Party Congress in December 1975 solidly endorsed the most strident of anti-American positions.

But it is Angola; that is, the presence of over 12,000 Cuban troops; that has radically altered the course of U.S.-Cuban relations, and it is that event which is worth examining in greater detail. The most important questions regarding this unprecedented Soviet-Cuban action are the following: Why was it done? Will the Cuban expeditionary force remain in Africa? Does Angola mean a change in Cuba's policy toward Latin America? What has been the effect on Latin America?

Castro himself has three explanations for moving into Angola. First, as he explained at a public rally immediately after the Party Congress in December 1975, Cuba has a common bond with African countries like Angola because "... we are not only a Latin American country, but also a Latin-African country. African blood runs abundantly in our veins and many of our ancestors came to this land as slaves from Africa."[2]

Second, Castro argued that helping the MPLA in Angola was a duty imposed on his revolutionary regime. In Castro's words, "... When the imperialist asks what interest we have, we would have to tell him to read a tract on proletarian internationalism ..."[3]

Third, Castro intervened upon the request of the MPLA after it had been attacked by the "... fascists and racists of South Africa" who had been unleashed, naturally, by the United States.[4]

Castro's reasons are, of course, rigorously self-serving. For example, it is quite likely that the decision to go in was made some time before the South Africans moved northward. But Castro's citing of an "international proletarian duty" is not mere rhetoric. He argued that line for years when assisting North Vietnam and quite clearly needed only an opportunity to carry it out on a grand scale. The civil war in Angola and generous Soviet logistical support provided just such an opportunity.

Castro's unstated reasons can only be surmised, but the following ones appear to be strong possibilities. First, the Soviet Union was anxious to displace Chinese Communist influence in Southern Africa, and assisting a pro-Moscow guerrilla faction to gain power in Angola would help serve that purpose. In order to avoid provoking a strong United States reaction and jeopardizing détente, the USSR asked Castro to act as Moscow's surrogate-mercenary force. Second, Castro knew that after the Vietnam fiasco, United States intervention in Africa was unlikely and support for the anti-MPLA forces would be restricted by public opinion. Third, the Cuban leader decided that the process of rapprochement with the United States would not produce the unilateral concessions (such as ending the U.S. trade embargo) that he demanded as a prior condition for serious negotiations with Washington. Thus, after deciding that he would lose little and gain prestige in Africa by challenging the United States in Angola, Castro agreed to provide the mercenary forces the Soviet Union needed to achieve its broader strategic objectives in Southern Africa.

The next question is: How long will the Cubans remain and will they intervene elsewhere in Africa? Judging from the MPLA's needs alone, full withdrawal in the near future is unlikely, despite recent Cuban claims to the contrary. The Cubans must provide substantial political and military training to the MPLA in order to complete the consolidation of the latter's authority over the country and protect Angola from outside threats. But beyond Angola, there are some other interesting possibilities. Even if the Cubans do not engage the South Africans in a conventional war, they may well spend a good deal of time and money on training the SWAPO—the South West African Peoples' Organization—which has not heretofore proved a particularly formidable force. That could take several years and eventually culminate in a serious insurgency in Ovamboland, the northern sector of South West Africa. While the Cuban-Soviet timetable for withdrawal is still unclear, it is unlikely to take place in the near future.

The Soviet-Cuban-African venture has renewed speculation over Castro's intentions for Latin America. Will he continue his policy of friendship for regimes that appear in any way anti-American or will he mount a more forceful campaign against all regimes which are not properly revolutionary?

At the moment, it is too early to say with certainty although a number of regimes previously friendly to Cuba are having second thoughts. Two things, however, are clear. First, Castro has so far publicly rejected the earlier demand for revolution throughout the region. Indeed, he advised General Omar Torrijos of Panama not to take the Canal by force.[5] Castro's statement, however, did not spring from a sense of moderation, but of prudence. Castro was arguing that while force could be used successfully in distant Angola where U.S. interests were not vital and obvious, force would be met by force in Panama where U.S. interests are substantial and its military presence already in place. This suggests, therefore, Cuba will only change direction in Latin America if an opportunity arises and the United States seems even weaker than it already is. In the meantime, the Cubans are cultivating extraordinarily close ties with the Guyana and Jamaican governments. Only Jamaica has an opposition party which is anti-Castro, and it may well be that Cuba as a first step would attempt to keep the current Jamaican regime in power.

But whatever course Castro follows, two major factors must be considered. First, the island is still under the control of the unpredictable Fidel Castro, a convinced Marxist-Leninist revolutionary, who wants to be a link between the Soviet bloc and Latin America. A lack of resources rather than a lack of commitment probably explains the recent diminution of Cuba's efforts at undermining "unprogressive" regimes in Latin America.

Second, the Soviet Union not only continues to keep an ideologically compatible regime afloat, it has used Cuba as an opportunity to increase its naval presence in the Caribbean. Moreover, Soviet military ties with Cuba are still a potential threat and source of conflict between the two superpowers.

Therefore, resumption of relations in the near future is not a likely event. However, within ten years some sort of rapprochement may begin again. At that time, the following critical bilateral issues will have to be considered:

1. *Guantanamo.* The Cuban regime wants to regain control of the United States naval base and related properties but the United States clearly cannot relinquish the naval base to a hostile Castro regime allied to the Soviet Union.
2. *Trade embargo.* The embargo should not be lifted unilaterally by the United States as a prior condition for discussions as demanded by Castro. Unilateral concessions to Castro will be interpreted in Latin America and the rest of the world as a sign of United States weakness.
3. *U.S. and Cuban property.* A settlement needs to be reached on expropriated United States property (especially the smaller claims) and frozen Cuban assets in this country.
4. *Immigration.* It is not in the interest of either country to foster a major population transfer to this country, but for humanitarian reasons it would be important to establish guidelines whereby families could rapidly be reunited.
5. *Political prisoners.* The United States should press for amnesty and safe conduct to the United States for political prisoners since a substantial number of American citizens are directly concerned.
6. *Human rights.* The United States should use its influence to ameliorate Cuba's gross and systematic violation of human rights (physical abuses of prisoners, inhuman conditions, and illegal detention).

U.S. Goals

The long range goal of U.S. policy towards Cuba should be the reintegration of a democratic Cuba into the Western Hemispheric system. It should be stressed that this is the ultimate aim of United States policy but there is little agreement about the best tactics to pursue in order to bring it about.

Impracticality and inconsistency are the objections usually raised. Western success in "rolling back" Communism has not been merely limited, it has been nonexistent. Nevertheless, Cuba is a test case for the United States. The most enduring of police states, the Soviet Union, still strongly resists the free flow of information and people within its borders and from the outside. Its leaders' fears, moreover, are probably justified. Therefore, if the Soviets have reason to be concerned, then how much more vulnerable is Cuba—far less remote, far smaller, and far more Westernized than Soviet Russia.

Making Cuba the Socialist camp's first true deserter is good policy because it is a possibility, and is perfectly in line with the axiom that the Communist world is not a monolith.

1. it fits into, rather than resists, present-day political currents in Latin America, and, indeed, the entire Western world;
2. it undermines a Marxist-Leninist police state, without resort to force, at its weakest point: its inability to withstand comparison between free societies and itself.

Current Policy

Present U.S. policy towards Cuba is rooted in a decision made more than a decade ago. After the October missile crisis, Cuba was no longer viewed as a direct military threat to the United States. But Latin America, it was thought, was a target for Cuban-sponsored guerrilla warfare. In the face of that threat, American objectives were twofold: (1) "to reduce the will and ability of the present regime to export subversion and violence to the other American states"; and (2) "to increase the cost to the Soviet Union of maintaining a Communist outpost in the Western Hemisphere."[6]

Since Latin America was the target, the United States chose to base its policy on cooperation with the OAS. The weapons selected to combat Cuban subversion were economic denial and political isolation. The first meant imposing a near-absolute trade embargo on Cuba which dealt a devastating blow to the island's economy since the United States had been Cuba's principal market and supplier. The second was accomplished largely through the imposition of OAS sanctions which included the breaking of diplomatic relations. At the time (1964) all OAS members except Mexico complied.

It must be made clear that U.S. officials did not think these measures alone would bring down the Castro regime. Short of military intervention (which we had forsworn) no policy, it was felt, could accomplish that.

For ten years, American spokesmen have insisted that Cuba has not changed its policy and consequently that any softening in U.S. policy would be interpreted in Havana (and Moscow) as a sign of weakness—that is, an admission of defeat on our part.

Until Angola, however, attitudes toward Cuba had softened on the part of many members of the OAS. The American response at first also seemed to suggest a new flexibility. While the United States would not unilaterally resume relations with Cuba (and thus flout the 1964 OAS decision), it promised to reexamine its policy, bilaterally and multilaterally, when the Organization voted to lift the sanctions. When the OAS agreed to allow each member to determine its own policy, this country was left free to change.

At first, the United States did make some cautious steps toward rapprochement. President Ford in an August 1974 news conference amended the Nixon formula. Previously, it had been argued that U.S. policy would change when and if the Cubans stopped subverting Latin America, and cut their military ties with the Soviet Union; that there were no signs that the Cubans were doing this, and therefore that there could be no shift in U.S. policy.[7] President Ford simply stated that the United States would consider a policy revision if "Cuba changes its policy toward us and toward its neighbors," and left it at that.[8]

Another indication of change was Henry Kissinger's March 1, 1975 speech in Houston. No specific proposals were made, but the secretary's much quoted "we see no virtue in perpetual antagonism" added to the ambiance of review and cautious adjustment that briefly seemed to characterize our Cuban policy.[9]

A year later, however, the situation had radically changed. Relations between the two countries were as bad as they had been in the early 1960s. The Cuban campaign to promote Puerto Rican independence, revived in the summer of 1975, was the first indication that the Castro regime had rejected rapprochement. The decisive step, however, was Cuba's armed support of the MPLA in Angola. The act of intervention ended, for this administration, any hope for improved relations in the near future, a judgment confirmed by President Ford's branding Fidel Castro "an international outlaw." In the same speech the president also added: "My administration will have nothing to do with the Cuba of Fidel Castro." As for any possible Cuban adventure in Latin America, President Ford stated bluntly: "I solemnly warn Fidel Castro against any temptation to armed intervention in the western hemisphere. Let his regime or any like-minded government be assured the United States would take appropriate measures."[10] For the moment, then, relations between the two countries are once again chilly, and a warming trend in the near future is unlikely.

Policy Options

The United States now has three broad options in dealing with Cuba. These options rest on different, even conflicting, assumptions which must be spelled out before the policies themselves are outlined.

Rapid Normalization of Relations. The main assumptions are that détente is real and probably permanent while the Angolan adventure will prove to be an aberration from the norm of recent Soviet and Cuban behavior. Moreover, in the much narrower context of U.S.-Cuban relations two other assumptions are included in this option. First, the Cubans were pressured into helping the Soviets as part of a repayment for the latter's economic and military aid. Second, while Castro did participate in the African venture, he has shown no signs of engaging in the promotion of guerrilla warfare in Latin America. With this in mind (and after an appropriate period of time which would let the Cubans withdraw) the following course of action should be considered.

1. initiate bilateral negotiations with Cuba by ending unilaterally our trade embargo;
2. pursue through negotiations the rapid resumption of relations with Cuba;
3. begin three-cornered talks between the United States, the USSR, and Cuba in order to remove this source of future tension between the superpowers. A strengthened public American guarantee of Cuban security, and perhaps the transfer of Guantanamo, would be the possible outcome in return for reduced Soviet military presence in the Caribbean.

Consequences. The benefits from such a policy would include the following:

1. the ending of the anomaly of continued U.S. hostility toward one small Communist regime;
2. the reduction of tensions with the Communist world generally;
3. the improvement of relations with much of Latin America, especially the governments of Mexico, Panama, Peru, and Venezuela.

The probable costs of such a policy, however, are considerable and must be carefully considered:

1. A sudden U.S. switch on Cuba would leave a number of Latin American supporters of the American position stranded, possibly embittered, and certainly skeptical of U.S. commitments, all the more so after the fall of Indochina.

2. It would throw away a number of bargaining chips that might have been used in subsequent negotiations with no clear return to us.

3. The resumption of trade relations would be of minor commercial value to us while of great importance to the Cubans.

4. A rapid reverse in policy would inevitably lead to a heavy pressure on Guantanamo without a quid pro quo.

5. This would probably also mean the surrender of any moral concern over the fate of Cuba's political prisoners.

6. Three-cornered negotiations tend to legitimize Soviet influence in Cuba, and by extension the hemisphere. And again there is no certainty the Soviets will withdraw in any way after an American guarantee of Cuban security.

7. Whatever benefits might be gained are even more questionable as long as Cuba pursues a sharply anti-American policy in Angola and toward Puerto Rico.

8. Finally, several key assumptions underlying this option are open to question. First, there is no evidence that Castro was forced into Angola. Indeed, there are a number of public statements by Castro which argue vigorously for the Cuban venture in Angola on the basis of "proletarian internationalism." Moreover, success in Angola is not likely to breed caution on Castro's part. In fact fresh opportunities have come up in Southern Africa, particularly in South West Africa (Namibia) and Mozambique. None of this, in short, suggests any kind of short-lived aberration. Second, Cuban plans for Latin America are not yet clear, and therefore require careful monitoring. We cannot now simply assume that Castro will not at some point carry out his international proletarian duty in the Western Hemisphere as well. He may well assume now that any overtly sponsored subversion on his part in the region will lead to an effective U.S. response. The United States was unprepared to counter a blitzkrieg securing of distant Angola for the MPLA. It is not likely that an easy success can be repeated in an area much closer, and more important to this country.

Limited, Conditional, Rapprochement. This option is based on the following assumptions:

1. détente, at best is limited, possibly ephemeral, and more akin to an armed truce than an *entente cordiale*, which is how it is often described;
2. moreover, even if détente with the Soviet Union and China were genuine, good relations with Cuba would not necessarily follow because Cuba (a) is not nuclear, (b) is overtly hostile and only recently and reluctantly a supporter of peaceful coexistence, and (c) is in an area of the world peculiarly sensitive to the United States.

Therefore:

1. the process of rapprochement would not begin until Cuba abandons its current foreign adventures;
2. any resumption of relations with Cuba would be the end product of a long and difficult set of negotiations;

3. such negotiations would proceed on a strictly quid pro quo basis. It would be recognized that there are three parties with substantial interests in the matter: the United States, the USSR, and Cuba.

This understanding requires a clear appreciation of what the Soviets want. Surely, they must want the preservation of a Marxist-Leninist regime, preferably at a lower economic cost to themselves. The first does not seem negotiable, but the Soviet military presence may be, and should be, if the United States is to make any concessions on Guantanamo.

Cuba's interest, aside from physical security, is in more normal diplomatic and trade relations with Latin America, and at the same time continued low-profile support for revolutionary groups and subversion in non-progressive countries. In addition, Cuba would want to remain an ally of the Soviet Union while acting as a spokesman for and supporter of "national liberation movements" throughout the Third World.

Direct Opposition to Cuban Interventionism. This option stresses that all talk of rapprochement must be suspended for the duration—that is, until the Cubans withdraw from Africa, abandon their Puerto Rican campaign, and shelve all possible plans for turning Latin America into another Vietnam/Angola. The strategy falls into four parts.

1. The United States will not force the Cubans out of Africa because there are no economic or political measures this country can take that would frighten Castro. However, the United States does have leverage over Cuba's partner, the Soviet Union; therefore we must split the Soviet-Cuban alliance in Africa by forcing the Russians to withdraw. Without their logistical support, the Cuban expeditionary force would wither away. The Soviets, of course, will not leave willingly. Only maximum political and economic pressure will compel them to do so, but the risk must be taken if Southern Africa is to remain free of communist domination.

2. In Latin America, U.S. officials should carefully monitor Cuban actions, and at the same time repeat President Ford's solemn warning against Cuban intervention in the hemisphere. The United States should also urge the OAS to resume its own survey of Cuban activity in the region. If the Cubans ignore the warnings and step up subversive activity, then the United States should extend bilateral assistance to any regime under attack. The United States might also consider promoting (once again) the use of OAS sanctions although this should be done as a last resort.

3. The most difficult problem would be Castro's backing of a regime intent on becoming more radical, that is, very unfriendly to the United States. This tactic was employed by Castro with the Allende regime, and he may be doing this now with Manley's Jamaica and Burnham's Guyana. Short of outright intervention, the United States can do little since its covert operations capability has been nearly destroyed. However, intervention must be accepted as a

possibility in case such regimes provide permanent military facilities of a strategic nature to the Soviet Union.

4. The primary purpose of United States policy is to discourage any further Cuban ventures before they are launched. No other policy will be considered until the Castro regime abandons its interventionist activities carried out under the guise of proletarian internationalism.

Consequences. A successful policy would force the Soviet Union and Cuba out of Southern Africa. It would also embitter relations between Cuba and Angola, and make Latin America more secure. It does, however, risk a major confrontation with the Soviets. It might drive the Cubans and Russians even closer together. And it may only enbroil the United States in yet another quarrel with any number of Latin American countries. But the issue remains the same from this viewpoint: neither the Soviets nor the Cubans are likely to alter their course until they are at sometime confronted by the United States.

Mexico

Background

Mexico, our only immediate neighbor in Latin America, shares with us a 1,946 mile border. Its very proximity has meant an extraordinarily visible American presence in Mexico—expatriates, tourists, private investment, and trade.[11] Proximity has also led to some extremely difficult bilateral questions, such as immigration and Colorado River salinity, which are unique in our relations with Latin America.

Despite (or possibly because of) this closeness, relations between the United States and Mexico have never been excellent over any period of time. Unlike Americans, Mexicans remember, always with bitterness, such confrontations as the 1846-48 war and Woodrow Wilson's armed intervention at Vera Cruz in 1914. Not surprisingly then, anti-Americanism has been endemic in Mexico and continues to color Mexico's relations with this country.

Although it is true that relations had been improving for a generation, a swing back to an older set of attitudes has occurred. For one thing, Mexico has begun to move away from its dependence on the United States by increasing its trade and diplomatic contacts, especially with the Second and Third Worlds. Mexico has also become far more active in Latin America, apparently aspiring to leadership of the region, which it had not done for a century and a half. On issues like Cuba, Allende's Chile, and raw materials cartels, Mexico has been openly critical of the United States. In recent months, high Mexican officials have also hinted at U.S. inspired "destabilization" schemes directed at Mexico because of its new foreign policy. Public statements have been made to the effect that the United States is responsible for Mexican right-wing criticism of the government as well as speculation against the peso, among other things. Henry Kissinger's June 1976 visit with Echeverría has helped ease the situation, but more of this type of criticism can be expected in the future.

Mexico would remain a sensitive problem for American diplomacy even if we were to ignore the rest of Latin America. Mexico's population is large (59.2 million, nearly four million more than France) and growing rapidly (3.3 percent per annum), which could mean a population of 84.4 million by 1985.[12] With so many people, so close, it is important to the United States that Mexico's economic development continue—and Mexico's recent record of slower rates of growth, inflation, and peso devaluation make this a problem. On the positive side, a prosperous country of that size would be a valuable trading partner for the United States through the rest of the century.

Critical Problems

For the long term, Mexico's burgeoning population is its most pressing problem. One estimate places Mexico's population at 135 million by the year 2000.[13] Despite recent official endorsement, family planning programs may well prove insufficient. Population pressure combined with economic stagnation may produce the worst-case situation: a violent, uncontrolled, and therefore unpredictable social and political explosion at our doorstep.

Lesser problems could certainly develop, however. The regime itself will continue to come under attack by left-wing elements, a situation that not only weakens its prospects for survival, but also encourages the Mexican government to take anti-American actions in order to mollify its critics.

Poverty and population pressure, especially in the northern rural areas, plus a lightly policed border, have promoted heavy illegal immigration to this country. Estimates vary from 4 to 12 million illegal Mexican aliens residing in the United States.[b] But whatever the number, it is quite likely to increase, and increase rapidly, if there is a slump in the Mexican economy.

In the international field, Mexico has recently made an effort to decrease its dependence on the United States. That, in itself, of course, is no critical problem, and should not be viewed as such. But the manner in which Mexico asserts its independence has caused difficulty. Mexico's outgoing president, Luis Echeverría Alvarez, showed a penchant for Janio Quadros-style gestures of independence which have strained relations with this country to no one's

[b]These are estimates issued at one time or another by the Immigration and Naturalization Service. Officials, however, have stressed that all estimates are at best rough guesses. The Service has requested $1 million to come up with a firmer figure, but so far the Department of Justice has been given only $50,000 to do a pilot study on a research design for another study that would make a census of illegal aliens.

apparent advantage. He has been particularly energetic in promoting his Charter on Economic Rights and Duties of States and the Latin American Economic System (SELA), both of which are intended to improve the economic fortunes of poor nations at the expense of the already developed. Moreover, Mexico's Third Worldism also seemed linked with Echeverría's campaign to be UN secretary general. But Mexico's new president, José López Portillo, will probably modify, but not abandon, this new foreign policy line.

Beyond that, Mexico now seems to have moved toward a position of leadership in Latin America. In part this has come about by default. Brazil, for example, cannot lead Spanish America because of its Portuguese heritage; Argentina has forfeited its chances by its chronic instability. That leaves Mexico and Venezuela, which, in fact, have been working in tandem on raw material questions. Now that Mexico has found significant, perhaps enormous, reserves of oil, their cooperation could well increase.

Mexico, like a number of other Latin American countries, has begun seeking links outside of the hemisphere. It is attempting to be yet another spokesman for the nonaligned, the poor, the raw-material-producing nations. Such a role, of course, has always invited demagogy, and the United States must be prepared to hear it from a near neighbor for some time to come.

But Mexico's attempt under President Luis Echeverría to lead the Third World has not been without setbacks. Echeverría's globe-trotting and his Charter on Economic Rights and Duties has garnered some publicity. So has his enthusiastic support for the SELA. But Mexico's approval of the anti-Zionist resolution at the UN backfired, and his apparent support for Guatemala on the Belize question was an unquestionable gaffe.

How much of this can be more than rhetoric or even international bumbling? The new administration may learn from the immediate past. Also it may understand that Mexico's diplomacy smacks of improvised amateurism because until recently that country felt no need for a far-flung foreign policy. Moreover, its apparently hearty support for the New Economic Order might well be tempered by the fact that Mexico's economy is not primitive and dependent on the export of one or two raw materials. Furthermore, it remains a neighbor of the United States. Therefore, while Mexico leaders cherish their independence from the United States, they have been relatively cautious on specific issues like OPEC which Mexico has not yet joined.

Current U.S. Policy

Over the last several decades, the United States has worked at being a good neighbor to Mexico. It has treated bilateral problems with patience, generosity, and, at times, skill. Current problems are also being handled well, for the most part. Some long-standing issues like narcotics control and the salinity of the Colorado River are in the process of being resolved. After a twelve-year controversy, the Colorado River began bringing potable river into the Mexicali Valley on July 1, 1974. At the time President Echeverría noted that the now salt-free Colorado was a symbol of good will and demonstrated the fact that international conflicts could be settled peacefully. He did not note that all the costs had been assumed by the United States.

By the early 1970s, U.S. officials had become greatly concerned about the mounting flow of narcotics coming over the border. Border inspection at American ports of arrival was tightened up in the 1970s, and Operation Cooperation was put into effect to elicit help from the Mexicans. Cooperation apparently has been forthcoming, but American agencies want more help.

Other issues have proved less tractable, although American policy remains insistent, albeit low key, on these matters. The most recent (and quite possibly the most important) concerns the discovery of oil in southeastern Mexico (La Reforma). Naturally, the United States would like access to this nearby petroleum at less than world prices. Since Mexico (so far) has adamantly proclaimed its intention of selling for cash at world prices to everyone, including the United States and Cuba, American policymakers have quietly expressed the hope that Mexico will stay out of OPEC and that this new increase in the world supply of oil will help break the current price.[14]

The problem of illegal immigration remains even further from solution. Since 1964 there has been no U.S. program permitting legal entry for Mexican farm workers, and there is little likelihood that any such program could be revived in Congress. In the meantime, the United States has begun to enlist Mexico's help on the problem. So far, there has only been an announcement of the creation of a joint commission to study the problem. At the same time, the United States, faced with an increasing number of illegal entries (between 500,000 and 800,000 Mexicans were returned in 1974), has reinforced the Border Patrol. But it has estimated that proper enforcement of immigration laws would require something in excess of $55 million—a sum that so far has not even been requested by the Justice Department.[c]

The United States' attitude has also been relatively low key on two other matters, until recently. The first involves some 600 Americans in Mexican jails, the majority on drug-related charges. Reports have already leaked out regarding gross mistreatment, and U.S. consular officials have complained that access to imprisoned Americans was delayed or denied. The matter was also discussed by Echeverría and Secretary Kissinger during the latter's June 1976 meeting in Mexico.

The United States has, however, begun to respond to President Echeverría's avowals of independence and Third World solidarity. Complaints have been

_____

[c]The funds would go for additional personnel and equipment including helicopters, which the patrol at the moment does not possess.

made about the Third World rhetoric at the UN and the United States has objected to certain portions of Echeverría's Charter of Economic Rights and Duties, especially the section dealing with multinational corporations. Secretary of State Kissinger's September General Assembly speech on economic coopera-tion with the LDCs was an open response to Mexican raw materials diplomacy. But while this move may well undercut Mexico's efforts, the latter are not going to cease altogether even with a new regime in office.

Policy Options

In the coming decade the United States should seek the following:

1. a stable, prosperous Mexico which has become less dependent upon, but not more antagonistic toward, this country;
2. a mutually satisfactory solution of the immigration issue which would involve commitments from both parties;
3. ongoing bilateral discussions of all economic issues with an emphasis on financial, trade, and investment questions;
4. a share in Mexico's oil exports on a long-term, fixed price basis.

The United States has two broad options in regard to Mexico. Each has its own assumptions and consequences as well as advantages.

Ad Hoc Problem-Solving. The first option is based on the assumption that there are no insoluble problems with Mexico. Despite past and current differences, all issues are suited to individual and separate negotiation. It also implies the assumption that Mexico will remain politically stable and economically prosper-ous and therefore should present no immediate security problem. Indeed, through continued trade, investment, and possibly U.S. access to Mexican oil, coinciding with an American modus vivendi with Cuba, U.S.-Mexican relations over the next decade could be the best in history. Under this option, presidential dialogue at the border would be a valuable tool in maintaining good relations.

Specific policies would be fashioned as the problems emerged. Agreements might be attempted on immigration and trade (including oil and the reduction of American nontariff barriers), and on the commonly accepted rules for United States private investment in Mexico.

The advantages of such an approach are obvious—flexibility is the most apparent. On the other hand, it may well be that no single issue will be resolved very easily since a number of problems (such as oil and illegal immigration) are of great concern to only one of the parties. Moreover, business conducted at the presidential level may be of less value than is often imagined. Success depends on the accident of personality, and serious discussions are limited by the lack of time. Such talks can only be useful for problem solving if detailed negotiations have already taken place.

Comprehensive Agreement on Outstanding Issues. Since no single issue is likely to be settled amicably, all problems should be handled in an interrelated fashion. The outstanding issues of the next decade are illegal immigration, the maintenance of Mexico's rate of economic development, and access to Mexico's oil exports. To handle these problems in a systematic fashion, a U.S.-Mexican Commission with broad authority to work out agreements on immigration, trade, and development might prove of value. The first item of business would be better policing of the border by both nations, while a fixed number of legal migrant workers would be permitted entrance. In addition, it would be assumed that the only long-term solution to illegal immigration is rapid economic development of Mexico, especially in the border areas. Agreements that would promote capital and trade flows within a designated region on both sides of the border should also be negotiated. Moreover, the commission could complete an agreement which would guarantee a secure U.S. market for Mexican oil at a fixed price below present price levels over a long period of time. This is especially important over the next decade because of Mexico's stability and proximity in glaring contrast to the Persian Gulf states.

It is not expected that any of these problems can be dealt with seriously over the short run. This is especially true of oil, since Mexico has already announced its interest in securing Third World markets and maintaining OPEC price levels. However, after two or three years, the advantages of a close (that is, low-transportation-cost), large, and secure market should become equally apparent to the Mexicans. Thus, by the end of the decade, a mixed commission may become a serious option for both American and Mexican policymakers.

Venezuela

Background

Although Venezuela's importance to the United States is of relatively recent origin, that country has now assumed a role far greater than might be expected from a nation of only 12.8 million people. Its importance is likely to continue through the coming decade. For more detailed analysis of Venezuela, see the Appendix in this volume.

Venezuela's first impact on the United States was economic, and dates from the discovery of oil in 1914. In 1975 Venezuela remained our principal foreign source of oil, supplying approximately 28 percent of our petroleum imports. Furthermore, major American investment in the mining sector has made Venezuela a prime supplier of high-grade iron ore. It is not surprising then that

U.S. direct investment in Venezuela was (until recently) the largest in Latin America.

Moreover, owing to its rapidly growing economy—its GNP in 1974 was $17.5 billion, and its per capita income, the highest in Latin America, was more than $1,300—Venezuela has proven to be a lucrative market for U.S. exports, ranking third in Latin America and thirteenth in the world. In 1974, Venezuela imported $1,768 million in American goods.[15]

Venezuela has also become politically important to the United States in recent years. Its importance is a result of our economic interests in Venezuela's geographic position. It has always, of course, been part of the Caribbean, an area long believed vital to the United States. In addition, contemporary interest in Venezuela was sharpened after the overthrow of dictator Marcos Pérez Jiménez in 1958, which suddenly reversed that country's nondemocratic political tradition. Since 1959 Venezuela has held four vigorously competitive free elections in which on two occasions power was peacefully transferred from the ruling party to the opposition—once from the *Acción Democrática* (AD) to the Christian Democrats (COPEI) in 1969, and then again from COPEI to AD in 1973. Thus, in contrast to most of Latin America, where military regimes have proliferated in the last decade, Venezuela has maintained and improved its civilian-led, representative democracy dedicated to social reform. It has become, in short, the kind of regime that the architects of the Alliance for Progress once envisioned for all of Latin America.

The accomplishment is all the more remarkable when one recalls that the Venezuelans were also forced to wage war in the 1960s against a serious guerrilla movement which was initially supported, if not controlled, by Communist Cuba. Furthermore, in facing this threat, Venezuela became one of the hemisphere's leaders against Cuban-sponsored subversion.

Critical Problems

Under the leadership of its president, Carlos Andrés Pérez, Venezuela is reshaping its political and economic role in Latin America, and indeed, the world. Its new strategy directly affects the United States, presenting both problems and opportunities in the construction of a genuinely balanced partnership where costs and benefits are mutually shared. Before that partnership can be achieved, the United States must confront the following forces and problems that may radically alter Venezuelan-American relations in the coming decade.

Venezuela's new strategy is to promote rapid economic development and the widest possible distribution of benefits. As such, this goal does not differ from that of most other poor countries, except in the seriousness of the commitment. But what makes Venezuela special is the means by which it hopes to accomplish this objective. Development is directly linked to exports, specifically, petroleum and, more recently, iron ore. In other words, development depends on the foreign sale of irreplaceable raw materials. Petroleum, of course, has been Venezuela's major export for years but proven reserves of high quality oil are dropping, and may well be exhausted within several decades.[d] Moreover, Venezuela's planners intend to stop exporting iron ore by 1985 in order to supply their own rapidly expanding steel industry.

But minerals not only have a habit of running out, they also are subject to sudden changes in price. Furthermore, the shift to exporting manufactured goods, the development strategy adopted by many underdeveloped countries (Brazil, Taiwan, South Korea), is not possible for Venezuela at present. The latter has a well-protected but high-cost industrial sector which recently managed to export a mere $11 million worth of goods from a fixed industrial investment of $450 million.

Venezuela's problem, in brief, is to squeeze as much export revenue as possible from its diminishing mineral assets.[16] It should come as no surprise, then, that Venezuela has led OPEC in insisting on higher prices for oil, which in turn has made production cutbacks possible. Thus, through 1973, Venezuela pumped 3.37 million barrels per day but in 1974 the average had dropped to 3.0 million barrels per day. Moreover, the government has recently announced a planned cutback to 2.2 million barrels per day for 1976, and 2.0 million barrels per day by the end of the decade.[17] These targets, of course, simply reinforce Venezuela's determination to maintain and, if possible, increase oil prices. Therefore, there is little chance that the Venezuelans, who are bitterly convinced that the price of petroleum was unjust, will settle for a price freeze, much less a price rollback.

Furthermore, the Venezuelans, in an effort to reinforce OPEC and perhaps allay poor-country criticism of rising fuel prices, have also announced support for other raw-materials-producer cartels. That support, which includes promised financial aid, would naturally increase their viability, and would result in even higher prices for a large group of raw materials.

Until recently, Venezuelan legislation decreed that foreign oil corporations had to surrender their leases in 1983. But the August 1975 law changed the date of surrender and nationalized the oil fields by the end of the year. The foreign companies are to be compensated, and most have accepted the terms (albeit reluctantly). Furthermore, Clause 5 of the new law specifically permits continued foreign participation in Venezuela's oil sector in the form of service contracts and even joint ventures. The results are obvious. In the late 1960s Venezuela attracted more U.S. investment than any other country in Latin America. By 1974, it had dropped behind Brazil and Mexico to a total of $1,722 million. If oil investments are subtracted from that figure, Venezuela would also fall below Panama and Argentina.[18]

---

[d]These estimates do not include any potential new finds of course, including the offshore oil discovered east of the Paraguana Peninsula.

Venezuela has not only moved against the private oil corporations; since joining the Andean Common Market, it has adopted the group's restrictive foreign investment guidelines set out in Decision 24, and in some cases has gone beyond them. Venezuela, in short, has shifted abruptly from being one of the few countries in Latin America open to foreign investment, to one of the toughest regulators of outside private capital.

Another issue that has caused trouble is section 502 of the new U.S. trade law. This excludes OPEC members from being eligible for Generalized Special Preferences and it included Venezuela. The Venezuelans protested vehemently, however, with some reason, since they did not join the Arab oil boycott of 1973. Furthermore, they have been successful in transmitting their sense of outrage to other Latin American countries which, despite their eligibility for GSPs, have also protested the trade law's provision against the oil cartel.

Venezuela has also changed in its foreign political policy in recent years. In the 1960s it was one of the strongest defenders of democracy in the region, and under the Betancourt doctrine refused diplomatic relations with regimes that had come to power by force. In addition, it was a leading critic of the Castro government. Now, however, it has adopted "ideological pluralism" as its diplomatic watchword, i.e., diplomatic recognition of all forms of government within the Western Hemisphere.

Naturally, this undercuts the belief that there are special factors which bring the hemisphere together, and for that very reason Venezuela's new position may well be more in line with reality than the old Pan-Americanist ideal. On the other hand, ideological pluralism can be merely a rationale for letting Cuba return to the American family without committing itself to nonintervention in the domestic affairs of others.

But despite the new problems arising from Venezuelan nationalism and will to develop, the United States still has opportunities worth exploring with Venezuela.

First, and most obviously, Venezuela no longer qualifies for bilateral or multilateral aid, which leaves more of that scarce commodity for others. Furthermore, Venezuela has become a capital exporting country, providing funds for the IDB ($500 million), the World Bank ($540 million), Andean Development Bank ($25 million), as well as bilateral credits to Bolivia, Costa Rica, Guyana, and Honduras. If any Latin American country, a decade ago, had actively promoted the economies of others, it would have been acclaimed as a triumph for the Alliance for Progress. Instead, almost nothing has been heard from the United States about this encouraging development.

Meanwhile, Venezuela, with its heady economy, will continue to be an excellent market for U.S. exports. And despite the surge of nationalism, most of the country's leaders are realistic about their need for technical assistance. Thus, with certain restrictions, they might borrow American technology, especially in the development of the Orinoco Heavy Oil Belt. The latter, however, can only be viewed as a long-term possibility.

Current U.S. Policy

Despite Venezuela's importance to the United States, there is little evidence that it has been given priority in our policy toward Latin America, much less in our foreign policy at large.

Oil, of course, is the major item of business between the United States and Venezuela. In 1970 the Caldera administration, faced with declining oil prices and exports to the United States, attempted to work out a long-term energy agreement ensuring the market stability of Venezuelan oil.[19] The United States, at the time, refused to make any such commitment. It did, however, attempt to negotiate with Venezuela a country-to-country treaty that would have guaranteed to American and other oil companies amortization of investment (including repatriation of profits) in developing the Orinoco heavy oil.

In the meantime, the United States was clearly caught by surprise by the recent moves of the Pérez administration. And now, since September 1974, the United States seems to have embarked on a harder-line policy toward all oil exporting countries. Although it has not singled out Venezuela for special treatment, the new American position drew an immediate and firm reply from President Pérez in an open letter published by the *New York Times* on September 25, 1974.

Policy Options

The United States should seek the following:

1. continued viability of Venezuela's democratic regime;
2. continued access on reasonable terms to its raw materials;
3. eventual joint development of the Orinoco heavy oil;
4. achievement of a balanced partnership in which costs and benefits are more nearly equally shared.

The United States has, in fact, very few options regarding Venezuela. It could, of course, simply let matters drift. This might not worsen Venezuelan relations but it would certainly overlook some opportunities that will come up in the next decade. On the other hand, the United States could attempt to counter Venezuela's oil and cartel policies and persuade Caracas to practice price restraint in the interest of world peace and stability. The chances for success, even in the short run, must be rated minimal, however, since obtaining maximum revenues from its minerals is considered by Venezuelan policymakers to be of vital national interest.

Broadly speaking, future American policy should rest on the assumption that Venezuela presents a clear opportunity for treating our friends very differently from our self-proclaimed enemies. If no distinction is ever made between them, what does it profit a nation to be our friend?

First, we can begin by acknowledging our differences, and then engage in wide-ranging, high-level bilateral talks on the following issues:

1. We must encourage Venezuelan investment in this country.
2. We should seek relaxation of Venezuela's overly strict and discriminatory interpretation of the Andean Group's Decision 24.
3. In return, the United States should offer Caracas a comprehensive agreement that would help overcome Venezuela's massive managerial deficiency through a major technical assistance program. This form of aid is eminently worthwhile since the payoff will be substantial.
4. We should continue to encourage Venezuela's capital assistance to poor countries on a bilateral and multilateral basis.
5. We should attempt to negotiate a joint venture with the participation of the Venezuelan and United States governments and the private oil and liquefied natural gas sector. We should also welcome third-country participation.
6. We must continue to support Venezuelan democracy.
7. The United States must begin developing alternative sources of iron ore within a decade. On this score, the Venezuelans have given us adequate lead time, and any shortages incurred after 1985 will be our own fault.

It should be pointed out that not all of these policy recommendations are feasible over the next few years. But they are worth examining periodically over the next fifteen years.

In conclusion, Venezuela presents another opportunity in Latin America to develop a balanced partnership. The success of such a relationship will do much to encourage other countries in the hemisphere to seek similar arrangements.

Brazil

Background

Brazil is emerging rapidly as a middle-level world power. Its physical size, population, resources, and rapidly growing economy mean that it can no longer be seriously challenged by Mexico or Argentina. Moreover, national rivalries make it extremely unlikely that a united Spanish America will emerge within the next decade to counter the Brazilian colossus.

By 1985, Brazil may well approach major power status in economic terms, and at the end of the century it may surpass Great Britain or France in both economic and military power. In the meantime, its present foreign policy elite is aware of Brazil's potential, and is making every effort to promote Brazilian greatness. But unlike some Third World countries, Brazil is not now overly ambitious: its leaders in the last ten years have not let their hopes exceed their resources in contrast to the tempestuous "independent foreign policy" of Jânio Quadros in 1961. Instead, the regime recognizes that its place in the world must come as a consequence of achieving its top priority—rapid internal development. This single overriding choice, the basis of Brazil's strategy, is more than a slogan for domestic consumption: Brazil maintained a growth rate of 10 percent until 1974.

Brazil's special position in the hemisphere has been complemented by its unique historical relationship with the United States. Almost from the beginning of their histories as independent nations, each saw in the other a natural complement to itself. That arch-republican, Thomas Jefferson, as president, welcomed by letter the Portuguese Prince Regent shortly after his arrival in Brazil in 1808. Jefferson expressed the hope that trade would be ". . . the true aliment of an unchanging friendship with the United States of America."[20] In addition, both Brazil and the United States shared the anomaly of being located in, but not quite belonging to the Western Hemisphere. The United States, of course, was English-speaking, but Brazil was Portuguese, and a monarchy to boot (until 1889). Neither could easily join in the many Spanish-American schemes of confederation, and neither did during the nineteenth century.

Decisions which tended to reinforce their natural rapport were made by both sides in that century. In 1889, the United States was among the first to recognize the new Republic of Brazil despite our good relations with the old Emperor Dom Pedro II. In fact, four years later, a U.S. naval squadron helped end a pro-monarchist revolt carried out by the Brazilian navy. In 1895, President Grover Cleveland awarded 14,000 square miles to Brazil in a territorial dispute with Argentina. In return Brazil supported this country in a serious quarrel with Chile that nearly led to war in 1891. During the Spanish-American war, Brazil, alone in Latin America, extended to us a friendly neutrality.

In the first decade of this century, a special relationship was consciously pursued, by the Brazilians at least, under the extraordinary leadership of Foreign Minister Baron Rio-Branco. The need for such a relationship had become obvious to Rio-Branco since the United States was rapidly replacing Great Britain as Brazil's major trade and investment partner. The Baron's policy meant, among other things, Brazil's acceptance of the Monroe Doctrine and American views on national responsibility and intervention in contrast to the well-developed Spanish-American doctrines on those subjects. In addition, Brazil began acting as an interpreter and mediator between the United States and Spanish America (without every trying to be the latter's leader). In return, Brazil expected to be treated as an equal, and to receive support from this country on issues considered vital to Brazil, for example, its physical integrity.

Given this background, it is no surprise that Brazil made the only significant military contribution during World War II in Latin America. (The principal political fallout of wartime cooperation was that a whole generation of Brazilian officers—many of whom held positions of power after April 1964—became convinced that Brazil's future depended on maintaining close relations with the United States.)

Brazil continues to play a well-defined role. Its potential and its historically benign relationship with the United States make it unique in Latin America. The United States, on the other hand, has never really had a well-focused policy toward Brazil. We have at times appreciated Brazil's uniqueness but we have not done so consistently and behaved accordingly. In part this has been because of a well-grounded fear of adverse Spanish-American reaction. But in the coming decade the choice will become even more clear-cut, and so will the need for a strategy to implement that choice.

Critical Problems

Compared to much of Latin America, Brazil would seem to present few critical problems. Nevertheless, the stakes are too high for complete confidence, and moreover, there are problems that could give the United States some difficulties in the years ahead.

Brazil still has a military-dominated regime. That should continue to be the case, barring a major upheaval, for at least the next ten years. Nevertheless, relations between the United States and Brazil are not likely to be so close as they have been in the preceding decade. That is because the officers dominating the armed forces will be more nationalist (though not leftist) than the moderate officers like Humberto Castello Branco who made the revolution of March 31, 1964. The moderate officers became the elite within the military because of their combat experience in Italy during World War II. Many of them were also American-trained, and almost all were admirers of the United States and firm believers in the western alliance. But through death or retirement most of these officers will have left the armed forces in a few more years.

The younger officers, in contrast, have no combat experience, are less often trained outside Brazil, and are firm nationalists with large ambitions for their country. They are also less tolerant of civilians and firmly anti-Communist, although that feeling is limited to local subversive groups. In any case, the new Brazilian military is likely to be more rigid in domestic affairs and more aggressively nationalistic in foreign policy.

Meanwhile, Brazil's rapid growth has caused apprehension in Spanish America. Charges of Brazilian imperialism are becoming common, and have even been made within official circles.[21] Accompanying this apprehension is the further suspicion that Brazil has been encouraged by the United States to be a junior policeman in South America. Indeed, the Nixon doctrine of low profile only encouraged such speculation about a Washington-Brasilia axis since it matches perfectly the scenario of U.S. withdrawal and Brazilian activism.

Some observers believe that the Brazilian miracle is over permanently. And there is some evidence to support that view. Brazil did not escape the world economic downturn in 1974-75. Growth rates in 1974 were only 6 percent and 4 percent in 1975. In 1976 there may be no growth at all. Moreover, it is also asserted that as the world's economy picks up Brazil's mounting fuel bill will still force a permanent slowdown.[22]

Others argue, however, that the bottleneck is only temporary, and that the petroleum, if anything, has stimulated greater effort in the export sector. Brazil's storehouse of raw materials in a raw materials-hungry world will prove a great help.[e] Moreover, Brazil's emerging capital goods industry—ships, chemicals, steel, aluminum—will just come into its own in the 1980s. On balance, the problems, though real enough, will not be prolonged, barring a complete collapse of the world economy.

One very serious consequence of continued slow growth is exacerbated social tensions. It is argued that while rapid growth has perhaps benefited the middle class, it has not improved the lot of the poor, and a slowing of growth would lead to unrest, followed by repression, and then vast social upheaval. Again, such a scenario is possible but unlikely. This chapter assumes that Brazil's slowed growth rate will last only a few years before it resumes a more rapid pace. Moreover, public services like education and health have greatly improved since 1964, although such benefits do not show up in individual income statistics.

Finally, brief consideration must be given to three problems that directly affect the United States. First, it seems clear that the United States will face increasingly stiff competition from Western Europe and especially Japan for markets in Brazil as well as for Brazilian raw materials. Thus, the United States can no longer take Brazil for granted as a trading partner, a partner that bought over $3 billion of U.S. goods in 1975 and sold $1.5 billion in turn.

Possibly even more important is the need for the United States to work out a better strategy in handling bilateral disputes, especially in economic matters. These, in the recent past, have proved far more acrimonious than American officials expected. A case in point was the soluble coffee dispute that broke out in 1967 in which Brazil wished to enter the American market with a considerably cheaper product. The State Department, under pressure from U.S. firms, attempted to restrain Brazil's exports, and after long and bitter negotiations managed to persuade the Brazilians to raise their prices slightly.

Why did it happen? Clearly, the United States misjudged the stubbornness of Brazil. The key to understanding Brazilian behavior is relatively simple. Its leaders are determined to make their country a major power. To do that, it must develop rapidly. Rapid development is best promoted through ever increasing exports. All attempts to inhibit that growth (especially by the already developed) will be strongly resisted. Moreover, this attitude is not likely to soften,

---

[e]Brazil has enormous deposits of iron ore, bauxite, manganese, and possibly uranium. It has also the world's largest reserve of unused arable land. Currently it is an exporter of basic foodstuffs like sugar, coffee, cacao, and soybeans.

especially in the next few years when Brazil's economic slowdown has forced it to even stronger measures at export promotion.

A new concern is Brazil's rapidly developing nuclear capability. Although for years Brazil's effort has been relatively modest compared to Argentina's, recently it has launched an ambitious program that should make it possible for Brazilian scientists to explode a nuclear device by the mid-1980s.

Until recently, Brazil, unlike Argentina, was also dependent on outside sources for services such as uranium enrichment. That will be changed, however, once Brazil obtains the nuclear facilities contracted for in a deal with West Germany that was announced in June 1975. Within ten years Brazil would have a virtually complete fuel cycle, and will no doubt remain outside of the Non-Proliferation Treaty as well as the Treaty of Tlatlolco.

Publicly, Brazil remains committed to using peaceful nuclear explosives and has denied interest in developing weapons. The latter position is, no doubt, dependent on the intentions of the Argentines. In the meantime, the Brazilians are doing advanced research in rocketry (again with West German help) which would also place them in a position to develop a relatively sophisticated delivery system by the mid-1980s.

Current U.S. Policy

Present policy is still pretty much in the doldrums following a period of very active and successful policymaking after April 1964.

The Brazilian armed forces on that date removed the corrupt, incompetent, and erratically leftist regime of João Goulart. Plagued by hyperinflation and negative rates of growth, Brazil plainly needed help not only to weather the momentary economic storm but also to master the much more difficult problems of great poverty in a country with even greater potential. Consequently, the United States committed itself to a massive rescue operation reminiscent of the Marshall Plan. The size of the American aid program ballooned until by the mid-1960s it was the third largest in the world (after Vietnam's and India's). Clearly, Brazil had become a priority worry, and almost any amount would have been spent to prevent it from sliding into economic chaos.

Once inflation had been tamed, and growth rates assumed, the United States, primarily at the embassy level, recognized the dangers of an extended and heavy commitment. Close American identification with the Brazilian regime was an increasing embarrassment to both sides. Moreover, the AID program was also being criticized in the U.S. Congress, especially those parts of it which funded "public safety programs" and became identified (probably erroneously) with Brazilian mistreatment of political prisoners.

The way out seemed to be "Operation Topsy" so initiated and so named by the then American Ambassador John Tuthill. Its object was simple: cut heavily into American personnel, especially in the AID program. Subsequently, reductions of up to 40 percent were made. This tactical move, carried out between 1967 and 1969 in Brazil, grew into the Nixon master plan for all of Latin America—namely, the lowering of the American profile in the region.

Once the profile was lowered, however, the United States was unable to "spell out a comprehensive program of U.S. government priorities in Brazil," as Ambassador Tuthill once suggested.[23] In testimony to a Senate subcommittee a recent American ambassador to Brazil asserted, "The importance of Brazil in hemispheric affairs, and indeed, in world affairs is indicated by its size, its population, its economy, and the rapidity with which it is progressing as a real economic power in the region."[24] But he could not go beyond that even under direct questioning.

But if the men in the field seem a little vague, what about officials at the top? On the basis of the public record alone, the last years have been very lean indeed until recently. Only two references by high officials are readily available. The first, from Richard Nixon, was directed at his visiting Brazilian counterpart, Emílio Garrastazú Médici in December 1972. In perhaps an unguarded moment, the then American president said, "As Brazil goes, so will go the rest of the Latin American continent."[25] Critics, here and abroad, like so many Talmudic scholars, have teased out so many wretched implications from these words that it is unnecessary to add any others. More important, they said almost nothing specific about American policy toward Brazil.

Far more revealing was then Secretary of State William Rogers' statement at a news conference held in Brasilia in April 1973, following talks with the Brazilian chief executive. The secretary, after describing their exchange of views, concluded, "We don't have any problems really, at the moment, at all between Brazil and the United States."[26] Nothing could indicate more clearly the present state of high policy. Brazil has no difficulties with us, or we with them. Future problems will be settled on the sort of ad hoc basis that is workable between mature partners. In short, Brazilian-American relations, after a period of storm and stress, have settled down to a comfortable, slightly dull domesticity.

There was, of course, reason for such satisfaction. A number of very nettlesome bilateral economic issues had been settled: Brazilian cotton textiles, U.S. wheat imports, and above all the soluble coffee controversy, which took nearly (and unnecessarily) five years to resolve.

In addition, President Nixon made a personal effort to keep in touch with his Brazilian counterpart. President Médici, for example, was one of only a half-dozen heads of government who were immediately consulted after the president's announcement of his August 1971 economic program.

Only one recent development needs mentioning. In February 1976, during Secretary Kissinger's stop in Brazil, the two countries signed an agreement for regular biannual consultations on a wide range of political and economic issues.

Table IV-1
U.S. Bilateral Assistance to Brazil
(millions of U.S. dollars, net)

	1960	1961	1962	1963	1964	1965	1966
AID, Total	11.9	7.0	84.5	86.3	178.6	230.7	242.3
Development Loans	−0.3	—	74.5	62.9	165.9	218.4	229.1
Grants	12.2	7.0	10.0	23.4	13.2	12.3	13.2
Food for Peace, Total	1.8	84.7	72.5	48.6	151.4	24.7	79.1
Total, Economic	13.7	91.7	157.0	134.9	330.0	255.4	321.4

Source: *United States Polices & Programs in Brazil* (Hearings Before the Subcommittee on Western Hemisphere Affairs of the Committee on Foreign Relations, U.S. Senate, 92nd Congress, First Session, May 4, 5, and 11, 1971, p. 162) and U.S. AID, Statistics & Reports Division.

The step was widely interpreted as U.S. recognition of Brazil's emerging role as a middle power. Although the criticism from Latin America was considerably less than anticipated, some press criticism is now being heard in Brazil to the effect that the February agreement will not be implemented owing to U.S. internal politics.[27] The criticism may be premature but there is no doubt Brazilian-American relations will be harmed if the United States reneges on its February commitment.

Policy Options

The United States should consider the following in the shaping of its policy over the next decade:

1. The United States should continue to stress partnership and help integrate Brazil more fully into the OECD group of countries.
2. The United States should also encourage economic growth, increased civilian participation in the democratic political process, and respect for human rights.
3. The United States should continue to help promote a favorable climate for foreign investment in Brazil.
4. The United States should attempt to dissuade Brazil from joining the nuclear club.

Three options face the United States in dealing with Brazil in the coming decade. First, we may continue the policy we have been following since about

1967	1968	1969	1970	1971	1972	1973	1974	1975
213.7	187.7	−11.7	61.2	117.6	21.0	53.8	17.2	14.6
119.0	176.3	−21.8	49.3	90.8	2.1	33.3	1.0	−
14.7	11.4	10.1	11.9	26.8	18.9	20.5	16.2	14.6
21.6	82.9	10.4	68.6	35.1	5.7	9.6	6.2	8.4
235.3	270.6	−1.3	129.8	152.7	26.7	63.4	23.4	23.0

1968; second, we may actively support desirable changes within Brazil; and third, we can attempt to integrate Brazil more completely into the Western community.

Maintaining the Recent Course. This implies:

1. maintaining a low profile diplomatically;
2. engaging in personal diplomacy on the highest official levels;
3. showing concern over political rights through behind-the-scenes diplomacy;
4. dealing with bilateral economic issues on a case-by-case basis. The assumption is that negotiations are between more or less equals where give and take can be expected from both sides.

Consequences. This policy is designed to let Brazil go pretty much where the Brazilians are intending to go. It would, among other things, do nothing to discourage the building of a nuclear explosive capability by Brazil. Moreover, letting Brazil alone would do nothing to convince the Spanish Americans that Brazil is not the surrogate Yankee policeman. Finally, such a policy would fail to take advantage of the fact that Brazil's economy is one of the most dynamic in the world, and is already predisposed to act within the Western community.

A Politically Activist Policy. This course implies heavy U.S. pressure on Brazil's political leaders to clean up the regime, in particular to end the use of torture, increasingly to civilianize the government, and to hold open competitive elections by the end of the decade.

Consequences. It is not likely that this kind of activism would work. It is likely that Brazil's leaders could draw on Brazilian nationalism and turn it against the meddling United States, needlessly straining our relations. Moreover, it would put those Brazilian moderates working toward changes in the regime in a difficult position.

Integrating Brazil into the Western Community. According to this policy:

1. Brazil is no longer considered just another Latin American country.
2. Brazil is gradually included in the Euro-American-Japanese community. Eventual membership in the OECD would be encouraged, and in general, Brazil would become part of the inner circle discussing trade, monetary, and energy problems.
3. In return, Brazil would be encouraged to abandon a wholly independent nuclear development policy.
4. Meanwhile, the United States would continue quiet diplomacy on political issues like repression.

Consequences. This policy would deliberately try to bring Brazil closer to the West. It might keep Brazil from siding with Third World countries on any number of political and economic issues. In addition, it would give the Spanish Americans another incentive to pull together faster, adopt the Brazilian economic model (instead of a quasi-Marxist autarkic one), and thus bring all of Latin America closer to the North Atlantic world.

Meanwhile, the United States can do little to stop Brazil's nuclear development. Placing pressure on West Germany to cancel the deal will not work but it will embitter relations with two friendly countries. However, there is some difference between doing little and doing nothing. The United States can insist on strict safeguards (the West Germans can hardly say no). And if this country chose to do so, it could urge a slow completion of the contract, especially for those parts of the fuel cycle that have not been fully worked out by the Germans and Brazilians.

Argentina

Background

Argentina is passing through a period of enormous political and economic turmoil. Moreover, despite the overthrow of the corrupt and inept Peronist regime, political violence and hyperinflation will not be ended soon. Despite this umpromising prospect for the medium term, however, Argentina possesses human and natural resources sufficient to make it eventually the leading country of Spanish America.

The United States has moderately important economic relations with Argentina. U.S. direct investment in Argentina (preliminary 1974 figures) was $1.4 billion, fifth highest in Latin America. Trade turnover in 1974 was $1,020 million. But Argentina's importance to the United States can be exaggerated. Buenos Aires is further from Washington than any of Western Europe's capitals, and Argentine leaders have tended to regard the United States as a rival, not a partner in the hemisphere.

Argentine diplomats, for example, vigorously opposed American schemes for closer hemispheric economic ties at the first Pan-American meeting begun in 1889. At subsequent inter-American gatherings Argentina continued to lead Latin America on questions dealing with U.S. intervention—usually at the expense of the United States. Argentina was neutral during World War I and remained sympathetic to the Axis cause until nearly the end of the last world war. In recent years, the two countries have avoided serious disputes—even Perón's return to power in 1973 did not damage American-Argentine relations as much as expected. While cultivating independent, "anti-imperialist" postures, the administrations of both Juan and Isabel Perón maintained relatively good bilateral relations with the United States. The new military regime clearly looks to the United States for help in solving its vast economic problems, and is unlikely to clash with this country unless all aid is denied.

Even close ties with the United States would have little effect on many of Argentina's domestic problems. Juan Perón, exiled for nearly twenty years, was thought to be Argentina's most intractable political problem. Powerful elements within the military refused to allow his return, while trade unions almost as powerful demanded it. But Argentina's revolving-door military and civilian regimes could neither preserve order nor cure the country's stagflation, and by 1974 Perón-the-problem had become Perón-the-savior. Only he, it was widely thought, could attract the support of Argentina's large well-organized lower and lower-middle classes that nearly two decades of middle class civilian and military rulers had alienated. It is a measure of Argentina's desperation that this near octogenarian was elected to the presidency by an overwhelming majority in an honest election.

Perón's new government provided only the most temporary political and economic stability. Indeed, the election of his wife as vice-president and his utter lack of interest in building a new generation of leaders demonstrated that Perón would never be capable of rising above petty political intrigue.

Perón's death was followed by economic crisis and political violence and polarization which his wife and advisers could not control. The March 1976 coup was thus considered inevitable even by hardened *peronistas.*

Argentina's inability to develop a stable, democratic regime despite its great natural and human resources must in turn color our expectations for the other countries of Spanish America. But the main question remains: why has Argentina failed?

Argentina's Political Heritage. In its early years, "Argentina" was hardly more than a geographical entity. The Argentine was ruled by regional caudillos, united only when one managed to impose his will upon the others by force of arms. But politically the caudillos were never more than robber chieftains: corrupt, cruel, and ignorant, they laid no basis for democracy or order whatsoever.

In fact, more than a half-century elapsed after independence before President Bartolomé Mitre suppressed interior insurrections and unified the country in the 1860s. The subsequent growth of Buenos Aires, stimulated by an influx of European immigrants and capital, led to the steady progress of the 1870s and 1880s unmatched in subsequent Argentine history.

The landed oligarchy that ran the country did pick competent chief executives and members of Congress. After 1880 an urban middle class grew up rapidly, becoming a third of the population of Buenos Aires by 1914. Heavy immigration from Italy and Spain, meanwhile, altered the composition of the working class, which shifted from mestizo or mulatto to European. By the 1890s the oligarchy had begun to lose control to new middle class parties.

One of them, the Radical party, was led by Hipólito Yrigoyen, a skillful demagogue, who claimed to represent the poor as well as the middle class. But his government was no more successful in assuring social peace than his predecessors. Yrigoyen's first term as president (1916-1922) was marred by labor violence, corruption, and irrational economic policies. His second term (1928-1930) ended in near chaos, with the military stepping in to restore order, and brought to a close Argentina's first experiment with civilian middle class government. It also brought the military to the center of political decisions—a position it retains today.

The military regime of 1943-45 effectively ended broad middle class participation in politics by dissolving the parties, censuring the press, and controlling the economy. These actions not only ended democracy in Argentina but also cleared the way for Perón.

First as secretary of labor and then as vice-president, Perón set about turning his own working class supporters into the nucleus of a single Argentine mass movement. In 1946 he was elected president with 56 percent of the vote and set to work reordering the Argentine way of life. Perón moved first against foreign investment, the railroads and utilities in particular, by nationalizing them. He redistributed income on a massive scale in favor of his supporters and to the detriment of agriculture. He also pursued indiscriminate industrialization by simple import substitution. The resulting increase in consumption without a corresponding rise in production resulted in inflation and the slowing of economic growth.

Despite Perón's widespread proletarian support, he was never a Marxist. Indeed, he attempted to develop a new idology, *justicialismo*, that would steer a third course between capitalism and communism. *Justicialismo*, over which many Argentine rhetoricians labored mightily in the 1950s, was also used to justify an independent foreign policy—independent of the United States and the Soviet Union.

But Perón's ideology was no more rooted in the economic facts of life then had been Hipólito Yrigoyen's musings on the dismal science. The result was a deteriorating economy, with declining agricultural production and exports. Politically, it meant increasingly arbitrary rule which finally provoked the middle class into a resistance movement that culminated in Perón's removal from power by the army in September 1955.

Perón's exile, however, did not end Argentina's political polarization or economic mismanagement. Nor is any other leader likely to emerge, for even this brief glimpse of Argentine history reveals a pattern of uncompromising social conflict and misdirected development. The oligarchy ruled well but the transition to middle class government was not smooth nor was the new leadership particularly competent. Moreover, there was no opportunity to learn from past mistakes because the military cut the civilians off from power and left the political arena open to Perón, the soldier-demagogue with a flair for organization. Perón organized another social class, the proletariat, into large, efficiently run labor unions. Union members have long come to expect a comfortable standard of living. But that has come at the cost of a vigorously expanding economy.

Stagnation has stimulated inflation and insured irregular and slower growth which in turn has alienated Argentina's large middle class. It has also exacerbated tensions between Buenos Aires, the capital and richest area in Argentina, and the provinces whose source of wealth is primarily agricultural—an economic sector long discriminated against by federal officials. The Argentina of the 1970s still resembles in some ways the Argentina of the 1820s—a nation of factions struggling for a larger share of a slower growing national product. No consensus as yet has been reached in order to take those admittedly measures of austerity that might bring that country out of its malaise, and none is likely in the near future. Furthermore, even if economic growth did pick up, there is certainly no guarantee that Argentina can have permanent social peace. However, continued economic difficulty almost assures continued strife.

Critical Problems

Argentina's political and economic problems are not likely to be resolved soon despite the new military regime's commitment to economic rationality. Inflation and stop-go growth will probably continue to foster political unrest including terrorism.

Argentina's lack of internal cohesion and leadership may keep it from playing a major role in Latin America, much less the world, but that will not prevent it from making occasional nationalistic gestures of a sort familiar to unstable governments anxious to win applause at home. The United States, of course, is likely to remain the major target of nationalist frustrations for some time. The extent of harm it can do this country, however, is limited. For example, although it supports the recently organized Latin American Economic System (SELA) it has not been one of its leaders due in large part to the lack of sustained, self-confident Argentine leadership. Nevertheless, any Argentine government may occasionally take positions contrary to American interests on a wide range of subjects (law of the sea, nuclear proliferation, trade policy, Panama Canal, etc.) making close relations with that country difficult for the long-term.

Political Decay. The government of the Peróns lasted far longer than anyone had anticipated. That fact raises two questions: how did Argentina come to be in such a fix and will the country get out of it?

The first is easier to answer than the second. At the time of the election that brought the Peronists back to power, Argentina had been under direct military rule by no less than three general-presidents for seven years. But the soldiers were no more successful in preserving order than had been their hapless civilian predecessor, Arturo Illía, a Radical party politician from Córdoba. Consequently, elections were decreed for March 1973. The Peronists were permitted to field a candidate—a reversal of long-standing government policy—although Perón himself was forbidden to run on a technicality. The result was a victory for the Peronist candidate, Hector Campora, who after being in office for barely seven weeks, resigned in order to pave the way for new elections. The *justicialista* candidate this time was Juan Perón and his victory (65 percent of the vote) was overwhelming. Even middle and upper class Argentines saw Perón as the only man able to restore order and economic prosperity. But the new president, at seventy-eight, was only a part-time leader. When he died after less than a year in office, the government remained effectively within the grasp of a small circle of conservative Peronists.

Isabel Perón's administration lasted longer than was generally expected. Thus, despite her government's inept handling of the economy, its corruption, and its inability to end the political violence, the military hesitated to move because of its own unhappy experience with direct rule. When it did, the new rulers found economic problems of larger scope than they had already feared.

The violence and drift cannot all be blamed on lack of leadership, or even on Argentina's labor unions, which are capable of simply defying government policy. In fact, economic self-interest aside, most union members as well as leaders tend to be moderate in their politics. Argentina's malaise (which is similar to Uruguay's) has now spawned a number of small but extremely effective terrorist groups that have done much to create the present atmosphere of perpetual crisis.

The oldest and largest is the so-called *Ejército Revolucionario Popular* (ERP).

Founded in 1964, the ERP (and several smaller splinter groups) have engaged in robbery, kidnapping, and murder, including attacks on military and police personnel. Its ideology is avowedly Marxist but it accepts no other "Marxist-revolution" as its model, although the press frequently describes ERP as Trotskyite. ERP's membership tends to be middle class students with a taste for violence and publicity led by a cadre of older revolutionary zealots.

Today, the ERP no longer enjoys a monopoly on terror. Its chief competitor is a faction of the Peronist youth organization, the so-called Montoneros, who adopted a similar policy of armed action after Perón's death. The Montoneros, however, are working class in origin and their prime targets are trade union leaders who have pursued a course of action entirely too moderate for them.

Meanwhile, the extreme Right has created its own mirror image of the ERP—the so-called Acción Argentina Anti-Comunista (AAA), which has so far specialized in the murder of people identified as leftist, including left-wing terrorists. It is widely believed in Argentina that the AAA continues to operate under quasi-official sanction and protection.

The result is that no one of any political significance in Argentina can feel safe—a situation with demoralizing consequences for the country's political infrastructure. In the meantime, the army has now joined the police in attempting to rid Argentina of terrorism. Both have recently enjoyed some success but it will take several years to eliminate the terrorists and may require a free rein for the military.

Argentina's political problem, then, has been a mixture of weak leadership, entrenched interests, and endemic violence, none of which is likely to disappear in the near future despite military rule.

The Argentine military government will continue to give the highest priority to eliminating the terrorist groups, the reestablishment of domestic peace, and the promotion of economic recovery. Success will require even harsher measures. These will divide the military itself and result in outside calls for respect of human rights. The latter would not ordinarily have much effect on Argentine actions but since they will probably influence the size and conditions of foreign aid, the matter must be considered seriously by the regime. It is likely, though, that if President Videla slackens the anti-guerrilla campaign he will be replaced by tougher, more nationalistic officers. In that case, Argentina's economic problems will be exacerbated although the guerrillas will probably be exterminated in a year or two. Argentina's return to civilian rule, however, may be long in coming, and the Argentine armed forces could adopt a "Brazilian solution," that is, a fixed routine which chooses a new military officer for the presidency every four years. In any case, a tranquil, prosperous, civilian-ruled Argentina is unlikely for the immediate future.

Economic Crisis. Argentina's economic crisis is closely linked to its political problems. Powerfully organized political groups, including those within the labor movement, are largely responsible for the recurring pattern of inflation, balance of payments crises, stagnation and recovery. By the early 1950s, the largest social group in Argentina, the urban workers, were organized into powerful unions coordinated by the General Confederation of Labor. The CGT can, as it has recently demonstrated, simply defy any government attempt to break hyperinflation, reduce monumental budget deficits, and promote agricultural exports. Excessive protection of inefficient national industry at the expense of agriculture has led to frequent balance-of-payments crises as exports (mainly agricultural) fail to expand rapidly enough to finance the imports essential for industry. This pattern has been repeated regularly in the last two decades.

In 1973 Juan Perón's Social Pact called for an incomes policy that would suspend wage negotiations and strikes for two years. Prices on hundreds of basic goods and services would also be frozen. At the same time, the government attempted to reduce expenditures while maintaining existing social programs. The Social Pact enjoyed some initial success but soon broke down. Price freezes led quickly to shortages and to a decline in product quality, while black marketeering flourished. Meanwhile, workers continued to agitate for higher wages and the government gave in to their demands.

Faced with the complete collapse of the Peronist plan, the regime cracked down on "economic crimes," while Minister of the Economy José Gelbard blamed the difficulties on "lawyers and agents of international monopoly" who were allying themselves with the national oligarchy in order to obstruct the *justicialista* new order. But exhortations did no good and the Social Pact did not survive Gelbard, who resigned after less than a year in office.

It would, however, be a serious mistake to blame the trade unions for all of Argentina's difficulties. For one thing, government policy has for decades ignored Argentina's traditional source of wealth: agriculture. Although it accounts for only 15 percent of GDP and employment, agriculture provides about 85 percent of exports as well as raw materials for Argentine industry. This sector has been punished by low government-fixed prices, inadequate research, and high tariffs on imports vital to farmers. As a consequence, Argentina imported 512,000 tons of wheat in 1973 and meat rationing has been imposed periodically for years to insure that surplus will be available for export.

Argentina can no longer satisfy the rising world demand for agricultural products. The sluggishness of its agricultural production, which falls far below potential, is documented in Table IV-2.

The 1985-86 estimates in the table above represent increases of only 30 to 150 percent over recent averages but could prove to be quite conservative if the government provided investment incentives to the agricultural producer. Since Argentina's population growth is low, most of the increase in output would be available for export. With large tracts of underutilized arable land and a large potential for raising yields, Argentina has opportunities to expand the production of cereals that few nations in the world possess.

Table IV-2
Production
(in 000/tons)

Year	Cotton	Corn	Wheat	Sugar Cane	Sunflower Oil Seeds	Sorghum
1967-68	230	6,650	7,320	9,500	940	1,897
1968-69	366	6,860	5,740	10,680	876	2,484
1969-70	458	9,360	7,020	9,700	1,140	3,820
1970-71	285	9,930	4,920	10,260	830	4,660
1971-72	337	5,800	5,440	–	820	2,350
1985-86	475	15,000	12,000	13,000	2,300	6,000

Beef is the other principal export with potential for considerable growth (see Table IV-3).

These years do not reflect the sharp rise in the price of beef in 1973. But while prices are dropping from their 1973 peak, the protein shortage in the world virtually guarantees a continuing market for higher-priced beef. For the period from 1967 to 1973 annual beef exports averaged 640,000 tons.

If the government promoted expansion of the cattle sector, a tripling of present beef production would not be impossible by 1985.[f] Argentine ranchers are experienced breeders constantly experimenting with higher yield strains, and there is scope for raising the yield per animal.

The country can also produce exportable surpluses of pork, lamb, and a variety of fruits and vegetables. But to achieve larger increases in output, Argentina will have to have adequate supplies of fuel and fertilizer as cultivation becomes more intensive. Currently, Argentina meets about 88 percent of its energy needs from domestic sources. In the early 1960s, when foreign private companies were welcomed, the country soon achieved self-sufficiency, which it retained until a new regime terminated the foreign contracts and production declined. Self-sufficiency in the field of energy would not be impossible by 1985 if private capital were once again allowed to run the necessary risks of offshore exploration. But as long as the government maintains its tight grip on petroleum (as it has since 1973), the prospects for reducing oil imports are not very good. To cover its current needs, Argentina has signed a long-term agreement with Libya at what seems to be a high price in order to supplement its normal imports from Bolivia and Venezuela.

In short, Argentina's agricultural production has not reached its potential and

---

[f]It is true that the government now lacks the resources to provide the agricultural sector much in the way of support. However, if a government were willing to engage in budget reform (for example, drastically cutting the huge subsidy paid to the nation's railroads), ample resources could be freed for agriculture.

Table IV-3
Beef

Year	000 of Head			000 of Tons of Processed Beef			Value of Exports $Millions
	Production	Export	Consumption	Production	Export	Consumption	
1970	12,815	3,086	9,290	2,610	735	1,868	349
1971	9,556	2,338	9,197	2,019	583	1,432	340

remains a great untapped resource. Tapping it would mean providing adequate investment incentives and credit and other facilities to the market-oriented Argentine farmer and rancher. In Argentina, however, such a program would be a reversal of decades-old practices. Moreover, even if production rose significantly, Argentina would find it difficult (though not impossible) to find new markets. The EEC, for the moment, has established strict quotas on meat. The United States has long kept out all but tinned beef from Argentina for sanitary reasons. Therefore, the Argentines will have to map out a detailed export strategy much as the Brazilians have done. It may well be the key to the sale of agricultural and some manufactured goods to those developing nations that are achieving some success: Brazil and Venezuela in Latin America; Nigeria and the Ivory Coast in Africa; and oil producing Middle Eastern states; Hong Kong, South Korea, and Taiwan in Asia.

Argentina's International Ambitions. Argentina's domestic difficulties have not entirely prevented its leaders in the past from promoting Argentine interests in the region and even the world. Severe internal distress and disunity, of course, limit the prospects for sustained, long-range foreign policy. Nevertheless, the Peronist theme of Third World nationalism will remain popular in an economy which, in the past, depended heavily on the capital, technology, and management skills of the European and American foreign investor.

Within the hemisphere, Argentina will always be concerned with its relations with the United States, its largest trading partner, chief source of capital, and major competitor in world markets. The United States will continue to be looked upon as a rival, particularly with respect to small neighboring South American republics which Argentina considers its natural sphere of influence. To the extent that U.S. leadership in hemisphere affairs and in the OAS can be diminished, Argentina's potential for leadership, like that of Brazil, Mexico, and Venezuela, is enhanced.

Argentina's rivalry with Brazil is particularly sharp at this time since Argentina aspires to leadership of Spanish South America at the expense of Brazil. It has recently bid for membership in the Andean Common Market and thus act as a counterweight to Brazil's expanding economic influence in the region. Argentina's ambitions, however, are not now acceptable to a number of the Andean countries, and therefore immediate membership does not appear likely..

In Latin America as a whole, Argentina has, at best, shared leadership with Brazil, Mexico, and now Venezuela. For example, in the Law of the Sea Conferences and the International Monetary Fund's C-20 Committee, the first three have represented Latin America as well as providing leadership for other developing countries. Argentina played no large part in the creation of SELA, but left that task to Mexico and Venezuela; nor has Buenos Aires been a conspicuous leader of the Latin American nations at the Geneva trade talks.

Argentina will also continue to show interest in the future of Antarctica, where it is a major territorial claimant. It will want to maintain both its naval capability, in order to patrol this area and its extensive Atlantic coastline, and the ground forces necessary to provide at least the illusion of protection from other South American nations, particularly Brazil.

Argentina's desire for economic independence and a "Third Position" has begun to show up in the trade area. Exports to the rest of Latin America, for example, nearly tripled between 1970 and 1974. Trade turnover with the oil exporting countries climbed from less than $100 million to nearly $600 million, and with the so-called centrally planned economies the figure rose from a mere $30 million in 1970 to $343 million with the Soviet Union responsible for one-third of it. In the meantime, Argentina continues its tradition of maintaining a favorable balance of trade with Europe, and continues to run deficits with the United States (see Table IV-4).

Nuclear Proliferation. Argentina may well be the second member of the nuclear weapons club in the Western Hemisphere—possibly by 1985. Its nuclear program began in 1950 when Juan Perón created the National Atomic Energy Commis-

Table IV-4

Argentine Exports and Imports, 1970 and 1974

(millions of U.S. dollars)

	World	U.S.	Other Western Hemispheres	Oil Ex-porting Countries	EEC	Asia	Centrally Planned
1970							
Exports	1,773	159	359	22	827	21	27
Imports	1,685	420	350	47	522	37	3
1974							
Exports	4,257	372	1,065	182	1,432	108	305
Imports	3,695	648	534	416	1,059	75	38

sion (CNEA). Despite numerous mistakes and erratic funding, the program is still the most advanced in Latin America after a quarter-century—although Brazil is now rapidly catching up.

Argentina has five research reactors and a functioning nuclear power plant of 600 megawatts. Similar reactors are coming on stream over the next decade. The country's nuclear facilities are manned by Argentine scientists who have received advanced training in the United States, Britain, France, and West Germany.

The military capability of this program is obvious. First, Argentina is committed to having a complete fuel cycle in the near future which would make it independent of all foreign assistance and materials and free of any suggestion of foreign control. Besides the reactor, Argentina has its own abundant sources of uranium, a small fuel fabrication facility (with a much larger one under construction), and a plutonium reprocessing plant. Moreover, Atucha is a heavy water reactor; it produces twice as much plutonium as the light water variety and the plutonium can be more easily removed. The Atucha plant has already produced about 100 kilograms of plutonium.

Argentina's nuclear capabilities are plain enough, but what are its intentions? In the first place, while there is no publicly announced policy of building nuclear weapons, there is interest in developing nuclear explosives for peaceful purposes. Argentina, for example, is not a party to the Non-Proliferation Treaty or Latin America's Tlatelolco Treaty. Indeed, Argentine diplomats showed no interest whatever in the concept of a Latin nuclear-free zone. Argentine officials have repeated their intention to develop nuclear explosives for peaceful purposes, and it will be as a peaceful nuclear power that Argentina joins the club—possibly in five years and probably within ten.

Several factors restrain Argentina from developing a nuclear arsenal. First, current production of plutonium is under IAEA safeguard. More importantly, Argentina has not developed a sophisticated delivery system (in contrast to Brazil) and therefore could only threaten its near neighbors unless a very expensive program were mounted soon—which is unlikely in the light of the country's economic problems. Finally, Argentina may hesitate because Brazil would probably follow suit—and Brazil has more resources to put into weapons and a more advanced delivery system. Nevertheless, the temptation will be there. Nuclear proliferation will certainly affect Argentine officials. And Argentina's frustrated nationalism and desire for sudden prestige could be decisive.

For the United States this possibility poses some difficult questions. Should we be concerned about nuclear proliferation in the area at all? Is there anything that can or should be done, beyond supporting more stringent international safeguards? To what extent will nuclear proliferation lead to increased risks for regional and global stability and peace? There are also other problems of a less complex nature. Argentina is no model of stability. It is peculiarly susceptible to terrorist attack and it is known that the Atucha plant has already been occupied by the ERP. Since plutonium removal is a fairly simple operation in a heavy water plant, the possibility of nuclear theft is a real one.

Any list of U.S. expectations for Argentina should be modest, since difficulties rooted in the character of the Argentine government will continue to beset U.S.-Argentina relations. About 65 percent of the electorate voted Peronist in the last election and strong Argentine nationalism will continue to mean "regaining" national sovereignty over the economy and eliminating the so-called domination of foreign capital and multinational corporations. Though this belief is rooted in myth it is nonetheless widely accepted in Argentina and a convenient scapegoat for political leaders unable or unwilling to make the hard decisions needed to pull Argentina out of its difficulties.

There will always be minor irritants in U.S.-Argentine relations but none of the problems on the horizon at present is very serious. In fact, U.S.-Argentine bilateral relations are better now than they have been in years. The United States, however, can expect some difficulty with Argentina on the following items:

1. request for support of Argentina's claim to the Falkland Islands—a British possession;
2. regular protests over the imposition of U.S. countervailing duties on selected Argentine exports;
3. continued complaints about U.S. sanitary regulations affecting Argentine beef;
4. disagreement on the dollar amount of trade permitted Argentina under the American system of generalized preferences;
5. fair treatment of U.S. investors in Argentina;
6. U.S. military sales and technology transfer.

Policy Options

If the worst is assumed, Argentina will drift into civil war within the next few years. Its immediate neighbors would be most affected, and Brazil would be greatly concerned about any repercussions on its own internal security. The United States can do little about this, nor can it do much except ignore Argentina's assertions of independence by its establishment of diplomatic relations with North Korea, East Germany, Albania, and Cuba.

The United States should pursue a friendly, even-handed policy towards Argentina that avoids the appearance of special treatment towards Brazil, its chief rival. The United States should attempt to cultivate, or maintain, good relations with all major political and social forces in Argentina.

For the immediate future, Argentina's task is to work its way out of difficulties that are largely of its own making. Ultimately, this means abandoning massive, illusory wage increases in favor of economic austerity and adopting a more effective policy toward terrorist groups. If Argentina adopts a rational economic course of action, which the current military regime has promised to do, the international capital markets and lending agencies should make available the necessary credits.

As elsewhere in Latin America, U.S.-owned multinational corporations are under constant attack in Argentina. The United States must continue to seek a variety of acceptable means of diminishing the impact and duration of such investment. However, the number of options available is limited by the need to adopt policies applicable to all, or nearly all, of Latin America. U.S. action on behalf of American Investors, as prescribed by U.S. law under the Hickenlooper or Gonzalez amendments, is categorized as intervention or economic aggression almost everywhere in Latin America. So are quotas and other nontariff barriers to Latin American exports, even though there may be valid "escape clauses" to which the United States can resort. Moreover, the extraterritorial application of U.S. law to American multinational corporations is rejected nearly everywhere in the Third World and is counterproductive. Indeed, it is a threat to U.S. investors. This was demonstrated in the case of the export to Cuba of automobiles manufactured by American companies in Argentina.

Finally, the United States has little choice regarding Argentina's nuclear capability. It can insist, of course, especially through agreement with other nuclear nations, that the safeguards be strictly maintained. But unilateral efforts are not likely to succeed, and any attempt by the United States to concern itself with Argentina's nuclear program, even a U.S. proposal for a cooperative venture with other nuclear nations, would probably be denounced as technological imperialism in Argentina.

Notes

1. Adrienne Koch and William Peden (eds.), *The Life and Selected Writings of Thomas Jefferson* (New York: The Modern Library, 1944), pp. 709-710.

2. Radio Havana, December 22, 1975, in *FBIS Latin America Daily Report*, December 23, 1975.

3. Radio Havana (international service), December 22, 1975, in *FBIS Latin America Daily Report*, December 23, 1975.

4. Ibid.

5. *FBIS Latin America Daily Report*, January 16, 1976.

6. George Ball, "Principles of Our Policy toward Cuba," *Department of State Bulletin*, May 11, 1964, p. 741.

7. Richard Nixon's views on Cuba were most succinctly stated in a televised conversation with Dan Rather on January 2, 1972, and were reprinted in the *Department of State Bulletin*, January 25, 1972, p. 84.

8. *Diario de las Americas*, August 30, 1974, p. 1.

9. Department of State Press Release, no. 108 (March 1, 1975), p. 6.

10. *Wall Street Journal* "Review and Outlook: Ford on Foreign Policy," March 3, 1976, and *Latin America* (London) March 5, 1976.

11. U.S. direct investment amounted to $2,825 million in 1974 while Mexico sent 62 percent of its exports ($3,386.2 million) and absorbed 66 percent of its imports ($5,340.3 million) from the United States also in 1974. Trade figures are from *Direction of Trade Annual* 1970-1974 (IMF and IBRD), and investment figure from *Survey of Current Business* (U.S. Department of Commerce: October 1975).

12. All figures taken from the 1973 *World Population Data Sheet*, Population Reference Bureau.

13. Frederick C. Turner, *Responsible Parenthood: The Politics of Mexico's New Population Policies* (Washington, D.C.: American Enterprise Institute, 1974), p. 16.

14. Mexican officials have been reluctant to disclose any figures, but U.S. estimates range from 10 to 20 billion barrels, *Oil & Gas Journal*, October 24, 1974, p. 73.

15. GNP and income figures are from AID, Statistics and Reports Division. Trade data taken from *Direction of Trade Annual* 1970-74 (IMF and IBRD).

16. Venezuela's estimated 700-billion barrel reserve of so-called heavy oil in the Orinoco Belt is still many years away from significant production, though it is now possible to recover 10 percent of that reserve at $5 per barrel. Among the other problems to be faced are heavy initial capital investment and better recovery technology. See Kim Fuad, "The Orinoco Challenge," *Business Venezuela*, number 22, 1972, pp. 5-11. The United States, along with other oil-hungry countries has shown a great interest in helping to recover the Orinoco oil. Venezuela has made no commitments as yet, however.

17. That figure is not entirely certain since extreme conservationists have urged a cutback to 1.0 m/b per day. Thus, despite Pérez's pledges, oil production is still an issue in Venezuela. See *Times of the Americas*, January 21, 1976, p. 1.

18. Investment figures are taken from Leonard A. Lupo and Julius N. Friedlin, "U.S. Direct Investment Abroad in 1974," *Survey of Current Business* (Washington, D.C.: U.S. Department of Commerce, October 1975).

19. See, for example, President Caldera's speech to the National Press Club, June 2, 1970, reported in the *New York Times*, June 3, 1970, p. 2, and his June 3, 1970 speech to a joint session of the U.S. Congress, reprinted in the *Department of State Bulletin*, June 29, 1970, pp. 796-799. A more complete account of the Caldera position can be found in Republic of Venezuela: *Official Oil Policy* (Caracas: Central Information Office, 1971), pp. 31-57.

20. Thomas Jefferson to the Prince Regent of Portugal, May 5, 1808, quoted in Adrienne Koch and William Peden, eds., *The Life and Selected Writings of Thomas Jefferson*, p. 588.

21. See, for example, the Buenos Aires daily *La Opinión*, November 16, 1975, p. 9, in a report dealing with official concern over Brazilian penetration of Argentina's Missiones province. *La Opinión*, which is Argentina's best newspaper, was quite specific: "But there can be no doubt that Brazilian officials approve this phenomenon (i.e., Brazilian migration) since it establishes an

important geopolitical beachhead for the progressive establishment of Brazilian culture in border zones. . . . In this regard we cannot disregard the connection between migration and maps absurdly claiming unquestionable Argentine regions, as Progressive Democrat deputy Angel Moral has reported."

22. Brazil imports approximately 80 percent of her fuel needs which may have amounted up to $3 billion dollars (IMF estimate). See Bernardo F. Grossling, *Latin America's Petroleum Prospects in the Energy Crisis* (Washington, D.C.: Geological Survey Bulletin1411, U.S. Department of the Interior, 1975), p. 24.

23. John W. Tuthill, "Operation Topsy," *Foreign Policy*, Fall 1972, p. 85.

24. United States Policies and Programs in Brazil, Hearings before the Subcommittee on Western Hemisphere Affairs: (92nd Congress, 1st Session, May 11, 1971), p. 290.

25. Quoted in the *Department of State Bulletin*, January 3, 1972, p. 13.

26. Quoted in the *Department of State Bulletin*, June 23, 1973, p. 915.

27. See *O Estado de São Paulo*, June 10, 1976, p. 3.

V Conclusions

What will United States-Latin American relations be like in ten years? Will they and can they ever improve? It must be said there is very little in the record that suggests radical improvement is possible, much less likely. At the least, the twentieth century reveals far more discord than harmony, and moments of genuine cooperation have proved fleeting indeed. It would be a brave and future policy architect who felt confident of his design being superior to all others previously drawn.

Nevertheless, precedent, although a useful warning to the innocent enthusiast, is not a fixed guide to the future. Moreover, other factors loom much larger in shaping tomorrow's hemispheric relations. Foremost is the effect political and economic trends will have on the region. The second is the kind of diplomacy the Latin American republics will continue to pursue in the coming decade.

The implications of the second are easiest to spell out. Short of a major war or worldwide economic collapse, Latin America will continue to seek out new economic and political partners. Few Latin American countries will remain as dependent on the United States as they once were in that half-century between 1915 and 1965. To be sure, the United States will never be insignificant but "hemispheric solidarity" may be much weakened in ten years, probably in fact, and quite possibly in rhetoric as well, particularly in the larger republics.

Latin America, at least that part which speaks Spanish, will continue to look inward also. Although integration will not develop along lines anticipated by those eager ECLA planners of the 1960s, progress will be made. Some forms of regional and subregional organization will exist. No doubt there will be no tightly bound political or economic union but the habits of cooperation and consultation may develop to an unprecedented degree.

It is usually assumed that Latin America's new diplomacy will give the region a sense of confidence, and therefore it will become less stridently critical of the United States. There is probably some truth to that although psychological interpretation of nation-state behavior is a risky business. Moreover, the belief that improving hemispheric relations depends on Latin America's entering into the world's mainstream neglects two considerations. First, it does not test the quality of the new relationships: are they meaningful or only superficial? Second, it does not ask which countries are being approached by Latin America. It is one thing for the region's republics to seek out Western Europe, it is quite another for them to join forces with the Third World, particularly those countries which are the most anti-Western, anti-democratic, and anti-capitalist. If economic development does take place, then in a decade much of Latin America would find itself allied with the developed and near-developed world. If, as this report suggests, Latin America's development is sporadic at best, then the region may well join the ranks of the viscerally anti-Western, and by extension, anti-American bloc.

That unhappy prospect raises the general problem of relating internal conditions to relations with the United States, which is both more difficult and more important to assess. As we have seen, most of Latin America will make some progress but only in fits and starts, and not enough to satisfy pent-up demand. Some countries will make no progress at all. This will not be because of a lack of potential—the region has natural resources in abundance. Latin America could be a major exporter of food, fuel, and minerals as well as manufactured goods of an increasingly sophisticated nature. But bad governmental management and political turmoil will continue to hamper the region economically.

Politically stable regimes will be the exception. In ten years, however, there may well be another swing back (albeit temporary) to civilian governments after a number of militaries discover that officers have no special taste or talent for government. But the new civilian regimes in most cases will be no more in control than their predecessors. They will continue to be plagued by periodic subrevolutionary violence which will be more than enough to turn out in most countries the fragile government of the day.

What will this development mean for the United States? Nations with economies desperate for development in general, and foreign exchange in particular, will engage in bitter disputes on trade issues. Any protectionist move made by the United States, though little noticed in this country, will be widely denounced throughout the region, even by our traditional friends. The issue will be further aggravated by the servicing of mounting foreign debt—a problem which may be Latin America's most serious international concern in the coming decade. It could, for example, result in a series of emergency meetings of governments, international agencies, and private banks by 1985 but it is unlikely any satisfactory arrangement short of continual debt rollover (a kind of creeping moratorium) will ever be achieved. Besides trade and debt, foreign investment will continue to be a sensitive issue. U.S. investment will probably stagnate but renewed interest in foreign capital will be shown by some countries which had earlier discouraged it through radical (and radically unsuccessful) social and economic experiments of their own. The wary investor, however, may be very difficult to coax back into the region.

On the political side the United States can expect trouble from several directions. First, if the civilians do replace the soldiers in some countries there will be considerable outcry directed at the United States for past "supporting" military dictatorships. Indeed, human rights may even become as sensitive an issue as it has been here. Democracy may become fashionable once more and talk of ideological pluralism will grow less frequent. The move to civilian regimes may be followed by a perceived drift to the left in those countries and old issues like U.S. corporations will again be ripe for expropriation or contract cancellation.

Thus, between the economic pinch and political turmoil, the United States is not likely to enjoy in 1985 the best of relations with the republics of the old Good Neighborhood. There will, no doubt, be great concern expressed over this in the United States, and if there is a new administration in 1984, a "fresh look" at Latin America will be taken. It should be pointed out, however, that much of what happens is beyond our responsibility and ability to correct. That should not prevent the United States from protecting its interests, and doing those things which are beyond immediate self-interest. The United States can, for example, keep its market open for Latin American exports. It can begin now to explore an equitable debt-servicing scheme. It can encourage military regimes to share power with responsible civilians, and take a firm position on human rights where it is necessary as long as no double standard of conduct is permitted: that is, to attack only non-Communist dictatorships when the region's only Communist dictatorship holds the record for the oldest, most repressive regime in the hemisphere.

The United States can also, unobtrusively to be sure, encourage economic rationality in the region. In the meantime it can and must resist those "reforms" of the OAS which are solely aimed at embarrassing the United States. It should refuse to accept the thesis advanced by left-wing partisans which hold this country accountable for all the region's political and economic ills. It must be resisted not only because it is false but because its articulation is inevitable. It is inevitable because the root of the problem is not generally what we have done or what we will do but what we are and will remain: the freest, richest, and most powerful nation in this hemisphere.

Finally, will the United States be confronted with a national security problem in Latin America over the next decade? Since 1960 that question has been directly linked to another question: will another Castro-style regime emerge in the area? That question, although currently unfashionable, is still appropriate because after more than fifteen years in power Fidel Castro's root convictions about this country have not changed. There is, to be sure, a possibility that some rapprochement may take place within the decade but even after twenty-five years in power, the Cuban leader's most cherished beliefs will probably remain unshaken.

Castro's success in making a duplicate Cuba will probably be limited. In any case, it will not come about as a result of a successful guerrilla movement whether urban or rural based. The only possibility lies with either left-wing officers seizing and retaining power or an elected regime suddenly bent on a radical change in policy at home and abroad. Neither possibility is welcome, but poses serious trouble for the United States only in the event that it takes place in the Caribbean and that it involves a close military alliance with Cuba and the Soviet Union.

And what of Cuba itself? Despite Angola or any further adventures in the more remote parts of the planet, Cuba is not likely to be a conventional military threat to any Latin American country. It will, however, while losing its pariah status, continue to act as a magnet attracting other regimes leftward, some of them desperate for answers to chronic social and economic problems, without necessarily bringing them into the company of the Socialist camp. This is most likely to occur in the Caribbean, and among the English-speaking states, in particular. Cuba therefore will remain, at the least, a nuisance to this country even if relations are reestablished.

Latin America has never been a part of the world that American policymakers have had much luck in influencing for the better. The problems have always been too great and our patience too small. The belief in our capabilities to solve them has been either smugly overestimated or caustically derided. Perhaps after this long and frequently bitter experience we will now be able to construct a more moderate and sustainable policy. Such a policy should reflect both our pragmatism and idealism, providing benefits for us and our friends in Latin America. The next ten years will provide us with that opportunity.

Appendix:
Venezuela in Change: Prospects and Problems in the Coming Decade and Beyond

Philip B. Taylor, Jr.

Long dependent on the political, financial, and managerial decisions of Americans located inside as well as outside its borders, Venezuela in 1975 was undertaking a sharply different role in both internal and foreign policy. In the past, Venezuela, like many of its fellows in the Latin America region, has been a country of largely unrealized possibilities. The abrupt vertical increase of world petroleum prices in 1973 and 1974 gave it the means by which to fund policy revisions and new types of activities, and its ambitions were focused by a sharp increase in nationalist mood.

These new policy areas include many interrelated aspects. Some were defined generally in policy statements and decrees announced during the first half of 1974 by the newly inaugurated government of Dr. Carlos Andrés Pérez.[a] A number of aspects are intended to be exclusively internal in outcomes; a few will be primarily external in effects. Yet in some respects virtually all will affect the capability of the country in the arena of international economic and diplomatic affairs; thus, the coming decade could be a period of continual and even of greatly heightened Venezuelan influence and power challenge throughout the hemisphere.

This special essay on Venezuela is included in this volume as a case study of a country in Latin America that has achieved a relatively stable democracy and has a relatively high potential for economic growth.

[a]Dr. Carlos Andrés Pérez assumed the presidency of Venezuela on March 12, 1974. He received 48.6 percent of the votes cast, and his party received 102 of 200 members of the Chamber of Representatives and 29 of 49 Senators. The second candidate, Lorenzo Fernandez, received 36.8 percent. In this essay, I lump these together as "social democratic" and middle-of-the-road constitutional parties, which have played the major role in the structuring of the present Venezuelan political system's values and styles of decision behavior.

On the other hand, with the passage of the decade other variables will come into play. It is not difficult to assume what these variables might be, but it is all but impossible to guess what their individual magnitudes might be, and what their interrelationships might become. Mineral resource depletion is inevitable, to point an obvious fact; oil has been cited as the most significant example, granted the world's and Venezuela's current technology. But while in 1962 it was widely propagandized that the proven reserves would be gone in about fourteen years at current production rates, in 1974 (production rates had increased somewhat during the period) it was still declared that reserves would endure, at that rate of use, about twelve to fourteen years. In effect, in this example as in many others, the merely physical circumstance is subject—often fundamentally—to technical interpretation and to the state of the technological arts. Consequently, conjecture is possible but specific prediction is likely to border on folly.

The Most Obvious Outcomes for the Decade

Responses to Internal Needs

These outcomes include:

a. accelerated efforts toward socially and economically distributive policies beneficial to the country's mass or lower class;

b. substantial adjustment of the size and direction of commitments to agriculture at both the large commercial and small individual levels;

c. major commitments of government funds, and offering of incentives for the investment of private funds, leading to the expansion of selected existing industries and the development of new industries; the selected industries will be predicated on Venezuela's natural resource base, on a need for further import substitution, or to fulfill planning decisions made by the appropriate agencies of the Andean Group;

d. heightened nationalism in internal economic affairs, in respect to foreign investors involved in Decision 24 of the Andean Group; these policies will not, however, presume a rejection of foreign technical or managerial skills, the need for which will continue to be great;

e. nationalization of the petroleum industry occurred in January 1976;[1] massive investment in new facilities for all aspects of the industry will occur, including accelerated training programs for technical and professional personnel, in order that Venezuela will remain competitive in the 1980s as United States policies of energy autonomy begin to be effective;

f. nationalization, with all possible speed, of all aspects of the remaining minerals industries, as well as of the service and processing industries integrally related to these fields.[2]

g. continued and probably expanding attention to national security needs, the substantial support of armed forces materiel and personnel needs (as defined primarily by the armed forces themselves), and the expansion of an intelligence capability;

h. the revision, on a major scale, of the tax base of the government, in the light of the nationalization of the principal sources of tax income; if done with appropriate attention to ability to pay as a criterion, this will possibly have some effects on the influence structure of national politics.

Responses to International Political and Economic Needs

Additionally, a number of policies will be undertaken which are intended to have international political and economic outcomes:

i. continual reduction of the level of production and export of both crude and processed petroleum products, with heightened emphasis on conservation practices; conservation will probably not be perceived as a goal for other minerals up to 1985, although there will be sharp concentration on exporting processed mineral products rather than raw materials;

j. continual increase in the short run, and probable maintenance of stability in the longer run, of prices of petroleum products exported from Venezuela; this policy may possibly involve preferential price treatment for less developed countries, especially those construed as located within Venezuela's potential sphere of influence;

k. a termination of the current (1974-1975) major unique contributions to multinational funds intended to assist the development of Third World and less developed countries, except possibly in the cases of members of development and market associations of which Venezuela is a member state;

l. selective bi-national credits and other developmental offers to less developed countries, with some preference for countries which, with this assistance, may be freed of some degree of economic or political control by industrialized and developed countries;

m. suggestions, probably implemented in some measure by suasion and the offer of loans, to other primary product producing countries of the "Third World," that their national interests will be better served by heightened nationalist attitudes;

n. highly pragmatic use of or recourse to the Organization of Petroleum Exporting Countries (OPEC);

o. use of Venezuelan membership within regional economic associations in order to increase the country's political and industrial/economic influence among the other members of these groups;

p. continuance of the recently reestablished diplomatic and economic relationships with Cuba on bases of self-interest, assuming continuing Cuban

commitment to a policy of nonintervention in the internal or external affairs of
Venezuela;

q. identification of Brazil's rising international aspirations as potentially
threatening to Venezuela's national and foreign policy interests; this may
possibly lead to a policy of informal or formal security association with
neighboring countries;

r. settlement of outstanding controversies with Colombia concerning the Gulf
of Venezuela; maintenance of the *modus vivendi* under the Protocol of Port of
Spain of 1970 concerning border disputes with Guyana; substantial interest in
the Dutch possessions in the Caribbean now approaching political independence,
but confinement of this interest to commercial and investment activities;
continued support for Panama's nationalist aspirations concerning control of the
Canal Zone and the Panama Canal;

s. the pursuit of policies tending to reduce the authority of the Organization
of American States, possibly through the aggrandization of an alternative body;
the employment of alternative forums for the statement of national views; this
will not, however, lead to reduced verbal commitment to the traditional
inter-American principles of self-determination, mutual respect and nonintervention;

t. continued, but somewhat more selective, political confrontation with the
United States; this policy will normally occur through indirect rather than direct
devices or issues.

In sum, the coming decade will encompass a heightened Venezuelan sense of
national identity, nationalism, autarky, commitment to internally distributive
social, economic, and political processes, and intent to take a leading role within
the Latin American region. The internal policy changes and advances will require
sustained improvement in the country's managerial and planning capability; in
past decades much of its underdevelopment has occurred because of the
shortcomings of its decisionmakers, and in 1974 and 1975 there was continuing
evidence of administrative inability and waste.[3]

Venezuela's foreign policy goals will almost inevitably cause some heightened
tension in international politics. Brazil has for at least a decade regarded itself as
the inevitable beneficiary of the developmental process in Latin America.[4] The
former dominance of the United States in the hemisphere, with special attention
to Venezuela, has been under sustained criticism by Venezuela and its colleague
states for a number of years; American response to Venezuela will be formally
careful but fundamentally firm; and this will be a probable cause of some
tension. It is not improbable that the greater sense of Venezuelan identity and
strength, which—if achieved—will more firmly base a bid for international
influence, may lead to a "new kid on the block" attitude, especially in the
Caribbean region, in which more than a hint of imperialism may seem visible.
This impression may possibly seem heightened in the short run, since the
Venezuelan decision elite has not had any opportunity to develop experience in

the analysis of national power and capability vis-à-vis national need and, surely, under the present extraordinarily heady circumstances of "oil bonanza,"[5] even the most experienced and sober leaders might find calm judgments difficult to make. On the other hand, among the new Caribbean states, the ground rules of politics are still being formed, and jockeying for internal advantage may cause their spokesmen to find offense even where none is intended.

The Policy Implications of Internal Change

Some review of factors relevant to the country's internal tasks is essential. Fortunately, there is an unusually detailed and analytical base-point volume available to inform the student of Venezuela's condition at the time the first constitutional social-democratic government in the country's history was established, in the report of a study mission of the International Bank for Reconstruction and Development.[6] In the period since that time, extraordinary tasks have been defined and undertaken, and much meliorative change has occurred in both social and economic areas. The country has, further, successfully passed through four heated democratic electoral processes since the fall of the last military dictator in 1958, and in the past two of these processes the principal party in opposition has won both the largest vote and the presidential office. Most notably, and in contrast to the generally discouraging condition of constitutional republicanism in the rest of Latin America, the margin of vote supporting social democracy has increased constantly; in the 1973 election, the *Acción Democrática* party (AD) was returned to office for a five-year term by a substantial plurality and with a clear congressional majority and, for the first time since 1958, the majority of votes in the national capital fell to the candidates of the two social democratic parties rather than to nominees of extremist, personalist, or transitory "parties."[7] The second party is the *Partido Social Cristiano* (COPEI).

The public ratification of the legitimacy of the regime is verified in a variety of other ways. The first AD government, of Rómulo Betancourt (1959-1964), was subjected to an extraordinary terrorist campaign which was aided by a variety of devices by the Cuban government of Fidel Castro. The following AD government, headed by Raul Leoni (1964-1969), was less heavily harassed, to be sure, but it was not until the presidential period of Rafael Caldera (1969-1974), leader of the COPEI, that the terror was brought to a virtual standstill.[8] The government inaugurated in 1974 now feels so confident of its ability to stand on a firm law-and-order position that it tolerates the open political action of virtually all the former terrorists and renewed its diplomatic relations with Cuba on December 30, 1974.[9]

The armed forces also have ratified the social democratic political order. The experience of the last military dictatorship, headed by Marcos Pérez Jiménez

(1952-1958), was harsh for many officers as well as for many early supporters of the military *golpe de estado* of 1948. While the social democratic governments since 1958 have more than adequately rewarded the armed forces for their obedience, the military commitment to constitutional practices became sufficiently strong to give Presidents Caldera and Pérez the confidence that renewal of relationships with Cuba, and the grant of partisan freedoms to extreme leftist parties, would not be met by overt acts of military opposition.[10]

One can suggest that "the rules of the political game" with regard to the "economic" or entrepreneurial sector have changed substantially since the late 1940s.[11] Many Venezuelans believe without qualification that this sector underwrote the Pérez Jiménez regime. There seems some evidence that members of this group, opposed to President Pérez's broad economic program, approached army generals in mid-1974; the suggestion is reported to have been rejected derisively by the officers.[12] Pérez felt confidence during his first months that tactics little known in Venezuela, but common in the more developed countries of the world, would be viable: that a political claim by the private sector could be treated as any other claim from an interest group, without special deference.[13]

The country does not lack for difficult socioeconomic problems which the Pérez government will be expected to confront. The population in 1973 was estimated at 11,520,000, and was believed growing at an annual rate of 33.9 per thousand; this would yield a population of about 14,100,000 in 1979, and 16,600,000 in 1984, if maintained. Venezuela has not established significant population planning goals or policies at this time, and continued growth will infringe upon the practical effects of the current cash inflows and their acquisitive possibilities from petroleum income.[14] Since 1958, when Venezuela started to attack its socioeconomic problems from a severe deficit of health facilities, housing availabilities, educational facilities, and social welfare provisions, great expenditures have had to be undertaken. Use of land was both socially retrogressive in terms of large concentrations in the hands of few owners and economically underproductive as expressed by the country's need to import large amounts of the most commonly used and basic foods. And while the country borrowed heavily abroad to build a modern economic infrastructure and to develop major modern industrial facilities capable of processing portions of its minerals, it also attempted to make the social investments that were indicated.[15]

Yet the sustained population growth rate, coupled with the initial deficit of facilities, tended to frustrate efforts. Whether the remark of David Nott is entirely valid ("Venezuela is not an underdeveloped country but an undermanaged country"),[16] the fact is that the Caldera government could be criticized in 1973 for inadequate reductions of the social deficits of unemployment, housing, and land use as well as income inequalities. These failures returned the AD to power in a significant electoral swing. Further, for the first time in over a decade, inflation had become a visible danger with a rate of nearly 15 percent at election time—at least triple that of the customary figure.[17]

Changed world oil circumstances have created a recent bonanza for Venezuela. In 1973, the gross domestic product (GDP) per capita, in 1970 dollars (at $1.00 = Bs.4.50) was $1,169. The figure places Venezuela statistically among the most affluent countries of the world. However, some perspective is given by the presidential statement in June 1974, that 1 percent of the population receives or controls 51 percent of the GDP, and that the remaining 99 percent share a monthly per capita income of 230 bolivares (in 1974, $1.00 = Bs.4.30).[18] National income data began to show explosive upward change in 1974, as the new price levels of petroleum took effect. While historically petroleum has contributed about 20 to 22 percent of the GDP, this percentage has been based on relatively modest market prices for the product. In the two-year period ending January 1, 1974, the average reference price of crude petroleum (which is fixed by government decree and serves as the basis for the calculation of official revenues from oil) rose from $2.63 to $14.08 per barrel, or 540 percent). Less spectacular increases continued as a result of the decisions made by the Organization of Petroleum Exporting Countries (OPEC) in subsequent months. The effect was that while Venezuela received $3,509 million dollars for oil exports in 1972, it received $14,990 million in 1974. The Venezuelan government has declared that it will seek even greater income per barrel from oil in the future. But since nationalization took effect on January 1, 1976, and the economic effects from this action are yet to be determined, the country's short-run pricing policies were not stated specifically.[19]

On May 1, 1974, President Carlos Andrés Pérez announced his policy priorities for his five-year term. Predicated on his certainty that government income will, if anything, be much in excess of the absorptive capacity of the country, the statement demarcates target areas for future budgetary appropriations. It continues the assertions in the planning documents of prior regimes concerning the linkage among levels of industrialization, the achievement of self-sustaining developmental growth, and the surmounting of social problems. The statement also contemplates substantial allocation of funds, through bilateral and multilateral agreements and organisms, to developing countries of the "Third World." Pérez asked Congress for a grant of emergency powers for one year with which to decree selected portions of the statement into force; this was granted in May. Although some sections of the statement are sharply nationalist in tone, and contemplate nationalization of selected portions of the economy, the major portion contemplates direct participation of the private sector in entrepreneurial and planning activities.[20]

Coupled with this statement of priorities there has begun a fundamentally promising reorganization of the executive branch of government. Both historical reasons generic in the Iberian heritage and reasons unique to the country in the present century, Venezuela has a record in even the recent past of administrative underachievement. There has been a growing dearth of trained administrative and supervisory personnel and, as the country moves into elaborate and complex plans for modernization, a notable lack of planners and professionals. It has been estimated that the present approximately 6,000 persons of some degree of experience and skill must be increased to about 40,000 by 1985.[21] Additionally, in the past the record of partisan-inspired spoils and peculation, with their implications of severe inefficiency, have been almost shocking even by Latin American customary standards. However, vigorous measures have been taken and are busy to reduce these practices.[22]

Probably the most important single event of early 1974, from the point of view of public administration, was the commencement of reorganization of the Central Office for Coordination and Planning (CORDIPLAN). The reform is based on studies and executive decisions begun under the Caldera government; CORDIPLAN's past record of preparing plans that were infrequently respected by government officials, and of timid negotiations with private sector planning groups that were often little more than charades in light of the agency's inability to enforce the agreements, should now be corrected.[23]

Under the reorganization CORDIPLAN has acquired control of the national budgeting process. While this adjustment had been a part of reorganization documents for a number of years in the recent past, the Pérez government now seems determined to fulfill the process. A substantial reform of the tax structure is planned, since the nationalization of oil will bring to a halt the era of easy government income pickings by the simple expedient of raising taxes on the foreign-owned oil corporations; the companies paid about two-thirds—or *more*— of the government revenues from the 1950s onward; the private sector will now be confronted by the kind of tax policy revisions that it forestalled by skillful political action in 1966 and 1967.[24]

Plans for the massive economic development program now must meet CORDIPLAN criteria. Existing public corporations will undergo substantial modification in some instances and new corporations, which will be wholly or partly government owned, will come into being to control petroleum, petrochemicals, steel, electric power, shipping, the Guyana region complex of industries, railroads, and a number of other activities. The planning and policies of these corporations will be coordinated with the executive branch ministries by CORDIPLAN. The agency also controls the statistical and census offices, so that data are more available for national planning purposes than in the past. In the future, no governmental unit, whether or not in the central administration, may draw on the credit of the state without its consent; this corrects a technique used flagrantly at times in the past, and especially by the military regime of Marcos Pérez Jiménez. CORDIPLAN drafts budgetary and program legislation submitted to the Congress, and executive decree powers become more centralized in terms of both formulation and execution.[25]

Building on the final months of the Caldera government, Pérez has imprinted his own innovations on policy. Assisted by the reorganization of the executive branch, his May presidential statement marks a wide area of priorities; he has set for his executive team a personal example of great activity that has tended to intimidate many of his critics.[26] Some 211 significant executive decrees had already been announced by the end of June 1974, only 110 days after his inauguration. From this activity has emerged a somewhat grandiose plan, but its clear intent to advance the country's economy, backed by the flood of oil income, makes it difficult not to share Pérez's optimism.

In 1975, while detailed plans were still in process of preparation, the bulk of new oil-based revenues were withheld from the internal economy; CORDI-PLAN's *Plan Nacional, 1975-1979*, was not announced until May 28, 1975.[27] The principal agency for application of moneys in public enterprises is the *Fondo Nacional de Inversiones* (FIV), which in 1974 received initial capitalization of 13 billion bolivares ($3.02 billion). FIV receives an established percentage of revenues from petroleum that are considered surplus to the government's operating budget and was initially scheduled to receive as much as Bs.70 billions by 1978, of which about Bs.50 billions would be fed into the industrial development of the country. By mid-1975 it was already realized that this amount would not be reached, as the groups in the country arguing for conservation of oil resources became more effective in reducing production of crude.[28] Through the end of 1975 most of the money under FIV control was actually held outside of the country, in loans, trust funds, short term deposits, purchases of foreign government securities, and common stocks. Undoubtedly, however, as the country's own absorptive capacity increases, these overseas activities will be reduced as the money is recalled.[29]

The FIV is not to be confused with a number of more modest (but still quite large in absolute terms) funds established for the furtherance of economic and social possibilities within the private sector.

Funds for Agriculture. Agriculture long has been viewed as the most deficient portion of the economy. The Caldera government had already proposed Bs.1,450 million in extraordinary credits, to be obtained by the sale of government obligations, for investment in 1974. But with the supply of new moneys, an agricultural development fund has been established, initially supplied with up to Bs.2 billions, and with expectations of spending up to Bs.4.5 billions by 1979. A *Fondo de Desarrollo Agropecuario* (Fund for Farm and Ranching Development) will administer revolving funds. Agricultural loans will be made for as little as five percent interest to landowners who submit viable projects. Commercial banks doing business in the country will be required to commit 20 percent of their loans to agricultural proposals. A primary goal of the plan is eventually to purchase self-sufficiency in food products and even to yield exportable surpluses of those crops for which there are unique advantages of soil or climate. The goal is a distant and difficult one, to be sure; the current deficits are large, and the prevailing birth rate, which yields a net population growth of about 33.9 per thousand per year is hardly encouraging. Beyond these factors there is also the need to encourage commercial agriculturalists by creating a market structure that will be rewarding. The country has actually had very little experience with real market mechanisms as yet, and this will have to be acquired.[30]

Other measures planned will draw on a variety of funding sources. Small farmers, whose share of the market is not large, will also be assisted by low-cost loans as well as by a substantial enlargement of the technical and advisory programs that have been a largely unfulfilled feature of the agrarian reform program of the country since 1960. An effort will be made to extend official minimum wage legislation, previously applied only in the major cities, to wage workers in rural regions; in May 1974, President Pérez decreed this national figure to be 15 bolivares per day or 450 bolivares monthly for full-time paid workers.

There will also be substantial use of FIV moneys when the planning is fully carried out. In April 1974, the government acquired control of about 1.5 million hectares (3.6 million acres) in Apure, Barinas and Portuguesa states. A portion of this land will be used for experimentation in drainage, pastures, and ground water control, so that the very large regions of the country's Orinoco river basin, hitherto almost useless because of major flooding or because of the lateritic soil, may be brought into effective use. Access roads, thirty-six dams, and many miles of control dikes are to be built. About 120,000 jobs will be created during the construction periods and as many as 46,000 jobs in permanent agricultural establishments are expected to be created. Additionally, a modest portion of the reclaimed lands will be made available for *asentamientos*, or land reform settlements.

Funds for Industry. A second internal development fund of Bs.2 billion was established in April 1974, the *Fondo de Desarrollo Industrial* (Industrial Development Fund). This is distinct from the FIV, in that these moneys are intended to encourage the private sector through loans normally negotiated through commercial banks but with government guarantees. While it is hoped that new entrepreneurs will enter the economy, or that current participants will undertake new ventures, there is no bar to the enlargement of on-going enterprises. There is a specified ceiling of Bs.1 million; interest rates are to range between 6 and 9 percent, and terms to run as long as fifteen years. The fund was the first to begin its operations, and appears to have set relatively generous principles.[31]

A number of variables will inevitably affect the role of private capital in the country's growth; all relate to its past or future expectations in the international sphere. The first issue is capital flight. Granted the semi-covert character of this phenomenon, its size and effects can only be the object of informed and usually inferential guesses.[32] The second issue is the role of Venezuela in the Andean Common Market, which was established by the Andean Subregional Integration Agreement signed at Cartagena, Colombia in May 1969.[33] The two issues are in some degree combined by Decision 24 of the Market's executive board, the common system for treatment of foreign capital within the territories of the member states. This common system came into existence on June 30, 1971; it was to enter into force for individual governments as they agreed to accept its terms. President Pérez announced its adoption by Venezuela on April 29, 1974; thus, the provisions of the system will come into force within a three-year period, and a number of effects can be noted.

The causes of capital flight are obvious in principle. Political instability and governmental incapability, when combined with a reputed or proven record of peculation and capricious seizure of private property by government leaders, easily provokes flight. None of these elements has been absent in Venezuela's past, at one time or another. Since the third decade of the century, one of the most obvious causes has not prevailed in the country, however: currency instability. Juan Vicente Gómez, whose tyranny from 1908 to 1935 united the country, made good his determination to stabilize the currency and to liquidate all foreign debts. But Venezuelans have found other reasons for exporting capital which, as petroleum income has been introduced into the economy in ever-increasing quantities, has become more plentiful. The possibility of the return of a military government has led to some flight; so has the election of social democratic governments, devoted explicitly to economic nationalism, when in fact these events ultimately would be beneficial to the private sector. Through all of this experience, the astounding stability of the currency, based on oil export income, has facilitated flight.

Despite the petroleum income, Venezuelan capital markets often have suffered from lack of funds. The suggestion that income tax rates—in recent years among the most generous in Latin America from the viewpoint of Venezuelan taxpayers—might be adjusted to weigh more heavily on the non-petroleum segments of the society has led to flight that is large in absolute terms alone and dangerously large in proportional terms. In consequence, foreign capital has played a larger role in the development of the country than might have been true. The Pérez regime thus has granted some priority to the task of correcting the condition. In effect the task is that of achieving a vote of legitimacy from the middle and upper classes as expressed by their willingness to invest in the country rather than to ship holdings abroad. The task in reality assures that the country's economic policies, especially toward private capital holdings, will be relatively conservative. The problem of balancing this interest off against the massive state capitalism that will result inevitably from the investment of FIV funds in industrial and infrastructure developments will remain a question of worldwide interest.[34]

The second issue for the role of private capital in industrial development is the role of the Andean Market. The common system provides that within a three-year period certain lines of activity shall be purged of specified percentages of foreign capital participation. Three categories are provided. Areas included in category one, defined as "national" or "domestic," must be owned at least 80 percent by nationals of the Andean Group of countries, Chile, Bolivia, Peru, Ecuador, Colombia, and Venezuela; this category includes natural resources, public utilities and such related enterprises as any individual government may choose to include. Category two, termed "mixed" or "joint," must be at least 51 percent nationally owned. Category three, "foreign," may be less than 50 percent nationally owned. The Common Market agreement provides for substantial trade liberalization policies for industries within categories one and two; products from these categories will ultimately be traded freely among the six member states. Only banks (in category one) may receive local currency deposits. Category three companies, on the other hand, may remit their initial investments at up to 14 percent annually on a cumulative basis and may not reinvest more than 5 percent of profits annually.

Under the Venezuelan decision in April 1974, to invoke Decision 24, by the end of 1974 only companies in category one ("national") may participate in any aspect of the electric power industry (eventually an FIV-financed government corporation will monopolize this activity), radio and television broadcasting, Spanish-language publishing, local and national transportation, publicity and advertising, supermarkets and department stores, commercial banks, and a number of other lines of business.[35] Since American investors have been active in many of these, and have dominated some, substantial shares of sales occurred in 1975. The Industrial Development Fund has helped finance some of the deals. The future use of the fund is yet to be defined, of course. One writer states:

With admirable candor, the manager of the industrial fund says he cannot foresee how the country will behave in the fact of the availability of such easy credit. He allows that many of the rules will have to be amended as experience dictates. Although no one has said so publicly, the FIV, too, will have to show similarly swift reflexes to the unknown ups and downs in its future course.[36]

Funds for Housing, Urban Development, and Construction Industry Tax Benefits. A third area of special funding concerns residential housing, urban improvements, mortgage guarantees, and tax benefits for the construction industry. A third internal fund, the *Fondo para el desarrollo de la construcción de interés social* (Fund for the development of social interest construction), capitalized at Bs.2 billion, was organized in August 1974. A fourth fund, the *Fondo de desarrollo urbano* (Fund for urban development), also capitalized at Bs.2 billion, was organized in November. In July 1974 the Ministry of Public Works announced a five-year commitment of Bs.1.5 billion for the construction of public services in some 350 villages and small towns throughout the country. Taken as a whole, these programs will be of immense benefit to the country's less spectacular and nonindustrial facilities; small commercial establishments may be built, but the emphasis is distinctly on dwellings, whether single or multifamily in nature. The provisions are exceptionally generous, however;

buildings of a value of up to Bs.140,000 per unit may be built, for example, and tax exemptions on income for a ten-year period may be given.[37]

The Nationalization of Minerals

President Pérez's priorities included early action to nationalize petroleum and eventually to take over the iron ore producing industry. Although there had been relatively little discussion of other minerals, it was accepted by the economic sector that government control or significant government participation would be inevitable in those industries once the first steps had been taken. Petroleum was expected to be the first target; it had been the target for nationalist thought as far back as the last days of Juan Vicente Gómez, and Rómulo Betancourt, acknowledged spokesman and leader of the political group that was to become the AD party, called for nationalization as early as 1939. The AD came to power in 1945 in a military-supported *golpe de estado*; despite the repeated demand for nationalization by Juan Pablo Pérez Alfonzo, minister of mines and petroleum, the country's acknowledged political expert on the petroleum issue, no action was taken. Finally, after the AD again came to power in 1959, Pérez Alfonzo was to admit that the country had too few knowledgeable specialists on the industry and too few resources for financing the industry, to take action.[38]

Throughout this period, talk of nationalization was always subordinated to AD's policy that no further concessions to the foreign companies would be granted. The military dictatorship of 1948-1958 did grant many more thirty-year concessions, however; since 1958 the social democratic parties have struggled with their consciences over their wish to respect legal contracts for the sake of the country's *bona fides*, and with the nationalists' desire to control this almost unimaginably huge resource.[39]

Many factors controlled the timing of the Pérez decision. Venezuela's lack of capital, technically knowledgeable personnel, and facilities adequate for proper handling of the post-production phases of the industry from transportation through refining, shipping, marketing, and retailing, all remained valid problems through the intervening years. The earliest investments and activities of the companies had been indispensable; without the large profit margins that had been allowed by Gómez and his immediate successors through 1945 there would have been far less enthusiasm shown by foreign investors and workers. Over time, however, the conflict of interest between the companies and the country grew more severe, with the companies outwitting the government repeatedly because of their size, worldwide operations, and greater knowledge of the multitude of factors involved. By the late 1960s the government was beginning to acquire at least the political sophistication and experience, as well as the information, needed to test and limit the managerial autonomy of the companies. And while this political shift occurred, an economic shift also occurred: payments to the government, in both absolute and proportionate terms, increased steadily.

In 1961 the government formed the *Corporación Venezolana del Petróleo*; under its basic law the companies were required incrementally to yield some areas of autonomy.[40] Although the industry continued in the hands of foreign managers, legislation was adopted that increasingly infringed the terms of the concessions of the 1950s. By the late 1960s it was clearly only a matter of time—and *not* the contractual dates of 1983 and 1984—when nationalization action would occur. Yet as late as May 1974, professional spokesmen recognized the country's unpreparedness for running the industry with the Venezuelans available.[41]

The Caldera government never enjoyed political control of the country; lacking a majority in either house of Congress, COPEI was forced in July 1971 to sign into law a reversion law not of its own definition. Concessions would revert to the government not later than 1983-1984 but, in the meantime, the companies were subjected to rigorous and nearly tyrannical management constraints. While Congress debated the bill the government reorganized the rules of the game concerning taxation and control of export prices, so that "reference prices," which are the bases for companies' royalty and tax payments, would be set by unilateral government action rather than by bargaining with the companies as in the past; current world demand would be the criterion for price, therefore, rather than management viewpoints or company profits.[42]

The Arab attack on Israel in October 1973 led eventually to united action on prices by the member countries of OPEC against the industrialized countries and others sympathizing with Israel. Venezuela refused to join the embargo, to be sure, but the other actions of OPEC demonstrated that Venezuela's active role in the establishment and strengthening of the organization had paid dividends.[43] The rising mood of nationalism in Venezuela, coupled with the heated campaign during the general election of December 1973, led the candidates of many parties (and, most notably, of COPEI), to promise the prompt nationalization of the industry. AD took a cooler position and remained noncommital. In his January 1, 1974 "State of the Nation" address to the Congress, Caldera counseled his successor to redeem his pledge; Pérez responded rather pointedly that he would make up his own mind.[44]

On April 28, 1974, Pérez announced that his first nationalization target would be the iron ore and the steel industry.[45] A National Steel Mill Council was established by decree to advise the president on all aspects of the industry. A wide variety of charges were laid on the Council. On April 29, Pérez announced his decision to make all aspects of the industry "national," within the meaning of Decision 24 of the Andean Market, beyond that portion of the industry that would be purchased by the government. The concessions to the United States Steel Corporation and Bethlehem Steel Corporation, located principally in the state of Bolívar, about 85 kilometers south of Ciudad Guyana on the Orinoco River, would revert to the state on January 1, 1975, rather than on the contract date of 2000. On May 21, the Steel Mill Council was sworn in and by the end of May 1974 the terms under which the companies would continue to operate the facilities and supply technical and managerial advice for a limited period of time were spelled out.[46]

The economies of the iron and steel industry in 1973, a relatively typical year, suggest the reasons for Pérez's actions. Twenty-two million tons of ore were produced for export by the two American companies which paid Bs.400 million in taxes and royalties to the government. In the meantime, the government-owned Siderúrgica del Orinoco, SIDOR, located at Ciudad Guyana, produced about one million tons of steel, principally from ore mined by national companies; in nonconcession regions several small privately-owned mills produced added amounts. But the country's total steel requirements were in excess of 1.9 billion tons, and the country paid about Bs.1 billion for the deficit. It was generally agreed that the cash deficit would increase over time if the concessions were allowed to run their full terms, even though SIDOR's capacity has been undergoing constant amplification since the first ingots were poured in the early 1960s. CORDIPLAN and the *Corporación Venezolana de Guyana* (CVG), which has a near monopoly of planning and capitalizations, as well as of management of the Guyana region, had for years planned to expand the region's total industrial capability. The new petroleum funds now permit the hastening of their project, and it is expected that about Bs.35 billion may be spent on the industry by 1985. In theory this will increase the steel producing capacity of SIDOR to about fifteen million tons annually, and Venezuela will become one of the world's principal steel exporting countries.[47]

In some respects, for all the size of the operation, the oil nationalization was anticlimatic. On March 18, 1974, COPEI and the former AD splinter *Movimiento Electoral del Pueblo* had introduced bills in the newly-inaugurated Congress. Although each bill called for the immediate nationalization of oil, MEP's bill approximated confiscation while COPEI's left the question of compensation in some doubt. AD's parliamentary control allowed the shunting of the bills into committee where they could be bottled up, and on March 22 Pérez decreed the establishment of a Reversion Commission of thirty-six persons to draft a bill. This decision seemed to flow from the 1971 law. The decree posed most of the problems to which the commission was to address itself and prescribed many of the terms within which it could work. The body was mixed in nature, with some members of the Congress, some of the executive branch, and some professional or economic groups represented. It was given six months in which to report. On May 1, Pérez announced that he would indeed nationalize the petroleum industry in the near future and, on May 16, the thirty-six members of the commission were sworn in.[48] The draft was published in August 1974, but it was not until March 12, 1975 that the bill, which was an amended version of the draft, was sent by Pérez to the Congress.[49] The bill was passed by the Congress on August 21, 1975, signed by the president on August 30, and came into force on January 1, 1976.[50]

From the viewpoint of foreign economic policy, the most obvious result of nationalization is that Venezuela will, during the coming decade, gain a high degree of financial and allocative autonomy. Although the government has declared repeatedly that it would not renege on contractual or historic obligations to help meet the United States market needs, toward which it exports an average of about 1.5 million barrels per day (bpd), it did reduce the production of crude to 2.3 million bpd, and it is anticipated that production will be reduced further. There is internal pressure to reduce production to the point that foreign exchange earnings equal current cash needs. If this is done, it is possible that production could fall much below two million bpd, assuming the world price does not fall; further, since there is no assurance that the OPEC countries will not continue to seek price increases (and, within this organization, no assurance Venezuela will not return to a circumstantial role as a lobbyist for higher prices, once the United States' economy has returned to a condition of relative balance).

Venezuela could meet its money needs with less production. At some point, Venezuela might well be unable to meet its historic commitments to the United States; further, if American energy independence policies and politically-inspired declarations continue, it may feel no need to meet them.[51] The result would be to free Venezuela to use its oil for trade and political influence within the Latin American region. This point will be discussed at a later time.

The principal political problem that arose for Pérez during the passage of the bill centered on Article 5, which provides that the executive may contract with foreign concerns for technical and material services, subject to approval by the Congress. The political and nationalist Left had demanded the termination of relationships with the American companies by January 1, 1976. But granted Venezuela's lack of personnel and facilities, these contracts are indispensable for an almost indefinite period. AD passed the law, to be sure, but only after it had invoked party discipline in the definitive votes in both chambers of the Congress. Many reports express some doubt that the relative good will that Pérez had been able to maintain with the Congress will survive in the future.[52]

The remaining internal problems that President Pérez must confront grow from the comparatively recent phenomenon of price inflation and the virtually permanent phenomenon of unemployment. Pérez's priorities statement of March 1974 placed greater emphasis on wage and price controls; a national minimum wage increase of 20 percent to 450 bolivares monthly was decreed for laborers and monthly paid salaries were raised by decrees that ran from 24 percent for salaries under 1,000 bolivares to 5 percent for salaries over 5,000 bolivares. The immediate response of many companies was to seek to discharge redundant employees, even to the extent of reducing their experienced employees in some instances. The government replied with a thirty-day freeze on the size of work forces: this has been extended subsequently in thirty-day increments. A bill was introduced into the Congress to preclude "unjustified discharges" in June 1974; employers' organizations, including the Federation of Chamber of Commerce and Industry, FEDECAMARAS, mounted an unqualified attack.[53] However, Pérez continued his policies. In April 1975, Pérez attacked the dangerously high unemployment and underemployment rate by submitting a bill to the Congress that would require employers to increase their work force by as much as 5 percent. This bill is simply to get the people off the streets.[54] Yet, despite the government's best efforts, workers were restive in light of the inadequacy of the minimum wage by the end of the year[55] and inflation in 1975 was expected to reach 21 percent.

Conclusions Concerning the Policy Implications of Internal Change

The policy statement of changes proposed through 1979, with its implications for the longer run, is ambivalent in many respects. It seems obvious, at least in theory, that the massive new oil income can be used to produce industrial, commercial, agricultural, social, and educational growth all at the same time. Provided the "Peter" (employees rise to the level of their incompetence), "Parkinsonian" (work always expands to take up all available space and funds) and other tongue-in-cheek principles of incompetence do not work simultaneously, Venezuela has a chance for both physical growth and politically meliorative change during a period of relative affluence and seeming government capability. But many adverse variables are also at work.

The tasks of management would be huge in any case. They are compounded by a dearth of knowledgeable and skilled personnel and an abundantly-proven national tendency to reject even the best advice if given by foreign specialists. While the 1973 election results were encouraging, in their apparent massive grant of public confidence to social democratic parties, the habits of some forty years of excessive partisanship make it difficult for "loyal opposition" to exist and for political legitimacy to be maintained. The Pérez government is clearly setting, at least in theory, an exceedingly broad table of possible investment opportunities and supports for the private sector, but, at the same time, it is proposing that the largely tax-free meal for the national private sector is over, and it is now up to the latter to cast its vote for economic legitimacy by demonstrating confidence in the future of the country per se and the nation's role by participating in the Andean Market. Finally, the government confronts the potentially very difficult task of establishing a new and massive state capital sector and of maintaining and perfecting an already-existing state sector of smaller size without overpowering, at the same time, a surprisingly still insecure private industrial and commercial sector through error or mistaken design.

It is this latter task, the hope of obtaining underwriting by a private sector which feels itself menaced, that causes the present national leadership to attempt to deal with so many widely dispersed viewpoints simultaneously. The government may go too far—and the planning for disposition of the oil moneys surely offers many indications of this—in search of private sector support. Yet at the same time, for the sake of the distributive principle, the government has sought by executive decrees and legislation to maintain or create jobs and to freeze or to support the costs of basic articles of general use at a level not responsive to market mechanisms. Finally, the current leaders are not so old as to forget the country's shabby experiences with rule by the dictates of a military tyrant; and there are some in the country who, unwilling to participate in the constitutional and republican interplay, would support a return to such a system.

National policy toward employment and worker rights also reflects this system's insecurity. In 1962 and 1969, "labor stability" laws were introduced into the Congress. Under their terms, employers would be unable to discharge workers at will, even though management might find them redundant. At neither time did the government seek such legislation. In fact it was severely embarrassed in 1962. In both cases the bills were bottled up in committee by business-oriented legislators, but the governments were the victims in terms of lost credibility in the political arena. In both 1974 and 1975, Pérez has taken similar steps for distributive reasons and employer reaction has been identical. There is no assurance that the new industrial developments will create jobs for the huge numbers of unskilled or semi-skilled persons in the labor force; rather, the reverse could occur, for abundant and generous funding, through credit that is actually cheaper than any available in the more industrial countries of the world, will surely encourage capital-intensive growth.

The Pérez-originated steps seem to revert to the country's authoritarian past, which often excused itself as motivated by a mixture of paternalism and Rousseauian theory. Entrepreneurial reactions may, in the future, assume vital importance for support and survival of the social democratic system. Organized labor in Venezuela has been, since its founding in the post-Gómez era, the mass-oriented instrument of the AD party. But it may lack the autonomy or will to provide the electoral and consensual support to the party and to the social democratic system needed in time of political crisis.

The armed forces' political intentions remain a potentially decisive uncertainty. The military's experience of several decades as an armed bureaucracy, as well as post-1958 efforts by some stubborn persons, both in and out of uniform, to make of it an armed political party, still cause nervousness. The ghosts are by no means all laid to rest.[56] The internal issues that might have caused direct military pressure have gradually been put to rest: guerrillas, organized unrest among the "available mass" of the *ranchos* or slums of the major cities, and political repression by the civilian-led government have all diminished or have disappeared. As will be shown, there are still a number of international border controversies and, in the past, there has been good evidence that the "die-hards" of the armed forces have sought to use these issues to cloak themselves in patriotism in order to gain leverage on the government. Thus great skill by leaders of the social democratic center will still be required.

In sum, the internal future of Venezuela rests on the skill with which its leaders direct the country's resources toward the resolution of internal needs. The massive oil moneys have provided breathing space in the past for the rise of constitutional republicanism. For the next decade this will probably continue. The current leadership, and those persons in both social democratic parties who will probably come to power in 1979, have gained enormously in partisan and policy experience and ingenuity since 1958. But it remains to be seen whether they will be able to confront the tasks of administering the country with equal success.

The Policy Implications of External Change

In the eighteen months since his inauguration (at this time of writing) President Pérez had led Venezuela toward a substantially more nationalist and autono- mous posture in international relations that it has taken previously. The country's present attitudes and activities may in some respect be judged as an exercise in exuberance, the "new kid on the block" syndrome. Or they may presage a more permanent change. In any case, the Pérez government has taken only a few foreign policy positions not relating directly to the topics already mentioned, so that internal factors, to some extent, serve as guidelines for future foreign policy.

Border Issues

It seems likely that the coming decade will see the resolution or definitive compromise of a number of relatively unimportant border problems. Vene- zuela's security concerns in the Caribbean and with its continental neighbors fronting on the ocean have never been great. In the past Venezuela has had substantial economic interests in the region, and the possibility that the bordering countries' submarine platform might include substantial petroleum reserves has led to some recent controversy. The limiting element that has prevented the deterioration of relationships among these countries, in some degree, has been the security interest of the United States; for more than a century the U.S. government has reacted to armed instability in these countries by some form of direct or indirect action and, on some occasions, it also has reacted to less serious disturbances as well. Although in all probability the United States government would now consider that the days of the "big stick" are gone forever—and it is clear enough that the Latin American countries wish sincerely they could have absolute guarantees to that effect—there remains some uncertainty.[57]

Venezuela's discontent over its eastern border has existed since its independence. In this instance, as in several others, common Spanish colonial control created ambivalence concerning the territorial claims of successor states. Before 1800, effective control of what became the region of British Guiana had passed from Spain to Great Britain, and the colony became the successor state of Guyana in the early 1960s.[58] Although arbitration presumably settled the border issue in 1899, Venezuela sought recurringly to reopen the matter and did so most recently in 1962. All the parties stood fast by the arbitral award; none of the parties to the settlement attempted to give Venezuela satisfaction of any kind, and appeals to the United Nations General Assembly were fruitless. After some years of controversy, and some threat by Venezuela, a modus vivendi was finally reached in the Protocol of Port of Spain in 1970. Although under the terms of this document Guyana or Venezuela are legally free to reopen the question at a later time, there is no likelihood that this will occur and the Pérez government has indicated that it will respect the Protocol.[59]

It can be presumed that the question might arise again should Brazilian pressure or interest, both of which have been noted, lead to a change of the Guyanan position. In recent years Brazil has shown interest in establishing settlements in the far southern region of Guyana, which is virtually empty save for tribal Indians. But, barring any concrete action, the matter seems settled as far as specific Venezuelan movement of personnel is concerned.

In one respect, however, Venezuela continues to cling to its claim, and this stubbornness might eventually cause some movement on the question. Guyana is not a member of the Organization of American States (OAS), although most of its former British colonial colleagues, as independent states, have joined: Jamaica, Barbados, Trinidad-Tobago, and Grenada. Article 8 of the OAS Charter provides that no country can be admitted ". . . whose territory became subject, in whole or in part, prior to December 18, 1964, . . . to litigation or claim between an extracontinental country and one or more Member States of the Organization, until the dispute has ended by some peaceful procedure." Guyana and Belize (against which Guatemala maintains an active claim whose tension is heightened by genuine threat of armed invasion) thus have been barred from membership. At this writing it is not possible to anticipate when the Venezuelan attitude will change.

Venezuela and Colombia have contended over a variety of issues for many years. The most sustained problem has been the flow of "undocumented" or illegal Colombian immigrants across the unmarked border into Venezuela for smuggling, in search of jobs, arable, and available lands, which is open and large-scale, or for less legitimate reasons. To be sure, there has been some reverse flow for similar reasons; historically, Venezuelan political exiles have found refuge in Colombia, while awaiting the appropriate time to return to action. However, the numbers of Colombians are probably second in the hemisphere only to the flow of illegal Mexican immigrants into the United States and, as in the case in the southwestern United States, individuals in the new host countries have found many ways of taking advantage of the situation.

There have been frequent intergovernmental meetings concerning the matter, some of them on the presidential level. Yet neither country has taken adequate steps to halt the flow of either persons or goods, and it is doubtful if these problems will be resolved in the future. Indeed, there is a strong implication that under the Andean Common Market agreements the movement of persons will be eased, for there will be increasing legitimate reasons and opportunities for skilled and semi-skilled migrants to seek jobs in Venezuela, which has both comparatively higher technical job requirements and substantially higher pay levels.

A more difficult current issue between the two countries has concerned sovereignty over the continental shelf to the west of the Los Monjes islands at the entrance of the Gulf of Venezuela.[60] Seismic exploration and verification by drilling indicate unmistakably the presence of oil. As a result of the recent rise in world prices and the approaching exhaustion of Colombian reserves, the issue has become more important for both countries and both have sought to solve it for more than a decade. Complex but unproductive negotiations have brought only repeated demands by Colombia for international arbitration proceedings; Venezuela has rejected all compromise. Discussions were broken off in 1973 when the Caldera government found that it and the Colombian government of President Pastrana had irreconcilable positions. The Pérez government has stated that it considers the settlement by negotiation to be a priority topic, however, and, in the first weeks of their existence the two new governments (Colombia's President Alfonso López Michelsen was inaugurated in August 1974), representatives met to declare that it would be inappropriate for fellow members of the Andean Group to remain in conflict over an issue of this kind.

It has already been noted, (supra, note 56) that in October 1974, a group of some five hundred retired officers, joined by the ambitious retired former chairman of joint chiefs and former presidential candidate, Martin García Villasmil, presented a manifesto to the Pérez government warning against giving away the disputed territory. The country reacted in a peculiarly mixed way. Many persons saw this as a possible military bid for renewed political power and were alarmed; others, from the same premise, were heartened. Radical nationalists, whose favorite whipping boy is, in any case, the United States, alleged that it was inspired by the Central Intelligence Agency. On the whole, it seemed both a peculiarly inappropriate issue and time for a manifesto, and the officers were rebuked by the government. However, this point should be made: a great many experienced specialists felt that the 1962 reopening of the Guyana border issue was designed to placate the armed forces. At the time the military was an active threat to the security of the Betancourt government and such a diversion was possibly useful. But the aftermath of the small adventure has been painful for nearly everyone involved. The initiative of Pérez, who would have known about the previous incident since he was a member of the Betancourt cabinet, has been a logical response to the problem.

Relationship with Offshore Islands and Caribbean Countries

Venezuelan relationships with the offshore islands and the countries of the Caribbean have not involved conscious clashes in most instances. The one severe problem that arose recently involved Cuba and this is discussed in detail later. Venezuela's relationships with the Netherlands West Indies, Aruba, Bonaire, and Curaçao have never posed security problems. It is possible that, since the islands will be granted independence by the Netherlands government sometime in the 1970s, the question of their own security might arise. However, these security issues would not endanger Venezuela unless a third party, either through actual invasion or through subversion of the successor island governments, intervened. In June 1973, representatives of the Netherlands met with Venezuelan officials in Caracas to discuss the political and economic future of the islands. Although no decisions were reached, there is a general assumption that Venezuela will assume a special role as protector of the islands after they become independent.[61]

The islands became economically important to Venezuela during the dictatorship of Juan Vicente Gómez. At that time, petroleum was gaining importance in Venezuela, and foreign companies were attracted to Venezuela. Gómez was antagonistic to the idea of locating a major refinery on Venezuelan soil, possibly because, some specialists believe, such action would create an industrial work force of large size which could be radicalized by agitators. Thus, the first refinery to process Venezuelan crude outside of the United States on a large scale was opened on Curaçao by the Royal Dutch Shell Corporation in 1917. By 1929, both Shell and Standard Oil Corporation of Indiana had additional refineries on Aruba.[62] For many years, the islands were the principal immediate shipping point for petroleum products into the United States. In 1975, a large new refinery was under construction in Curaçao, in part with Arab financing.[63] However, in the 1960s major new refineries were built in Venezuela.

The Netherlands government generally considers the continued possession of the islands a luxury from the colonial era. It would like to grant independence but, since no responsible Dutch government considers the cluster economically viable, there is unwillingness to cut them loose abruptly. The islands were originally scheduled to be independent as early as 1974. However, in May 1974, the islands' government demanded the postponement of the step by six years.[64] The Dutch government agreed to a delay but seems unlikely to stand still for the entire period requested. In the meantime Surinam, formerly Netherlands Guiana, was scheduled for independence before the end of 1975. Although there have been some delays, it is moving gradually toward this break although there are severe internal problems to be resolved.[65]

The suspension of Cuban membership in the OAS in 1964 was precipitated by proof of Cuba's interference in Venezuelan internal affairs and of that country's support of guerrilla forces seeking to overthrow the Betancourt government. The successor Leoni government moderated Venezuela's official antagonism toward Cuba somewhat but, in general, continued to support the hard American line toward Cuba. Caldera, on the other hand, softened Venezuela's position toward Cuba considerably; he had had reasonable luck with his pacification program directed against the guerrilla groups, many of which were having severe difficulty replenishing their "dropouts" and losses. Caldera felt that he could not allow himself to be frozen in a position picked by his political opposition and, by the end of his administration, Venezuela seemed ready to renew relations with Cuba—provided that satisfactory understandings could be reached on questions of mutual respect and trade and an end brought to Castro's intermittent propaganda attacks on the Venezuelan government.[66]

The Pérez government continued the generally friendly attitude toward Cuba and bilateral diplomatic relations were renewed on December 30, 1974. However, there is still some ambiguity in this relationship from the Venezuelan viewpoint. In early 1974, for example, Marcos Falcón Briceño, who was Rómulo Betancourt's minister of foreign relations, made what was believed to be a statement on behalf of President Pérez. Falcón said that Cuba should rejoin the OAS and seek its future in the inter-American system within that organization. Castro repeatedly has rejected the OAS as an organization largely controlled by the United States, and thus the Falcón statement seems to lack meaning. In the immediate future, it seems unlikely that trade between the two countries will extend much beyond an exchange of Venezuelan oil for miscellaneous Cuban primary products.[67] Since Cuba has developed its own industrial processing plants for its minerals, and Venezuela is now making major investments to achieve autonomy in sugar production, logical trade possibilities are reduced.

The opening of full trading and diplomatic relationships with Cuba will be attractive for virtually all countries. The long economic blockade of Cuba has been difficult for that country. The door to trade with Latin America-based subsidiaries of American trans-national firms was opened by the United States government only with harsh restraints and some ill-will. The prolonged negotiations in 1973 and 1974 that were necessary before American automobile manufacturing companies in Argentina could accept contracts with Cuba, illustrate an attitude that is viable in neither economic nor diplomatic terms. Venezuela was severely critical of the American attitude and played an active if somewhat frustrating role in the prolonged Latin American effort to persuade the United States to pronounce itself in favor of renewed Cuban relationships for the hemisphere. At the 15th Meeting of Consultation of Foreign Ministers in November 1974, held in Quito, Ecuador, it clearly overcommitted itself. After his return to Caracas, Foreign Minister Efraín Schacht Aristeguieta denounced the American delegation for insidious pressure on all who wished the renewal. This position was adopted by a number of other delegations as well, although it was not based on substance. Finally, as a result of this embarrassing position, as well as internal political problems, Minister Schacht resigned his portfolio in early 1975.

There has been some recent relaxation of Cuban relationships with colleague states in recent years. There have been a number of agreements among the Latin American countries with Cuba against aerial and ocean hijacking, for example. The Cuban deputy foreign minister attended the Territorial Seas conference in Caracas in July 1974, and a large number of informal conversations with both Venezuelan and other Latin American representatives took place. Finally, the two countries have had specific discussions on prices of raw materials and terms of trade in international commercial relationships.[68] With the renewal of broader Cuban relationships after the 16th Meeting of Consultation at San José, Costa Rica, the possibility of Cuba's returning to its place in the American regional trading system seems open. Venezuela played a significant role in this renewal and will doubtless continue to be a partisan of Cuba in the future.

In the past decade Venezuela has played an active role in the Commonwealth Caribbean island republics, a cluster of small states singularly open to sphere-of-influence politics at this time. As a consequence, Venezuela has played a role in the economic decision process of the island countries but has found itself in competition with other mainland Latin American countries.

The Caribbean Free Trade Association (CARIFTA) was organized in 1965; this significant first step toward jointly-based economic autonomy became, in July 1973, the Caribbean Common Market (CARICOM) under the Treaty of Chaguaramas, Trinidad.[69] Venezuela was admitted to membership in the Caribbean Development Bank, CARICOM's affiliated agency, and made a contribution of $10 million to its Special Development Fund; this money is to be re-loaned to government financial institutions on the smaller islands. In August 1975, FIV signed an agreement with the Development Bank establishing a $25 million trust fund to support expansion programs in the CARICOM member states.[70] The Venezuelan funding through these means is not all that is available in the region; a $500 million trust fund established through the Inter-American Development Bank on February 27, 1975 is also available to countries in the Caribbean and several loans had been made from it by the end of the year.[71]

Apart from this series of events involving official funds, the activity of private Venezuelan interests in the Caribbean seems significant. As early as 1972, for example, a number of major Venezuelan firms and conglomerates had signed contracts for commercial and industrial operations in the minor states of the

Caribbean. The Eugenio Mendoza interests planned cement and concentrated foods production on five islands; eleven contracts have been signed and construction has begun on other islands for activities as diverse as furniture production, breweries, cosmetics and detergents, as well as a host of others.[72] In September 1975, plans were completed for a processing plant for Guyanan bauxite, to be built with mixed public and private funds from both Guyana and Venezuela.[73]

Finally, a number of diplomatic and presidential-level meetings were held in the 1970s at the initiative of Venezuela. A Consultive Conference of Caribbean Foreign Ministers was convoked by the Venezuelan Foreign Ministry in November 1971, to discuss the common interests and problems of the island countries. Additionally, Venezuela invited the Latin countries of the mainland from Guatemala to Colombia. The agenda was largely technical and commercial, and presaged later cooperation in other areas.[74] During 1974 the new government of President Pérez sought to establish Venezuelan influence more firmly and, in December 1974, the Venezuelan foreign minister again met with his counterpart officers from Barbados, the Dominican Republic, Guyana, Haiti, Jamaica, and Trinidad-Tobago to prepare a later chiefs of state meeting held in January 1975. At the second meeting, the agenda ranged more widely, to include commercial, transportative, industrial and political cooperation.[75] The reaction of the individual former British colonies has varied because of their historic interests, however. Jamaica's collaboration with Venezuela promises to be close, with joint processing of Jamaican bauxite a key issue; in this respect, Venezuela finds itself in competition with Mexico. On the other hand the population of Trinidad-Tobago, the larger island of which was once a part of the Spanish empire, has been subjected for decades to varying degrees of harassment by Venezuelan officials. Consequently its government has taken a much more difficult position. Trinidad's prime minister, Eric Williams, was preoccupied for many months in 1975 with denouncing the "imperialist" schemes of the larger country in the Caribbean. Many commentators dismissed this as the talk of a disappointed politician who had hoped to develop his own sphere of influence in the Caribbean and was frustrated by Venezuela's wealth and energy, but it is true that Venezuelan influence is increasing among the former colonies.[76]

Venezuela's policy toward the five mainland Central American countries has been similar in many respects to that toward the island republics. Despite their longer historic record of political independence, these five present similar problems and opportunities from the Venezuelan viewpoint.[77] They are all larger in territory and population than the English-speaking island states, but their experiences of political instability and counter-productive economic behavior have left them in some respects hardly more advanced than the others in terms of general developmental criteria. The five joined in creating the *Mercado Comun Centroamericano* (MCC), with an associated *Banco Centroamericano de Integración Económico*, in 1960; earlier that year the *Asociación Latin Amer-*

icana de Libre Comércio had been established, and the MCC was to some extent
a product of the emotionally-inspired optimism of that effort. The MCC has not
prospered for a number of economic and political reasons, including a war and
the absence, in general, of reasons for internation commerce.

A number of Venezuela's Caribbean-wide diplomatic and commercial initiatives, undertaken in the late 1960s and early 1970s, involving the island
countries were also designed to include the mainland nations. The feeling among
the Central American governments that they could hope for sympathetic
hearings by Caracas led the five to send their ministers of economics in February
1974 to seek special consideration on the importation price of petroleum. The
Caldera government, then in its last weeks, honored Venezuela's explicit pledge
to maintain OPEC-decreed price levels, however. While the Central Americans
complained that the new prices would raise their annual energy costs by at least
$250,000,000, Venezuela responded only with improvised suggestions: Caracas
might help Costa Rica finance an oil refinery, Honduras a paper mill, the
banana-producing countries a banana cartel, the coffee-producing countries a
price maintenance arrangement.[78]

During 1974, Venezuela's policy matured under the leadership of the
newly-inaugurated AD government. Apart from the prospect that the Central
Americans would be able to draw on a trust fund to be established jointly with
IDB (Costa Rica was one of the first to do so, in April 1975),[79] in December
1974, the presidents or their representatives from the five countries, plus
Panama, met with Pérez at Puerto Ordaz, Venezuela. The host government
announced its decision to contribute moneys paid, over a basic $6 per barrel, to
a special fund to be granted by the FIV. It was estimated that at current
consumption levels this would yield about $400,000 daily. The money would be
placed in special development accounts in the respective Central Banks; FIV
would agree to accept an interest rate of less than the 8 percent demanded of the
IDB trust fund. The banks could, in turn, lend the funds for internal
development projects at advantageous interest rates and repayment terms. The
FIV also agreed to purchase $40 million in bonds of the BCIE and to loan it an
additional $60 million at 8 percent interest.[80] Further, Venezuela would
underwrite 70 percent of the cost of a coffee retention program, up to a
commitment of $80 million, for the benefit of the Central American pro-
ducers.[81] In May 1975, Venezuela joined with and gave major support to the
establishment of the *Naviera Multinacional del Caribe, S.A.*, a shipping company
which will be capitalized at $100 million, for a 99-year term, and which will
offer shipping services throughout the Caribbean. Ultimately as many as sixteen
countries may be members of this multinational agency.[82]

These various multinational institutions and Venezuela's relationship with
them may foretell some aspects of future Latin American cooperation, as well as
of the Venezuelan approach to solving problems. There has been a distinct
effort, not only by Venezuela, but by other countries of the Latin American
region, to depict the United States approach as predicated on a bilateral basis

that they allege is invidious to the smaller partners. It seems most doubtful that there is much that is deterministic in either approach; the behavioral pattern of a dominant country may become objectionable even if it is screened by the involvement of third states in an agreement. In any case, for the present the multinational approach enjoys a certain vogue; one can hardly make more than this tentative judgment.

Panama has benefited from these economic and commercial agreements, as well as from some additional (bilateral) agreements not extended to the other mainland countries.[83] There is an additional factor in Venezuela's attitudes toward Panama because of the extremely nationalist and politicized attitude that country has taken concerning the Panama Canal and the Canal Zone. Although the United States-drafted treaty of 1914 was at one time acceptable to the Panama government (the circumstances were obviously not those of negotiating between peers), the Panamanian government began almost immediately to seek modification of the provisions. By the end of the Second World War the pressure had become more intense, but it was not until 1964 that the current series of negotiations opened. American internal politics have prevented much freedom of movement on the part of the United States negotiators, while the almost perpetual disruption of Panamanian politics, very frequently internally generated, has played a parallel role. The current government of General Omar Torrijos has been able to maintain itself for a number of years, however, and has pressed the United States very hard on the issue. In early 1973 a United Nations Security Council meeting, held in Panama as a special symbol of worldwide "Third World" sympathy for the Panamanian position, would have voted a resolution censuring the United States had that country not exercised its veto.[84]

In March 1975, President Pérez met with the presidents of Colombia, Costa Rica, and Panama to discuss the canal issue. It could hardly have been expected that the meeting would resolve the issue; no devil's advocate was present to argue the American position and no commitment to action was produced. It was, however, a useful exercise from the viewpoint of the participants; a joint declaration was published by the four governments in the leading newspapers of the hemisphere.[85] As in the commercial agreements, this approach also seems to forecast the multilateral or cooperative approach that Venezuela hopes to maintain in future relationships with its Latin American neighbors. In this more politicized instance, of course, the approach is not only desirable for its contrast of style, but also because it serves to focus the views of many against the one antagonist. Whether the technique can be maintained indefinitely is another matter; it may in fact break down over the issue of Brazil.

Brazil's Future Role in Venezuelan Foreign Relations

Brazil's future role in Venezuelan foreign relations may place the latter country in quite a different position. Venezuela may become an important petroleum supplier in the future, although Brazil's interest in Middle East sources appears in early 1976 to be increasing. In abstract terms, the aggressive Brazilian efforts of the past two decades to stabilize and expand its internal economic structure, and to broaden its areas of economic and political influence in both Latin America and the world, are quite understandable in light of its large and rapidly growing population.[86] Yet the frictions caused by its neighbors on the South American continent are hardly easy to bear. Further, and probably more alarming to the neighboring countries, is the peculiar Brazilian mixture of nationalist ethnocentrism, militarism, and professed anti-Communism that has been brought to bear, not only on its own people, but also in the countries that have come explicitly within its sphere of influence. This mood is at least in part based on a rising level of military influence within Brazilian life since the fall of the "First Republic" in 1930; it now verges on the hysteria so well experienced by Americans during the (Joseph) McCarthy experience of the 1950s. While today the Brazilian military controls the government and hunts down and condemns its critics, it also remains receptive to Soviet bloc overtures for technical and financial aid for its industrial growth.[87] While it is "conventional wisdom" among anti-United States ideologues in both North and South America that Brazil is the South American agent of Yankee imperialism, in fact Brazil proves repeatedly that it is an independent actor and increasingly self-directed.[88]

The nervousness of Brazil's neighbors is not lessened by the increasing efficiency apparent in Brazilian army-directed adventures. Brazilian arms purchases and its own arms industry account for approximately 40 percent of the weapons of the holdings of the region. And Brazil has exploited this capability.[89] In 1973, the Brazilian navy announced its intention of organizing a Pacific ocean force. Brazilian military aircraft gave air cover to forces of the Bolivian army in a civil war in 1974. Brazilian border posts on the Venezuelan frontier were construed by that country as intended to intimidate, and Venezuela commenced a similar program in 1970 on its own side of the border. The major Brazilian Amazon highway project was viewed by neighboring countries as an extension of military capability as much as an access road for regional economic development.[90]

Venezuela's response to these Brazilian initiatives has been one of preoccupation. Some Brazilian actions could be viewed as friendly; for example, after negotiation in 1973, Brazil ceded claims to about 4,000 square kilometers of territory on the northern edge of the Amazon basin to Venezuela, let contracts for construction of a portion of highway between Brasilia and Caracas on the Brazilian side of the border and concluded several commercial contracts. On the other hand, the border settlements program which was integrated with the siting of Brazilian army units was viewed as so threatening that the Venezuelan government undertook the CODESUR project, which was announced publicly as a search for mineral resources and research concerning the indigenous peoples of the region. However, in fact, the project was used in part as a cover to airlift military equipment in the period 1971-72.[91]

The relations between the two countries are officially low-keyed; a prominent Brazilian political figure, Herbert Levy, first vice-president of the national Chamber of Deputies, has called allegations of Brazilian threats to its neighbors "rubbish."[92] Yet the possibility of an inadvertent clash over national interests remains good in this writer's judgment. Bailey and Schneider point to Brazil's substantial advantage over Venezuela in case of conflict. Apart from its preponderant size, Brazil's technical-military infrastructure has been carefully coordinated over many years of planning. The Brazilian armed forces have had actual combat experience in this century, and have begun to develop an independent doctrine as well as substantial technical ability. There is, on the contrary, no evidence that any of these points could be made about Venezuela; this is surely true in light of the performance of Venezuelan military units in the last armed challenge of any size that had to be confronted, the abortive leftist-inspired uprisings of 1962 at Puerto Cabello and Carúpano. Apart from the expendable wealth from oil, Venezuela appears only to have a kind of brashness of inexperience. Actual conflict would have only a one-sided result.[93]

Venezuela's Role in the Less Developed Latin American Countries

In the decade under consideration, and in the longer term, it is probable that Venezuela will have a major role in assisting the development of the less developed Latin American countries and may possibly extend its assistance to development on other continents as well. The priorities statement of President Pérez in April 1974, as well as policy views expressed by the preceding Caldera government and by leading private sector spokesmen of the country, suggest that the Andean Market grouping will play a significant role. Venezuela will also employ its FIV for multilateral trust fund advances to international institutions and for bilateral loans.

The Venezuelan role will be, in some respects, virtually revolutionary. Venezuela has undergone more than a mere politically revolutionizing experience since 1959. While it is true that its apparently definitive passage from military tyranny to constitutional republicanism was change enough in some respects, it is more important that before the death of Gómez in 1935, the flood of foreign capital, technology, and ideas had blanked out whatever might have survived of the "Iberic-Latin" tradition of the colonial period. Venezuela had to be converted to a syncretism in which success would be measured in ways more understandable to the Western European and Anglo-American world.[94] Had Venezuela had a nineteenth century experience like that of Colombia, this might not have happened; the elite of Colombia's colonial period survived the wars of the first century of independence with little real difficulty. Venezuela, on the other hand, administered recurring shocks of blood and culture to its never especially prestigious colonial elite, and the unification of the country was accomplished by a successful and grossly crude rural adventurer.[95] For practical purposes, therefore, Venezuela has become a logical agent for the modernizing revolution that contemporary technology, in potentially very large doses, can administer to those countries upon which it seeks to exercise its influence.

Petroleum income is the base for Venezuela's ability to play an international role in the future. At this time, Venezuela's national economy cannot absorb the flood of funds without very disruptive effects. Measures intended to keep the money outside the country will thus not only benefit the internal structure, but they will serve as a counterpart of the "sow the petroleum" policy of the late 1930s since it will be a savings account against which withdrawals can be made at a future time.[96] Capital goods which the country could not itself produce can be obtained abroad. Contracts can import technology and information, as well as high technical skills, and thus selected sectors of the economy can be stimulated, but much of the disbursement of funds can occur outside the country. Loans and investments abroad can stimulate markets for future Venezuelan raw materials and manufactures, and thus have invisible beneficial effects. Future feedbacks of principal and interest payments can occur at some indefinite time when natural resources may be approaching exhaustion. And in the meantime, Venezuelan political influence can be enhanced.

The Andean Market has been mentioned as possibly having central importance for future Venezuelan international economic policy in South America. Although Venezuela was a participant in the presidential-level meeting in Bogota in August 1966, thus laid the groundwork for the Andean Subregional Integration Agreement, and took an active role in defining the terms of the final document that was signed in May 1969, at Cartagena, it did not join immediately. The private sector assembled almost overwhelming opposition to participation in the Congress and the Caldera government, elected in 1968 by a plurality of less than 1 percent of the votes (which had been assembled in part with explicit support from the same private sector), did not feel able to act. Finally, in the last year of his term, Caldera was able to accede to the treaty, and Venezuela became a member on January 1, 1974.

The Market Agreement establishes a common market, with ultimate free passage of goods among the member states. This will be achieved by stages; 1980 is the full target date for the four countries with stronger economies, and 1985 is the date set for Ecuador and Bolivia. Full common external tariffs will be negotiated among the six, in stages, by 1985; some implementing steps have been taken already. The Andean Development Corporation is associated with the Market for financial support of industrial and commercial development within the region; both governments and private citizens may subscribe to its shares. The agreement establishing the ADC entered in force January 1, 1970; Venezuela is an original member, and its seat is in Caracas. The seat of the Market itself is in Lima.

Membership in the Market has substantial effects, to be sure, but the private sector in Venezuela imagined them to be more profound than most government specialists felt likely. The conservatives on the issue have some cause. The country's economic stability is among the highest in the world. Its price structure historically has been very high—although the extraordinary inflation in other countries and the high stable purchasing power of the bolivar have combined to reduce Venezuela's relative costs of production in recent years. The concept of a free internal flow of goods did concern Venezuelans, however. The possibility that other member states, unable to import because of the weakness of their own economies, might try to import into the market through Venezuela with the use of its currency, was an issue that was hard to settle. It also was feared in Venezuela that, with the attractiveness of Venezuelan industrial jobs and goods, there might well be a flood of nationals from other countries which would result in more severe unemployment for the already underemployed Venezuelan labor force.

While it is true that Venezuela, left to its own devices, is potentially capable of producing a wider variety of manufactures than the other members, the decisions of the Market executive have tended to reduce competitiveness. As the wealthiest member of this six-nation group, Venezuela's views have always weighed heavily in the decisions of the Market executive and technical organs. Yet, the executive may decide to grant semi- or full monopolies to countries in such areas as new business or industrial lines; this can be especially advantageous to the less developed countries. Decisions also may reduce the ability of a country to export an easily-produced article, in favor of another member state, although the first may continue to produce for its own market. In 1975, Venezuela has been involved in very hard and not especially successful bargaining over petrochemicals and automobile and truck manufacture; thus a Venezuelan nationalist businessman probably would complain that his country has given him relatively little protection from other member states of the Market.[97]

The Decision 24 accession by President Pérez on April 29, 1974, began the three-year period during which foreign firms must divest themselves of shares in order to comply with the percentages of national participation required in terms of the line of activity.[98] Decision 24 demarcates a region, the Market area, within which entrepreneurs who are nationals of the six countries shall enjoy special preferences.

The Andean Development Corporation, initially capitalized at $100 million in 1970 and now seeking an expansion of funds to $400 million, is intended to support capital formation in lieu of foreign sources. The ADC promotes projects through seed money in a number of ways; it will make grants for feasibility and market studies, and will then fund up to 25 percent of the total costs of projects undertaken under the industrial planning program.[99] It thus supports the goal of Decision 24 of making the capital involved *national* (in contrast to *nationalized*) within the Market group of countries. It is intended to work for the benefit of entrepreneurs, but the literature does not report any guarantee that a radical government would not expropriate a resulting investment. A state's adherence to the Cartagena agreement implies a political obligation to adhere to conventional standards of behavior, and it could be supposed that expropriation is less likely to occur.[100]

Venezuela's Attitude toward the United States

The final point to be made concerning changing aspects of Venezuela's foreign economic policy deals with its increasing aggressiveness toward the United States. It is true that the principal flag-bearers in this respect have been either Peru, which seems bound by a leftist ideology that is unique to itself to take extreme if not abusive positions toward the United States, or Mexico. The latter has had good historical reasons for an anti-United States attitude: the war of 1846-1848 is by no means entirely forgotten and there is a continuing record of exploitation of Mexican nationals in the southwestern United States. But Peru's rather devious tactics have led many of its fellow Latin American countries to turn away from its leadership,[101] and in 1974 Luis Echeverría of Mexico was beginning to emerge as a self-announced spokesman on the world scene for the Third World countries.[102] Together with Venezuela, those three have become the principal organizers of the *Sistema Económico Latinamericano*, SELA. This has been described by Latin American nationalists as a kind of inter-American system without the United States, within which economic independence from exploiting industrialized countries could be achieved. While this claim is, in the short run, obvious hyperbole and may be assessed against the difficulty that Latin America has in collaborating for any purpose, there also is the fact that collaboration within the Andean Market is well begun, and that the ALALC could become a larger base for long-term collaboration.

Venezuela has supported these initiatives in the hemisphere arena. It also has supported Mexico and Peru in bilateral actions. Pérez and Echeverría met in each others' capitals on two occasions in 1975. The statements which were issued after the meetings bristled with rhetoric concerning past and present exploitation, including the dependence imposed upon the countries of Latin America and the Third World.[103] Pérez visited Lima in December 1974, on the occasion of the 150th anniversary of the Battle of Ayacucho. He and two others, among several heads of state who were invited, joined the then president, General Juan Velasco Alvarado, in the Declaration of Ayacucho. The language employed was similar to that which later appeared in the joint statements with Mexico.[104] Finally, acting only with the support of Ecuador, Venezuela took the lead in the cancellation of a special meeting of the Foreign Ministers of the American Republics scheduled for March 1975 in Buenos Aires. The action was based entirely on the recently enacted Trade Act of 1974 of the United States; the Act's Title V barred all OPEC countries from the benefits of a trade preferences extension system established elsewhere in the Act. This exclusion, which had been placed in the Act in the conference committee stage of enactment by the Congress and over the expressed opposition by the president and Department of State, was nevertheless viewed as sufficient cause to continue the nationalist course on which Venezuela and its supporters had embarked.[105] It is not possible at this time to suggest the long-term outcome of this Venezuelan mood.

It should be noted in passing that another evidence of Venezuelan antipathy toward United States economic policy (which obviously cannot be distinguished in many ways from its political policies) can be found in the decision to establish the $500 million trust fund now administered by the Inter-American Development Bank. Under the IDB's rules, loans sought under certain circumstances are subject to the requirement that two-thirds of the executive directors approve. Since the United States' ordinary capital contribution (which determines the weighting of its vote) exceeds one-third total, in effect that nation, in some instances, possesses a "veto." In ordinary questions, a simple majority of either the executive directors, or the governors, as appropriate, controls a decision. The Venezuelan trust fund is explicitly not subject to the two-thirds vote; and while the 1974 annual meeting, to which Venezuela first offered the fund, did not accept the proposal with specific reference to this condition, yet the statement of the Venezuelan governor referring to loans allegedly denied the Allende government of Chile was suggestive enough for the point to be made. In a press conference on July 10, 1975, IDB President Antonio Mena argued that this interpretation was without basis, however.[106]

Conclusions

Introducing his chapter on contemporary Venezuelan history, Hubert Herring wrote, "Only in the Americas, under the restraining shadow of the United States, could so rich a nation and so defenseless a people have retained sovereignty against nineteenth-century imperialism."[107] The record of the 1970s that has been reported in this essay demonstrates that this is at least a simplistic statement. Nationalist Venezuelans would be likely at least to argue that the restraining shadow was rather more substantial, and that the country's current policies are intended to remove it. More critical students of the present would suggest that these current policies could be viewed logically as expressive of a Venezuelan desire to play a central role in the hemisphere, and possibly even one that would cast its own shadow.

The current policy is a fascinating blend of inchoate and relatively inarticulated theory and of hard economic facts. Venezuela's mineral resources give it the economic edge needed for both internal economic "take-off" in the Rostovian sense and to establish influence over its immediate neighbors. Alone among the countries of the South American continent, Venezuela has the massive exportable volumes of oil needed for the region's drive toward industrialization and economic autonomy. While Ecuador has an export capability at this time, no one can be sure that its reserves will permit it even to approximate a tiny part of the larger country's influence and wealth in the long run. And, in the immediate future, its internal political instabilities and ambition tend to nullify its best efforst to achieve respect and influence abroad. So far as is known in 1975, only Mexico is now able to plan on petroleum-based greater affluence or energy-induced influence in its neighboring regions, and this may be able only to meet the needs of the area of the Caribbean.

But apart from the minerals—and one surely cannot ignore the possibility that the tar belt of the Orinoco will continue Venezuela's petroleum predominance well into the twenty-first century[108]—Venezuela is now also struggling to define its view of itself as a developing country among the countries of the Third World. Within this almost undefinable community, Venezuela looms as a somewhat improbable champion. Except for Iran, Venezuela is alone among the OPEC countries in terms of its physical and social, let alone political, development. Alone among them all, for example, Venezuela is a constitutional and republican democracy. Save for Iran, it is manifestly a more distributive system; and in Iran, at least, distribution is a gift of the ruler rather than an economic and legal right. Beyond the OPEC countries, many of which are still (in the classic phrase once applied to Bolivia) beggars seated on a golden throne, rank the Third World countries in terms of affluence, distribution, and distress. A few possibly are capable of significant steps toward operable constitutional political institutions, but the great majority are not. Further, Venezuela, through its price-supporting pledges within OPEC, contributes substantially to creating a "Fourth World" of countries without either sources of energy, or fertilizers, or hope of survival.

A portion of the inchoate theory is to be found in Venezuela's partial subscription to the concept of "dependency." This school of interpretation of economic relationships among countries suggests that the early-achieving industrial states (principally those of Western Europe and North America), which in varying degrees are all committed to private entrepreneurial systems, achieved economic and cultural control over the Latin American countries and over the Third World countries as a whole. Events contributed to the tightening of the control. Local elites-oligarchs, called variously national bourgeoisie and *compradors* by different authors, emerged from their early *status*/prestige ownership roles to become *class*/prestige managers and agents of the exploiting countries. The exploiting-industrial countries fixed upon the dependent countries the trading patterns that provided markets for manufactures while continuing their reliance on the export of primary products with which to pay for the manufactures. The *agent-compradors* often became the local officers of transnational company branches, which made use of local investors and securities markets for their working capital. But since the parent companies remained domiciled abroad and imposed upon their subsidiaries the technology and management that characterized their operations, the transmission of fees came to replace the transmission of profits.[109]

The adequate presentation of the view of the dependency school would require more time and space. But depending on the degree of commitment to the school, policymakers who accept it become variously merely nationalistic, nationalistic with more than a passing commitment to state capitalism and/or socialism, or quasi-Marxist revolutionaries. The rhetoric has undeniable attraction, possibly because it seems to say much while concretely offering little. At the very least it identifies a style designed to imply anti-United States views when employed in Latin America. Thus, the Declaration of Ayacucho of December 1974, to which Pérez and Velasco subscribed together with several presidential representatives, states in part, "... our countries' ... incorporation into the world economy ... created various forms of dependency which explain the obstacles to our development ... We reiterate ... a prohibition on ... economic, or financial aggression in relations among states. ..."

The Declaration of Ayacucho continues with strongly suggestive language for future economic policy, however.

... Our countries have the inalienable right to the full exercise of sovereignty over their own natural resources, the defense of the price of their raw materials, the regulation of foreign investment and the control of the activities of the trans-nationals. The joint efforts of all of our nations are essential for the creation and strengthening of associations of countries which produce and export raw materials to attain the most favorable terms for our products in international markets; to obtain the best possible conditions for the transfer and exchange of technology adapted to our individual realities, to insure the best regional supply of essential products—especially foods—to create Latin American multinational concerns; and to cooperate with regard to monetary, transportation and communication problems, foreign financing and Latin American financial organizations.[110]

The future of Venezuelan policy is clouded by mutually conflicting statements. The level of rhetorical militancy against the United States is at times very high. For example, on May 6, 1975, Foreign Minister Ramón Escovar Salom commented in a press conference: "We consider the [Panama] Canal to be a humiliation not only to Panama but also to all of Latin America."[111]

The decision of the government to reduce petroleum production by a third in the last twelve months (at the time of writing) while continuing to support the upward movement of world petroleum prices cannot be viewed except in its consequences for both the United States as the largest importer of Venezuelan oil exports, and for the other oil importing countries. President Pérez commented in his July 5, 1974 speech commemorating the country's declaration of independence: "... We will be significant in the Continent and in the world in which we live. We neither wish nor will we accept being a marginal or discounted country that participated in international meetings only to ratify decisions taken by the great centers of power of the world."[112]

On the other hand, Venezuela played the role of mediator on behalf of the industrialized countries in the bargaining over price levels at the Vienna OPEC meeting of September 1975, and Foreign Minister Escobar's address to the 30th Session of the United Nations General Assembly on October 8, 1975 was notable for its moderation toward the major industrialized countries at a time when immoderation caught the notice of the world.[113]

A number of variables suggest the possibility that in the medium to long run, Venezuela may become substantially more important to the other countries of the hemisphere than has already been suggested. There has been some shifting by Brazil away from petroleum importation from Venezuela and toward Middle Eastern suppliers, but antisemitic pressure by Arab states against Latin Americans, with the strong implication that oil sales will be affected if they do not accede to Arab demands, will probably have some counter-productive effect in time.[b] Venezuela will, in time, become one of the hemisphere's major exporters of iron and steel products as well as of ore and with its increasing interest in the production of aluminum from its own and Caribbean ores, it will become a major supplier of this metal as well. And lastly, although it is probable that conservationists will be able to bring about a reduction of the production of petroleum—and thus reduce both the petroleum products available for export and the amount of funds that will flow through FIV for overseas investments and loans—Venezuela will be able to contribute substantially to capital flows needed in the developing countries.[114]

All of these elements will be of smaller importance if the present government is unable to overcome its severe deficit of competent leadership. The complexity of the plans that have been developed and announced by the Pérez planning team, and their sheer volume of diverse detail, call for skills and experience that are in short supply. Congressional debates in October on the budget proposals for 1976 pressed the government hard on this point and wrung the admission that administration will be as great a task in the next few years as any other that has faced the country in the past several decades.[115] Venezuelan governments in the past have frequently offered to the public national development plans notable for their breadth of imagination, soon followed by scanty fulfillment. While in the past these failures or partial achievements have deprived the constitutional republic of public support and thus of legitimacy, yet there has been some sense of movement among most of the people. And at the same time,

---

[b]Moises Cohen was Uruguayan minister of economics and director of the Office of Planning and Budget until his removal in June 1974. His removal had been demanded some months earlier by the armed forces, but a simultaneous suggestion by Arab representatives that Uruguay would have difficulty obtaining petroleum unless its Jewish economics minister was removed had the effect of prolonging his tenure briefly. Nigeria has on one occasion warned Brazil that it could not purchase oil unless a cooler attitude were taken by the latter toward Portugal's policy concerning its African colonies.

a substantial majority of the people can remember when distributive benefits were accorded on a basis of personalism and were accompanied by some cruelty. That condition now has changed; the country as a whole is aware of the bonanza that has become available and its appetite for both distributive benefits and for national influence has been whetted. The Venezuelan system faces a decade of real challenge; in some respects its foreign policy outputs will be only a minor part of the whole.

Notes

1. The petroleum nationalization law was signed by President Carlos Andrés Pérez on August 30, 1975. It entered in force on January 1, 1976. The text of the bill submitted to the Congress appears in *Comercio Exterior* 25, 3 (March 1975):303-307. The text of the law, which differs from the bill only in minor respects, was published by *The Daily Journal* (Caracas), September 1, 1975.

2. Nationalization of iron ore production activities became effective on January 1, 1975. Details of the law appears in *Latin America Economic Report* (London), *LAER*, January 17, 1975.

3. *LAER*, February 28, 1975, reports in detail the critical views of Dr. Juan Pablo Pérez Alfonzo, former minister of mines and petroleum under Rómulo Betancourt, and long considered Venezuela's magisterial figure in petroleum and general economic matters.

4. Norman A. Bailey and Ronald M. Schneider, "Brazil's Foreign Policy: A Case Study in Upward Mobility," *Inter-American Economic Affairs* 27, 1 (Summer 1973):3-25, is a useful summary of Brazilian views and ambitions.

5. David Nott, "Venezuela, The Oil Bonanza and the New Government," *Bank of London and South America Review* 8, 5 (May 1974):196-204. This short article is the best currently available overview of the Pérez statement of priorities.

6. IBRD, *The economic development of Venezuela* (Baltimore: The Johns Hopkins Press, 1961). Other general sources, for more up-to-date information are Venezuela, Oficina Central de Información, *Ahora* 1, 3 (June 17-24, 1974):2; Inter-American Development Bank, *Economic and Social Progress in Latin America. Annual report 1974* (Washington, D.C.: The Bank, 1975), pp. 427-434; Population Reference Bureau, Inc., *Population Data Sheet*, 1974 (Washington, D.C.: The Bureau, 1975). Apart from the IBRD report, the following general works are useful: Robert J. Alexander, *The Venezuelan Democratic Revolution. A Profile of the Regime of Rómulo Betancourt* (New Brunswick: Rutgers University Press, 1964); John D. Martz, *Acción Democrática. Evolution of a Modern Political Party in Venezuela* (Princeton: Princeton University Press, 1966); Rómulo Betancourt, *Venezuela: política y petróleo* (Bogota: Editorial Senderos, 1969, 3rd printing); David E. Blank, *Politics in*

Venezuela (Boston: Little, Brown and Co., 1973); Daniel H. Levine, *Conflict and Political Change in Venezuela* (Princeton: Princeton University Press, 1973); Frank Bonilla and Jose A. Silva Michelena (eds.), *A Strategy for Research on Social Policy* (Cambridge: M.I.T. Press, 1967); Frank Bonilla, *The Failure of Elites* (Cambridge: M.I.T. Press, 1970); Jose A. Silva Michelena, *The Illusion of Democracy in Dependent Nations* (Cambridge: M.I.T. Press, 1971); John Duncan Powell, *Political Mobilization of the Venezuelan Peasant* (Cambridge: Harvard University Press, 1971); Philip B. Taylor, Jr., (ed.), *Venezuela: 1969. Analysis of Progress* (Houston: University of Houston, Office of International Affairs, 1971).

7. David E. Blank (ed.), *Venezuela Election Factbook*, December 1, 1968 (Washington, D.C.: Institute for the Comparative Study of Political Systems, 1968), p. 35 (for 1958 election results) and p. 38 (for 1963 results). In the 1968 election a split in the AD party led to a majority of anti-AD/COPEI votes in the capital, although it is possible that without the split the majority might have fallen the other way. The mood of the 1973 campaign is reported in George W. Grayson, "Venezuela's Presidential Politics," *Current History* (January 1974):23-27,f.

8. Representative items in the bibliography on the Fuerzas Armadas de Liberación Nacional (FALN) include James L. Lalley, *Castro—Communist Insurgency in Venezuela: A Study of Insurgency and Counter-insurgency Operations in Venezuela, 1960-1964* (Alexandria, Va.: Georgetown Research Project, 1965); James Petras, "Guerrilla Movements in Latin America—I," *New Politics*, 6 (Winter 1967):80-94; and Philip B. Taylor, Jr., "Venezuela, 1958 until 1963," in Doris M. Condit, Bert H. Cooper, Jr., and others, *Challenge and Response in Internal Conflict*, vol. III, *The Experience in Africa and Latin America* (Washington, D.C.: Center for Research in Social Systems, 1968), pp. 464-499.

9. Relations were broken in 1961. The circumstances leading to Cuba's suspension from the Organization of American States in 1964 are reported in detail in Organization of American States, Council, *Report of the investigating committee appointed by the Council of the Organization of American States*, acting provisionally as Organ of Consultation (Washington, D.C.: O.A.S., 1964), document OEA/Ser.C/IV, C-i-658, February 18, 1964.

Readmission of the Communist party to legal activity is reported in "Venezuela: Communist Party Regains Its Legality," *World Marxist Review* 12, 5 (May 1969):41-42, among other sources. In the 1973 campaign the party was splintered, and its most active wing was the *Movimiento al Socialismo*. See Eleazar Díaz Rangel, *Como se dividio el P.C.V.* (Caracas: Editorial Domingo Fuentes, 1971).

10. The military traditions and attitudes of Venezuela are discussed in a variety of works. See, for example, Robert L. Gilmore, *Caudillism and Militarism in Venezuela, 1810-1910* (Athens: Ohio University Press, 1964); Philip B.

Taylor, Jr., *The Venezuelan golpe de estado of 1958: The Fall of Marcos Pérez Jiménez* (Washington, D.C.: Institute for the Comparative Study of Political Systems, 1968); Winfield J. Burggraaff, *The Venezuelan Armed Forces in Politics, 1935-1959* (Columbia: University of Missouri Press, 1972).

11. Levine, *Conflict and Political Change*, pp. 231-255, discusses the concept of "rules of the game" in useful detail.

12. For example, see Bonilla, *Failure of Elites, passim*, and Silva Michelena, *Illusion of Democracy, passim*, for essentially ideological interpretations of the middle class and elites. The 1974 approach to the armed forces is reported in "How Venezuela Spends Its Oil Riches," *Forbes* (July 15, 1974):45 ff. The incidents have been confirmed by two other private sources, independent of each other, as well.

13. Nott, "Oil Bonanza," observes Pérez' refusal to be rushed in reaching decisions concerning petroleum and other issues. *El Nacional* (Caracas), June 30, 1974, reports Pérez' policy speech to the 30th annual conference of the Venezuelan Federation of Chambers and Associations of Commerce and Production (Fedecamaras); *LAER*, June 6, 1975, reports briefly some of the government's policy statements to the 31st annual conference. *El Nacional*, May 17, 1974, publishes the text of Pérez' appointment of the Oil Reversion Commission.

14. Andrés Ladino L., "Venezuela: actitudes nacionales hacia el problema de población," a leaflet article published by Population Reference Bureau, Inc., Bogota, January 1971, discussed population planning attitudes of the country.

15. IADB, *Economic and Social Progress*, pp. 427-430, 434; Enrique A. Baloyra, "Oil Policies and Budgets in Venezuela, 1938-1969," *Latin American Research Review* 9, 2 (Summer 1974):28-72. *LAER*, May 9, 1975, reports some evidences of severe agricultural shortfalls now and for the future, if land use and population growth patterns do not change rapidly.

16. Nott, "Oil Bonanza," p. 197.

17. Ibid., p. 203; "Venezuela," *Bank of London and South America* 8, 6 (June 1974):369. "How Venezuela Spends . . ." (*Forbes*), notes inflationary rates in Venezuela normally have run to about 2.5 to 3 percent annually in the past five years.

18. President Pérez to Fedecamaras, June 29, 1974. The per capita income datum is from IDB, *Economic and Social Progress*, p. 441.

19. Venezuela's attitudes toward OPEC price policies have been subject to much change. In the June 15, 1974 quarterly meeting of the OPEC conference at Quito, for example, Venezuela wished substantial increases in the reference price, as well as in royalty demands on the operating companies, while several of the Middle East states wished to lower the reference price. In compromise, for a period of three months the reference price was maintained without change, but royalty figures were raised by two percent. After the meeting, Venezuela decreed an average increase of its own reference price from $14.08 to $14.43 per

barrel. *Latin America* (London), June 14, 21; and July 5, 1974. Still discontented, Venezuela announced its intention of returning to the issue in the September 1974 quarterly meeting.

In contrast, with nationalization now scheduled and the marketing implications highly uncertain, Venezuela played a mediating role at the Vienna September 1975 meeting, which voted a 10 percent world price increase, *LAER*, October 3, 1975.

20. Especially see Nott, "Oil Bonanza," *passim*; and "How Venezuela spends . . ." (*Forbes*), *passim*, for details concerning the atmosphere of the official statement.

21. David Nott, "Venezuela: The Apportionment of Oil Wealth," *BOLSA Review* 9, 1 (January 1975):2-12, at p. 5. The Gran Mariscal de Ayacucho scholarship program was established in June 1974 under the supervision of the planning agency, CORDIPLAN. Up to 10,000 special scholarships were established for advanced technical and professional training in institutes and universities in Venezuela and abroad. The plan is a major expansion and upgrading of the *Instituto Nacional de Cooperación Educativa*, INCE, for technical and vocational training, as well as of the higher education facilities of the country. By September 1975 ten foreign countries had received about 5,000 students, mostly at the university level; 1,900 of these were enrolled in United States universities. *Times of the Americas* (Washington, D.C.), October 1, 1975.

22. The historical experience concerning corrupt and irresponsible practices in the Ibero-American region is suggested in, among other sources, Benjamin Keen (ed.), *Readings in Latin-American Civilization, 1492 to the Present* (Boston: Houghton Mifflin Co., 2nd ed., 1967), pp. 134-137; and J. Frank Moreno, "The Spanish Colonial System: A Functional Approach"; *The Western Political Quarterly* 20, 2 (June 1967):308-320. Under the 1945 *Ley contra el enriquecimiento ilícito de funcionarios públicos* (Law against the illicit enrichment of public officials) a permanent investigative commission is established. During study trips to Venezuela this writer frequently has been told by respondents of their certainty of massive peculation by former presidents. Although the AD governments of 1945-48 and 1959-64 found evidence against former heads of government, the record seems to indicate that at least at the presidential level actions occur for political rather than evidentiary reasons.

23. Alexander, *The Venezuelan Democratic Revolution*, pp. 63-66, indicates the commitment of social democratic regimes in Venezuela to planning for development purposes. Also, see John Friedman, *Venezuela: From Doctrine to Dialogue* (Syracuse: Syracuse University Press, 1965). The relative neutralization of CORDIPLAN in the past is suggested in Lloyd Rodwin and Associates, *Planning Urban Growth and Regional Development: The Experience of the Guyana Programs of Venezuela* (Cambridge: M.I.T. Press, 1969), *passim*, and Blank, *Politics in Venezuela*, pp. 252, 259-261.

24. Gertrude G. Edwards, "Foreign Petroleum Companies and the State in

Venezuela," in Raymond F. Mikesell and others, *Foreign Investment in the Petroleum and Mineral Industries. Case Studies of Investor-Host Country Relations* (Baltimore: The Johns Hopkins Press, 1971), pp. 101-128; R. Lynn Kelley, "The 1966 Venezuelan Tax Reform," *Inter-American Economic Affairs* 24, 1 (Summer 1970):77-92.

25. Nott, "Oil Bonanza," pp. 197, 199-201; and Nott, "Apportionment of Oil Wealth," pp. 10-11.

26. *Latin America*, January 11, 1974, reports Caldera's "State of the Nation" address recommendations to his successor, January 1, 1974; *Visión*, April 30, 1975, reports Pérez' activity and concentration on his job, at pp. 16-17; also, see Nott, "Apportionment of Oil Wealth," pp. 11-12.

27. *LAER*, June 20, 1975.

28. *LAER*, October 3, 1975. For the first eight months of 1975 oil production was off 19.1 percent to 2.47 million barrels per day (bpd), as against 1974 figures. In the month of August production was 2.28 million bpd. In the first six months of 1975, exports were off 12.2 percent.

IBD News 2, 7 (August 1975):8, reports briefly a speech at the Inter-American Development Bank, Washington, D.C., by Constantino Quero Morales, FIV president, concerning his country's plans for the money.

29. Nott, "Apportionment of Oil Wealth," p. 3; *LAER,* June 27, 1975. *El Nacional*, July 7, 1974.

30. *LAER*, June 7 and 21, 1974; and May 9 and October 10, 1975. Nott, "Apportionment of Oil Wealth," pp. 2-3; *Venezuela Ahora* 1, 5 (July 1-8, 1974):4-5. Bs.1 billion are reserved for small agricultural loans to Bs.500,000.

31. Nott, "Apportionment of Oil Wealth," p. 6.

32. John P. Powelson, "La fuga de capital en Venezuela, 1961-1962," *El Trimestre Económico* 31, (Jan.-March 1964):93-105. Now somewhat dated as to data, the causes of capital flight from Venezuela are reviewed usefully. They are supported by this writer's extensive interviewing in 1962.

33. Among useful articles are Edward S. Milensky, "From Integration to Developmental Nationalism: The Andean Group, 1965-1971," *Inter-American Economic Affairs* 25, 3 (Winter 1971):77-91; Milensky, "Developmental Nationalism in Practice: The Problems and Progress of the Andean Group," Ibid. 26, 4 (Spring 1973):49-68; Kenneth A. Switzer, "The Andean Group: A Reappraisal," Ibid. 26, 4 (Spring 1973):69-81; William P. Avery and James D. Cochrane, "Subregional Integration in Latin America: The Andean Common Market," *Journal of Common Market Studies* 11, 2 (December 1972):85-102.

34. Nott, "Oil Bonanza," p. 204, comments, ". . . few recall the President's warning, given during the election campaign, that if in the next five years the Government fails to achieve the progress to which the people aspire, non-democratic forces will intervene and the parliamentary system will be discredited."

The Caracas press, with the support of the nationalist business organization *Pro-Venezuela*, in June 1974 began an attack on the rising number of offers of opportunities for investment abroad, especially in Europe and the United States. Sales offices had been opened, and some new holders of surplus funds (even of small scale) had sent their money out of the country. It was alleged by some writers that this was actually a conspiracy by more conservative entrepreneurial groups in the country to weaken Pérez's plans for diversification of private holdings. The government undertook to investigate. *Latin America*, June 14 and July 5, 1974. While the observer may well feel there is a touch of paranoia in some of this record, it must be added that the evidences of both fact and attitude are relatively typical.

35. *Venezuela Ahora* 1, 4 (June 24-July 1, 1974):4-5, publishes a synopsis of a statement by CORDIPLAN Director Gumersindo Rodriguez concerning the conditions under which foreign investments may operate in the country.

36. Nott, "Apportionment of Oil Wealth," p. 7. Additionally, a smaller fund of Bs.360 million, has been established for small and medium industry, the *Corporación de desarrollo de la pequeña y mediana industria*, which is to be an autonomous government corporation. *Venezuela Ahora* 1, 7 (July 15-22 1974):5-6.

37. *Venezuela Ahora* 1,13 (Aug. 26-Sept. 2, 1974):5, reports the first fund mentioned; Ibid. 1, 28 (Dec. 9-16, 1974):7, announces the second fund; and Ibid. 1, 8 (July 22-29, 1974):5-6, announces the Ministry of Public Works program.

38. Edwin Lieuwan, *Petroleum in Venezuela. A History* (Berkeley: University of California Press, 1955), pp. 107-108; Juan Pablo Pérez Alfonzo, *Petróleo: jugo de la tierra* (Caracas: Editorial Arte, 1961), pp. 11-41.

39. Betancourt, *Venezuela: política y petróleo, passim.*

40. Franklin Tugwell, "Petroleum Policy in Venezuela: Lessons in the Politics of Dependence Management," *Studies in Comparative International Development* 9, 4 (Spring 1974):84-120, is an exceptional able treatment of the problem of strategies; Ruben Sader Pérez, *The Venezuelan State Oil Reports to the People* (Caracas: Corporación Venezolana del Petróleo, 1969), *passim;* Arturo Uslar Pietri, *Petróleo: de vida o muerto* (Caracas, 1966).

41. *El Nacional*, June 23, 1974, reports a speech by the president of the Association of Venezuelan Petroleum Engineers.

42. *LAER*, October 26, 1973, reports details of the policy changes.

43. Useful general works on OPEC include Zuhayr Mikdahsi, *The Community of Oil Exporting Countries–A Study in Governmental Cooperation* (Ithaca: Cornell University Press, 1972); Mikdashi, "Cooperation among Oil Exporting Countries with Special Reference to Arab Countries: A Political Economy Analysis," *International Organization* 28, 1 (Winter 1974):1-30; Fuan Rouhani, *A History of O.P.E.C.* (New York: Praeger Publishers, 1971).

44. *Latin America*, January 11, 1974.

45. Sources for this discussion include *LAER*, May 31, 1974; *Latin America*, May 10 and June 14, 1974; Nott, "Oil Bonanza"; "How Venezuela spends . . . " (*Forbes*); and *Venezuela Ahora* 1, 3 (June 17-24, 1974):3-5.

46. *LAER*, January 17, 1975, offers a concise account; also, Nott, "Apportionment of Oil Wealth," p. 7.

47. *Latin America*, July 19, 1974; *LAER*, March 7, 1975; Nott, "Apportionment," pp. 4-5.

48. *Venezuela Ahora* 1, 1 (June 3-10, 1974):3-5; *New York Times*, May 18, 1974, lists the groups represented in the commission.

49. *New York Times*, August 20, 1974, summarized the draft reported out by the commission. The text of the bill sent to the Congress by Pérez appears in *Comercio Exterior* 25, 3 (March 1975):305-307.

50. *Daily Journal* (Caracas), September 1, 1975, publishes the text of the law.

51. *Latin America*, September 26 and October 3, 1975, discusses the most recent exchange between President Gerald Ford and President Pérez. Latin America described the exchange as if the American message were sharply critical and somewhat overbearing; this is not possible to say, since as of this writing neither message had been released to the public. There is precedent for harsh exchanges between the two executives, however, granted the exchange that occurred in September 1974. At that time President Ford and Secretary of State Henry Kissinger warned that the oil producing countries should not keep prices "artificially high," nor use oil supplies as a blackmail weapon. President Pérez replied sharply, in a message printed in full in the major newspapers of this country and Venezuela. *Venezuela Ahora* 1, 18 (Sept. 30-Oct. 7, 1974):3-5.

52. *LAER*, February 28, 1975, reports extensively on the severe misgivings expressed by Juan Pablo Pérez Alfonzo concerning the decision to proceed on nationalization, in light of the lack of facilities and personnel. For example, with an estimated 100 petroleum and mining engineers in the country, the Rector of the Central University estimated that about 50 petroleum engineers would receive their degrees from the country's universities in 1977. *LAER*, August 1, 1975.

The acrimony over the parliamentary tactics employed by AD, and over the issue of article 5 of the nationalization bill, is reported in *Latin America*, March 2, June 6, July 18, August 25 and September 5, 1975, and in the *New York Times*, June 20, 1975.

Additional useful descriptive articles include one by Kim Fuad for United Press International, published in the *Houston Chronicle*, August 29, 1975, and by Nigel Cumberland for the Associated Press, ibid., October 12, 1975.

53. *Semana* (Caracas), No. 322 (July 4-10, 1974):5-7, 13, 41.

54. *Latin America*, May 2, 1975.

55. At the beginning of Pérez's term, semi-official estimates had placed unemployment at about 20 percent of a working force of 3.1 million persons. *Venezuela Ahora* 1, 1 (June 3-10, 1974):2, reports the work force size. In August 1975, CORDIPLAN reported a reduction of unemployment to about 18 percent. *Andean Report* (Lima), No. 3 (September 1975), p. 18.

56. In October 1974 some 500 retired military officers published a manifesto warning against undue concessions to Colombia in an ongoing dispute over the

188   LATIN AMERICA: STRUGGLE FOR PROGRESS

Gulf of Venezuela. The government reacted with some apprehension and reprimanded the senior signers. The declaration was most notable for its irrelevance at the time; but its occurrence suggested an essentially antidemocratic state of mind among the signers. See *Latin America*, October 25, 1974.

57. Gordon Connell-Smith, *The Inter-American System* (London: Oxford University Press, 1966), is a comparatively recent and highly detailed summary text concerning inter-American relations, with a critical approach to United States policy. Concerning the American position in the Caribbean, see p. 24 for the probably critical reference in President John F. Kennedy's 1961 speech concerning the lessons of the Bay of Pigs invasion in Cuba and continuing American interests.

58. Among useful sources are Otto Schoenrich, "The Venezuelan-British Guiana Boundary Dispute," *The American Journal of International Law* 43, 3 (July 1949):523-530; United Nations, document UN/SG Doc. A/C.4.536, February, 1962; Guyana, Ministry of Foreign Affairs, *Guyana/Venezuela Relations* (Georgetown 1968); Leslie B. Rout, Jr., *Which Way Out? A Study of the Guyana-Venezuela Boundary Dispute* (East Lansing: Michigan State University, 1971).

59. *Latin America*, March 15, 1974.

60. Useful sources concerning the territorial waters claim are Eduardo Zuleta Angel, *El llamado Golfo de Venezuela* (Bogota, 1971), a collection of legal documents on the matter; *Visión*, February 13, 27 and July 17, 1971, and December 30, 1974; *LAER*, December 7, 1973.

61. *Latin America*, June 29, 1973.

62. Lieuwen, *Petroleum in Venezuela*, pp. 17, 47-49.

63. *Christian Science Monitor*, May 17, 1974.

64. *Latin America*, June 7, 1974.

65. *Latin America*, October 17, 1975. Also, see *El Nacional*, February 11, 1971.

66. *Visión*, January 30, 1971; *Latin America*, February 16, 1973.

67. After the Castro seizure of power in 1959 the oil industry was nationalized; since then it has been operated by the government. For the most part the refineries built by the American companies were designed for use with Venezuelan crude stocks; the conversion of the plants to Soviet crude in the 1960s was not technically successful because of the much heavier sulfur content, and vehicles using the resulting fuel have had much difficulty.

Monthly refinery runs averaged about 1.8 billion barrels monthly in 1960; a small portion of this was based on Cuban-produced crude. The refining capacity at that time was about 2.4 billion barrels monthly, largely among plants built by Jersey Standard, Shell and Texaco. Wyatt MacGaffey, Clifford R. Barnett, and others, *Twentieth-century Cuba. The Background of the Cuban Revolution* (Garden City, N.Y.: Doubleday & Co., 1962).

68. *Latin America*, February 22, March 8, 15 and 29, June 21, and July 5, 1974.

69. *Comercio Exterior* 23, 6 (June 1973):501-502; and ibid., No. 8 (1973):741-742; *LAER*, May 24, 1974; *Visión*, January 13, 1973, discusses other aspects of planning for international cooperation in the Caribbean. A detailed account of recent developments in CARICOM is found in *Comercio Exterior* 24, 12 (Dec. 1974):1239-1240.

70. *LAER*, September 12, 1975.

71. *IBD News* 2, 2 (March 1975).

72. *Visión*, October 7, 1972.

73. *Latin America*, October 3, 1975.

74. *Visión*, December 8, 1971.

75. *Latin America*, December 20, 1974.

76. *Times of the Americas*, June 25, 1975; *Latin America*, June 27, 1975.

77. *Visión*, January 13, 1973, is a useful short summary article of the commercial links among the countries within the Caribbean zone, including Mexico and Colombia.

78. *Latin America*, February 8, March 1 and June 21, 1974.

79. IDB Press Release NR-23/75. A combination of two loans totaling $13.6 million was released to Costa Rica for fisheries expansion.

80. *Comercio Exterior* 25, 2 (Feb. 1975):130.

81. *Times of the Americas*, December 25, 1974.

82. *Comercio Exterior de Mexico* 21, 6 (June 1975):185-187; this is the English language edition of the publication. Ibid., No. 7 (July 1975), p. 230.

83. *LAER*, April 25, 1975 reports a visit by Minister of Economy Hector Hurtado to Panama to inaugurate joint operations of two official banks, the Banco Sudamericano de Desarrollo of Panama, and the Banco Nacional de Descuento of Caracas. Hurtado observed that this might become the first of many such arrangements.

84. *Visión*, April 7, 1973, summarizes the events. Other sources, apart from a rapidly growing assortment of books of both scholarly and polemic natures, include "U.S. Policy toward Panama, 1903-present." Questions of Recognition and Diplomatic Relations, and the *Department of State Bulletin*, April 22, 1974; "Panama Canal Treaty Negotiations: Background and Current Status," The Department of State, News Release, January 1975; "Panama and the United States: Toward a New Relationship," The Department of State, News Release, May 22, 1975, text of a speech by Ambassador Ellsworth Bunker, the principal U.S. negotiator in Panama.

Following the failure of the Security Council resolution, on March 21, 1973 Security Council voted Resolution 330 (1973), "requesting" the member states "to refrain from using or encouraging the use of any type of coercive measure against states of the [Latin American] region."

85. *New York Times*, April 10, 1975; *Visión* April 15, 1975.

86. See, for example, Domar Campos, and other, *Paz, seu nome e desenvolvimento* (Rio de Janeiro: Editora Fundo de Cultura, 1968), in which six economists who have held ambassadorial rank at one time discuss economic

development problems from the viewpoint of Brazil's mission to motivate continental change. Also, Peter B. Evans, "The Military, the Multinationals, and the 'Miracle': The Political Economy of the 'Brazilian Model of Development'," *Studies in Comparative International Development* 9, 3 (Fall 1974):26-45.

87. *Latin America*, December 7, 1973, reports censorship controls over leading Brazilian newspapers. Thomas G. Sanders, "The Brazilian Model," *American Universities Field Staff Reports* (East Coast South America Series, 27, 8, TGS-7-'73), reports the heightened level of fascist practice, by which the entrepreneurial elite is linked to the military planning and strategy structure. Also see Bailey and Schneider, "Brazil's Foreign Policy," *passim*; and Stanley E. Hilton, "Military Influence on Brazilian Economic Policy, 1930-1945; A Different View," *Hispanic American Historical Review* 53, 1 (February 1973):71-94.

Other sources from a literature that is surprisingly candid in view of the harshly authoritarian public face and fact of the regime since 1964, include Augusto Fragoso, "A Escola Superior da Guerra," *Problemas Brasileiros* 8, 88 (Dec. 1970):19-34; the author, who was commandant of the ESG, explains its structure, goals and philosophy. A similar article is Coronel ***, "El Ejército del Brasil, sus problemas y políticas," *Estrategia*, No. 2 (July-Aug. 1969):62-77. The author's nationality is not stated, but presumably is Brazilian; the reader's interest is heightened by the fact that the article appears in a semi-official publication of the Argentine army. Joviniano Soares de Carvalho Neto, *Nacionalismo em fato novo: perspectiva do nacionalismo, autoritario no Brasil* (São Paulo: Edições Loyola, 1973), discusses the uses of nationalism by authoritarian regimes such as Brazil. The annual reviews of Brazilian affairs by the French research institute, La Documentation Francaise, "Problemes d'Amerique Latine," are also exceptionally useful. See its "Bresil: 1972-1973, les deux dernieres annees de la presidence Medici," *Notes et Etudes Documentaires*, No. 4084-4086, April 30, 1974; and Michel Foucher, "La mise en valeur de l'Amazonic bresilienne," ibid., Nos. 4110-4111, Sept. 15, 1974.

88. Possibly the most critical issue is that of Brazilian nuclear policy. See H. Jon Rosenbaum and Glenn M. Cooper, "Brazil and the Nuclear Non-proliferation Treaty," *International Affairs* 46, 1 (January 1970):74-90; *LAER*, June 20, 1975; *Latin America*, March 14, 1975.

89. Brasil, Exército, Centro de Relações Públicas, *O seu exército* (Rio de Janeiro, n.d.); this is a glossy public relations presentation of the Brazilian army, with strong focus on doctrine, training institutions and equipment. Luigi Einaudi, Hans Heymann, Jr., David Ronfeldt, and Cesar Sereseres, *Arms Transfers to Latin America: Toward a Policy of Mutual Respect* (Santa Monica, California: Rand Corporation report R-1173-DOS, 1973); *Latin America*, December 21, 1973, reports on the Brazilian submarine force. Marlise Simóns, "The Brazilian Connection," *Washington Post*, January 6, 1974, reports the role of Brazilian financing and subversion in the overthrow of the Chilean government of Salvador Allende in 1973; since that time there has been a variety of

incidents of Brazilian secret police who have acted to detain and/or dispose of political refugees within Chilean territory.

90. *Latin America*, March 2 and June 8, 1973, reports the meeting of Venezuelan President Caldera with Brazilian President Emilio Garrastazú Médici, and Venezuelan concern as a result of the Brazilian attitudes. Earlier in February, on the other hand, Caldera had completed a swing around the Spanish-speaking countries of the continent and Brazil had been reported concerned at the implications of "encirclement." *Latin America*, February 16, 1973.

91. *Latin America*, March 2, 1973; Walter Coppens, Roberto Lizarralde and H. Dieter Heinen, "Indian Policy," prepared for a forthcoming volume edited by John D. Martz and David J. Myers, *Venezuela, the Democratic Experiment*.

President Médici met with President Richard Nixon in Washington in 1972. Nixon afterward remarked, to the deep concern of nearly all Latin American countries (and Caldera spoke forthrightly in protest at the statement) that he considered Brazil the proper model for Latin American development. During the meetings, a Brazilian senior officer accompanying Médici remarked to a counterpart American officer that Brazil considered its security required that it maintain close intelligence surveillance of uranium deposits in the Venezuelan state of Bolivar and in its Amazonas territory. He said Brazil would expect American understanding should at some future time Brazil declare its paramountcy in the area.

92. Levy is quoted in a *Washington Post-Los Angeles Times* syndicated article published in the *Houston Chronicle* on October 18, 1975.

93. Concerning Venezuelan troop behavior see Taylor, "Venezuela, 1958 until 1963," *passim.*

94. Howard J. Wiarda, "Toward a Framework for the Study of Political Change in the Iberic-Latin Tradition: The Corporative Model," *World Politics* 25, 2 (January 1973):213-237; Richard M. Morse, "The Heritage of Latin America," pp. 123-177 in Louis Hartz and others, *The Founding of New Societies. Studies in the History of the United States, Latin America, South Africa, Canada and Australia* (New York: Harcourt, Brace and World, 1964); and this writer, "Is 'development' for everyone?", pp. 1-14 in Philip B. Taylor, Jr. (ed.), *Problems of Law, Politics and Economic Development in Latin America* (Houston: University of Houston Latin American Studies Program, 1975).

95. Domingo Alberto Rangel, *Los andinos en el poder* (Caracas, 1964); Robert L. Gilmore, *Caudillism and militarism in Venezuela, 1810-1910* (Athens: University of Ohio Press, 1964).

96. Lieuwen, *Petroleum in Venezuela*, p. 83.

97. *LAER*, August 1, September 5, and 12, 1975. The Market executive Decision 91 allocates petrochemicals rights and markets, and makes tentative adjudications for production of automobiles and trucks. See also, The Andean Report, September 1975. *BOLSA Review* 9, 9 (September 1975):499-501, reports Andean Market events.

98. *Latin America*, May 30, 1975, reports that the International Basic Economy Corporation has completed the sale of 51 percent of the shares of its supermarket chain in Caracas. *LAER*, July 18, 1975, reports that automobile manufacturers are now seeking local purchasers for shares.

99. "The Andean Group, A Progress Report," *BOLSA Review* 8, 5 (May 1974):251-258.

100. Germanico Salgado Penaherrera, "El grupo andino y la inversión extranjera," *Comercio Exterior* 23, 2 (Feb. 1973):154-160; and ibid., No. 3 (March 1973):223-233. Dr. Salgado is a member of the executive committee of the Market.

101. Mexico played a central role in the adoption by the United Nations General Assembly (29) of resolution 2381, the Charter of Economic Rights and Duties of States, document A/RES/3281 (XXIX), January 15, 1975.

Concerning Peru's ambitions, see *Visión*, August 11, 1973, and *Latin America*, March 14, 1975.

102. *Comercio Exterior* 25, 4 (April 1975), published a special supplement, "Visita de estado del Presidente de Venezuela a Mexico: documentos," which includes a large number of documents of the Pérez visit of March 17-22, 1975.

103. *Latin America*, August 15, 1975, offers the text of the resolution establishing SELA, voted at Panama on August 2, 1975. For other details concerning the politics and the diplomacy of the issue, see ibid., February 21 and 28, March 14 and 28, August 8 and October 8, 1975. For additional information see *Comercio Exterior* 25, 8 (Aug. 1975):847-850.

104. *Venezuela Ahora* 1, 29 (Dec. 16-23, 1974), contains the text of the Declaration of Ayacucho. Also, see *New York Times*, December 13, 1974, and *Latin America*, December 13, 1974. The signatories of the Declaration are Peru, Bolivia, Venezuela, Panama, Argentina, Colombia, Chile and Ecuador.

105. H.R. 10710, The Trade Act of 1974. The Latin American view is summarized in a lengthy special supplement that accompanies *Comercio Exterior* 25, 5 (May 1975), "La ley de comercio de 1974 de Estados Unidos. Análisis y documentos." The American position is summarized in "Latin America and the Trade Act of 1974," Department of State, Special Report no. 18, May 1975. Also see *Latin America*, January 17, 24 and 31, 1975.

106. Details concerning voting in IDB boards are offered in *Inter-American Development Bank. Fifteen years of activities, 1960-1974* (Washington, D.C.: The Bank, 1975). *Noticias del BID* 1, 4 (May 1974):4, reports the first Venezuelan discussion of the trust fund proposal, and summarizes its position. *IBD News* 2, 7 (August 1975), includes the text of the press conference.

107. Hubert Herring, *A History of Latin America: From the Beginnings to the Present*, 3rd edition (New York: Knopf, 1972), p. 513.

108. While the quantity of oil possibly contained in the tar belt can only be guessed, estimates run from 700 billion barrels upward. See the *Christian Science Monitor* (midwest edition), August 29 and September 3, 1974; and the *Washington Post*, December 5, 1973.

109. Among works frequently cited in the dependency school are Andre Gunder Frank, *Latin America: Underdevelopment or Revolution. Essays on the Development of Underdevelopment and the Immediate Enemy* (New York: Monthly Review Press, 1969); Theotonio dos Santos, "The Structure of Dependence," *American Economic Review* 60, 2 (May 1970):231-236; Suzanne Bodenheimer, "Dependency and Imperialism: The Roots of Latin American Underdevelopment," in K. Fann and D. Hodges (eds.), *Readings in U.S. Imperialism* (Boston: Porter Sargent, 1971). Recent useful statements of the thesis include Octavio Ianni, "Imperialismo cultural en América Latina," *Comercio Exterior* 25, 7 (July 1975):749-753; and Ianni, "Imperialism and Diplomacy in Inter-American Relations," pp. 23-51, in Julio Cotler and Richard R. Fagen (eds.), *Latin America and the United States: The Changing Political Realities* (Stanford: Stanford University Press, 1974).

110. Declaration of Ayacucho, text presented on Peru official radio transmission, December 10, 1974.

111. United Press International dispatch, Caracas, May 6, 1975.

112. *Venezuela Ahora* 1, 7 (July 15-22, 1974):3-4.

113. Venezuelan Mission to the United Nations, "Press Venezuela," release 612, October 8, 1975. *LAER*, October 3, 1975, reports the Venezuelan role at Vienna.

114. *LAER*, September 19 and 26, 1975, reports in some detail concerning reductions between 1974 and 1976 due to reduced petroleum earnings. The initial budget estimate for 1976 proposed no allocation to the FIV at all, in contrast with the Bs.13 billion received in 1974 and Bs.7,457 million received in 1975.

115. *Latin America*, October 17, 1975. Under Article 6 of the Oil Nationalization Law, the Corporación Venezolana del Petróleo was reestablished as PETROVEN, a public corporation, to manage all aspects of the petroleum industry after January 1, 1976.

Index

Index

197

About the Authors

JAMES D. THEBERGE is currently U.S. Ambassador to Nicaragua. From 1970-1975, he was Director of Latin American Studies at Georgetown University's Center for Strategic and International Studies. He is an international economist who has served as adviser to the State Department, the Inter-American Development Bank, the World Bank, the United Nations (UNCTAD and UNIDO) and the Andean Development Corporation. He was a Research Associate at the Latin American Centre, St. Antony's College, Oxford University in 1969-1970. His recent books include *Russia in the Caribbean* (1973) and the *Soviet Presence in Latin America* (1974). He is also an editor of and contributor to the *Economics of Trade and Development* (1968), *Soviet Seapower in the Caribbean* (1972), and *The Western Mediterranean* (1974).

ROGER W. FONTAINE is the new director of Latin American Studies at Georgetown University's Center for Strategic and International Studies. Dr. Fontaine received the B.A. from Valparaiso University in 1963, and the M.A. (1965) and the Ph.D. (1970) from the Johns Hopkins School of Advanced International Studies in Washington, D.C. He has taught at Middlebury College in the Department of Political Science, and has done economic and political research on Latin America at American University, Research Analysis Corporation, Resources for the Future, Inc., and the Institute for Defense Analyses. In 1972/73 Dr. Fontaine was a Rockefeller Fellow attached to the Washington Center for Foreign Policy Research. His publications include a study of U.S.-Brazilian relations: *Brazil and the United States: Toward a Maturing Relationship*, and *On Negotiating with*

Cuba, both published by the American Enterprise Institute for Public Policy Research in Washington, D.C.

PHILIP B. TAYLOR, JR. is Director of Latin American Studies at the University of Houston. He has taught Latin American politics at Northwestern, Michigan, Tulane, the Johns Hopkins School of Advanced International Studies and two Latin American universities: University of Montevideo in Uruguay and the Universidad de los Andes in Colombia. Dr. Taylor has written the *Venezuelan Golpe de Estado of 1958: The Fall of Marcos Pérez Jiménez* (1968) and *Government and Politics of Uruguay* (1962) and his articles have appeared in the *American Political Science Review, Western Political Quarterly*, and *Journal of Politics* among others.